The Rise of Ethnic Politics in Nepal

The relationship between ethnic politics and democracy presents a paradox for scholars and policy makers: ethnic politics frequently emerge in new democracies and yet are often presumed to threaten them. As ethnic politics is becoming increasingly central to Nepali politics, this book argues it has the potential to strengthen rather than destabilize democracy.

Drawing on years of ethnographic fieldwork, Susan Hangen focuses on the ethnic political party, the Mongol National Organization (MNO), which consists of multiple ethnic groups and has been mobilizing support in rural east Nepal. By investigating the party's discourse and its struggles to gain support and operate within a village government, the book provides a window onto the processes of democratization in rural Nepal in the 1990s. This work presents a more nuanced understanding of how ethnic parties operate on the ground, arguing that ethnic parties overlap considerably with social movements, and that the boundary between parties and movements should be reconceptualized. The analysis demonstrates that ethnic parties are not antithetical to democracy and that democratization can proceed in diverse and unexpected ways.

Providing an in-depth discussion of the indigenous nationalities movement, one of Nepal's most significant social movements, this work will be of great interest to scholars and students of Asian Politics, South Asian Studies and Political Anthropology.

Susan I. Hangen is Associate Professor of Anthropology and International Studies at Ramapo College, NJ, USA. She is the author of *Creating a New Nepal: The Ethnic Dimension*. Her current research investigates transnational politics in the Nepali diaspora.

Routledge contemporary South Asia series

The Rise of Ethnic Politics in Nepal

Democracy in the margins

Susan I. Hangen

Routledge
Taylor & Francis Group

LONDON AND NEW YORK

FIRST INDIAN REPRINT, 2010

First published 2010
by Routledge
2 Park Square, Milton Park, Abingdon, Oxon OX14 4RN

Simultaneously published in the USA and Canada
by Routledge
270 Madison Ave, New York, NY 10016

Routledge is an imprint of the Taylor & Francis Group, an informa business

© 2010 Susan I. Hangen

Typeset in Times by Wearset Ltd, Boldon, Tyne and Wear
Printed and bound in India by Nutech Photolithographers, New Delhi.

British Library Cataloguing in Publication Data
A catalogue record for this book is available from the British Library

Library of Congress Cataloging in Publication Data
Hangen, Susan I.
The rise of ethnic politics in Nepal: democracy in the margins/Susan I. Hangen.
p. cm. – (Routledge contemporary south asia series v. 25)
Includes bibliographical references.
1. Political anthropology–Nepal. 2. Politics and culture–Nepal. 3. Indigenous peoples–Nepal–Politics and government. 4. Nepal–Ethnic relations–Political aspects. 5. Nepal–Politics and government. I. Title.
GN635.N425.H365 2009
954.96–dc22   2009026550

ISBN10: 0-415-77884-0

ISBN 978-0-415-77884-8

FOR SALE IN NEPAL ONLY.

Contents

Figures

All photographs are by the author, except for Figure C.1, courtesy of Man Kumar Gurung.

Tables

Acknowledgments

Over the many years that I have worked on this project, many people have offered me many forms of assistance. My greatest debt is to the people of Ilam and Jhapa, who opened their homes and their lives to me. This project would have been impossible without their support. I am particularly grateful to Gopal Gurung, Kiran Akten and his family, and all of the people of the village in Ilam I call Maidel. I also thank MNO supporters in Kathmandu for their assistance.

I thank all of the activists in the indigenous nationalities movement in Kathmandu who have shared their time and ideas with me, including Ganesh Man Gurung, Om Gurung, Arjun Limbu, Bal Krishna Mabuhang and Parsuram Tamang.

Tika Gurung made major contributions to this project by assisting me with research in Ilam and Jhapa in the 1990s, and our conversations have influenced this book in countless ways. Sangita Gurung helped me by transcribing taped interviews in 1997 and by conducting interviews with activists in 2006. For research assistance in 2008, I thank Rashmi Tamang.

My initial field research between 1994 and 1997 was generously funded by the Fulbright Foundation (IIE), Sigma Xi Society Grant-in-Aid of Research, a Social Science Research Council/American Council of Learned Societies Dissertation Research Fellowship and a Wenner-Gren Foundation for Anthropological Research Pre-doctoral Grant. Funding for research between 2003 and 2008 was provided by Ramapo College of NJ SBR Grants. The Faculty Resource Network at New York University supported my work during the summers of 2004 and 2005, when I was a summer scholar in residence there.

Many colleagues have played an important role in shaping my ideas in this book. I am very thankful to people who read and offered detailed critical comments on part or all of the manuscript: David Gellner, Laura Kunreuther, Mahendra Lawoti, Anne Rademacher and Anna Stirr. Many other people have influenced my thinking through their invaluable feedback on my conference presentations and articles, including Krishna Bhattachan, Mary Des Chene, Bill Fisher, Jim Fisher, Arjun Guneratne, Krishna Hachhethu, David Holmberg, Lauren Leve, Kath March, Pratyoush Onta, Tom Robertson, Sara Shneiderman, Seira Tamang, Mukta Tamang and Deepak Thapa. The shortcomings of this book are my responsibility, of course.

Finally, I am grateful to Tika Gurung and Jaya Gurung for their love, patience and support during the many years I have devoted to this project.

Permissions

I thank publishers of my earlier monograph and articles for granting permission for me to use those ideas in this book. Parts of Chapter 2 of this publication were originally published as East–West Center Policy Studies 34, titled 'Creating a "New Nepal": The Ethnic Dimension.' Other parts of Chapter 2 were published in the article 'Race and the Politics of Identity in Nepal' in *Ethnology*, 44(1), copyright © 2005 by The University of Pittsburgh. Parts of Chapter 6 were originally published in the article 'Boycotting Dasain: History, Memory and Ethnic Problems in Nepal', in *Studies in Nepali History and Society*, 10(1), 2005. Some ideas from my article 'Between Political Party and Social Movement: The Mongol National Organization and Democratization in Rural East Nepal', in *Contentious Politics and Democratization in Nepal*, published by Sage Publications, 2007, appear in various places in this book.

Notes on Nepali transliteration

Nepali is written in the Devanagari script. I have transliterated Nepali words into English by following Guneratne's (2002) adaptation of Turner's (1931) system of transliteration from *A Comparative and Etymological Dictionary of the Nepali Language*. Like Guneratne, I transliterate Turner's c as ch, ch as chh, and s, ś and ṣ as s.

The official calendar system of Nepal is the *vikram sambat* calendar. This calendar is roughly 57 years ahead of the Gregorian calendar, and its new year begins in the middle of April in the Gregorian calendar. Dates that are given in *vikram sambat* are marked with 'v.s.' following the date. Sources that are published in Nepal typically list the *vikram sambat* date as the year of publication. For these sources, I use the *vikram sambat* date.

Villages and individuals in this book are identified with pseudonyms. I have only used the real names of widely-known political figures such as Gopal Gurung.

Introduction

Democracy and ethnic politics

In April 2006, hundreds of thousands of people flooded the streets of Nepal to demand the restoration of democracy. This 19-day movement, now called the second people's movement, was in many ways a political watershed for the country. After ten years of a Maoist insurgency, an alliance of seven major political parties and the Maoists launched the movement to end four years of direct rule by the king. The contrasts between the first people's movement of 1990, which ushered in a multi-party system, and the 2006 movement are striking. Whereas the 1990 movement was confined largely to the capital city of Kathmandu and the other cities in the valley, in 2006, people throughout the country, including rural areas, staged protests. In 1990, people demanded a democratic form of government; in 2006, they sought not merely to restore multi-party politics, but to completely transform the state and create a 'new Nepal'. The outcome of the 2006 movement was unprecedented: the king was forced to relinquish power, and the new ruling coalition declared Nepal a secular state, created a new interim constitution, and held elections in 2008 to a constituent assembly to write a new constitution. The Constituent Assembly abolished the monarchy, declaring Nepal a federal democratic republic.

The 2006 movement and its aftermath revealed that a dramatic transformation had taken place since 1990: people became more politicized, especially in rural Nepal, and they began to make more radical demands. Yet the scholarly record offers little insight into how these changes occurred. This book sheds light on these political shifts and the democratization process by examining one of the most significant social movements to emerge since 1990 – the indigenous nationalities movement. This movement brought numerous politically and culturally marginalized ethnic groups together to end the political and social dominance of high-caste Hindus, demand greater representation in the political system and revive their own waning cultural practices. By focusing on an ethnic political party within this movement, the Mongol National Organization (MNO), and its mobilization in rural eastern Nepal, the book provides a view of the democratization process after 1990 beyond the political center in the capital city.

Scholarly and popular attention to Nepali politics has concentrated on the Maoist People's War that the Communist Party of Nepal (Maoist) waged from 1996 to 2006 (Hutt 2004; Onesto 2005; Thapa 2003, 2004). The Maoists gained control of most of the countryside through this insurgency, became part of the ruling coalition after the 2006 people's movement, and won the largest block of seats in the Constituent Assembly elections in 2008. During the decade-long war, 13,000 lives were lost in battles between the Maoists and the state forces, and hundreds of thousands of people were displaced from their rural homes.

Although the role of the Maoists in Nepali politics is significant, numerous other political parties and social movements have also been part of the process of political and social change in the post-1990 era. Unlike the Maoists, many of these other forces did not employ violence and coercion to create changes. This study of the indigenous nationalities movement is a step towards understanding these other political forms.

Ethnic politics have become increasingly central in Nepali politics. In 1990, issues of ethnic rights were ignored in the mainstream political discourse. Over time, the state became more responsive to the indigenous nationalities movement, most notably by establishing the National Foundation for the Development of Indigenous Nationalities in 2002. After the April 2006 movement, the ruling coalition implemented changes that matched many of the indigenous nationalities movement's long-standing demands to remove symbols of high-caste and royal privilege. They changed the state from a Hindu to a secular polity, curtailed the power of the monarchy, wrote a new interim constitution that gives more rights to marginalized groups, and held elections to a constituent assembly in 2008. These changes demonstrate the indigenous nationalities movement's considerable influence on contemporary political discourse.

These legislative changes, however, have not resolved ethnic political demands. Protests by ethnic political groups, who include the Madhesi peoples from the Tarai, Nepal's southern plains, as well as the indigenous nationalities, became increasingly vociferous and violent after 2006. Adamant that they should not be excluded from the new political system, these groups demanded that the new constitution grant regional autonomy to ethnic groups, create a federal rather than unitary polity and institute a proportional system of representation in all public institutions, including the Constituent Assembly. Protests by these groups continued after 2008 and have delayed the country's efforts to regain political stability. Many of the biggest challenges that the Constituent Assembly faces concern ethnic political issues. Ethnic politics will play a major role in Nepal's political future.

This book traces the rise of ethnic politics and the democratization process in Nepal since 1990. It focuses on the mobilization of the Mongol National Organization, an ethnic political party based in rural Nepal, primarily during the mid-1990s, drawing from ethnographic fieldwork. The book sheds light on how people in the margins interpreted and engaged with the democratic political system that was instituted in 1990. To understand the changes in the political structure and in political practices that occurred after 1990, the book explores the strategies and experiences of the MNO as it maneuvered through the political system in its bid for power. I consider the structural challenges the MNO faced as a new ethnic party, and its capacity to create cultural and political changes.

Centered on the experiences and roles of individuals in the party, the book analyzes democracy from a cultural perspective and provides a grounded view of ethnic political organizing outside the capital city. I investigate why the party's discourse about ethnic inequality made sense to rural people in eastern Nepal and how people's cultural practices and interpretations of their lives changed as a result of their involvement in the party.

Ethnic parties like the MNO frequently emerge in new democracies around the world, and yet scholars and policy makers often presume that they threaten democracy. Ethnic parties are often a response to the discourse of democracy and to democratic institutions; they may have the potential to strengthen democratic political systems.

Ethnic parties like the MNO elicit a deeply personal engagement in politics. They give people compelling reasons to become affiliated with them: they offer historical narratives about ethnic divisions and inequality that people use to explain their own social position and problems, and to frame their lives. Through their participation in these parties, people adopt new cultural practices and change how they identify themselves. Thus, these parties lead people to reshape their visions of society and, in turn, to view themselves as political actors who have the capacity to change society.

By connecting political change with the transformation of everyday practices, ethnic political parties can develop and deepen the participation of people in the political realm. Such participation and involvement of citizens in politics is a necessity for a democracy. Through examining these aspects of the MNO, this book shows that ethnic parties can be compatible with democracy and that democratization can proceed in diverse and unexpected ways.

The MNO

In September 1994, just four years after a multi-party political system was restored in Nepal, a group of 25 men and women who belonged to a political party called the Mongol National Organization came to meet with me in their village in the hills of far-eastern Nepal. As we crowded on the porch of a local activist's home to escape the rain, these people told me why they joined the party and what they hoped the party would achieve.

An elderly Rai man said Mongols were like *sinkī*, pungent fermented radishes that are buried for a month or more before they are unearthed. Things had changed since 1990, he proclaimed: 'These days, we are starting to get a little air!' A middle-aged Rai woman who worked at the health care post continued this theme: 'These days, since democracy (*prajātantra*) came, we have a little light. We can at least call ourselves Mongols.' Another man asserted, 'The 20 percent are oppressing the 80 percent. The MNO was formed to bring up the Mongols. Our goal is for the Mongols to have power. We also hope to let the international arena hear about our cause.' A Limbu woman who ran for election in the village government as an MNO candidate lamented the fact that not all Mongols supported the MNO, because it lacked cash. 'If the Congress Party were holding this program they would have had a budget of 20,000 rupees for it! The MNO party pays for nothing,' she exclaimed, as everyone laughed. Before the meeting disbanded, the prosperous Rai man who hosted the event urged me to send my book to the Nepali government, explaining, 'Those who have dirt in their eye can't see it themselves but others can see it. It's up to America to show the Nepali government that there are no human rights here.'

At this gathering, one of my first meetings with MNO supporters and activists, people enthusiastically expressed many of the themes that I would hear repeatedly over the next three years of fieldwork in eastern Nepal. Foremost, people from dozens of ethnic groups, including Rais, Sherpas, Gurungs, Tamangs, Limbus and Magars, stated that they were Mongols who together formed the majority of the population, while the Hindus who had long ruled the country were a minority group. They linked the Mongol identity to the emergence of the democracy, which gave them the freedom to call themselves Mongols. They spoke of the exhilarating possibilities of political change in the new democracy, using metaphors of light and air, but were somber about the challenges that their young, cash-poor party faced in competing with well-established parties like the Nepali Congress Party and the Nepali Communist Party. They were acutely aware of the international arena and its discourse of human rights – a political realm beyond the Nepali state that they hoped to connect with in order to gain leverage for their movement; they also expressed their expectations that I, as a US citizen, would provide this link for them by documenting the oppression of Mongols and their lack of human rights.

The MNO emerged when ethnic politics gained momentum after the political changes of 1990. Marginalized ethnic groups came together and formed many different organizations in order to demand an end to the long-standing dominance of high-caste Hindus. These diverse ethnic groups forged new collective identities, calling themselves indigenous nationalities (*ādivāsi janajāti*) or members of a Mongol race, and emerged as a critical political force. Their organizations aimed to increase the social, economic and political power of these ethnic groups, and to revive their cultural practices, which waned during the Panchayat era (1962–1990) when the state worked to create a homogeneous Hindu Nepali nation. This movement also worked to make sweeping changes to Nepal's political structure, so as to end ethnic inequality and achieve a more democratic state.

The MNO was initially one of the few ethnic political parties in this movement, and one of the smaller of the dozens of political parties that emerged after 1990. It aimed to gain political power for a collective of over 60 linguistically and culturally diverse ethnic groups. As a way of uniting this heterogeneous population, the MNO called these people 'Mongols', reviving a racial term that originated in nineteenth-century British ethnology. The MNO argued that Mongols, the indigenous peoples who form the majority of the population, have been politically and culturally dominated by high-caste Hindus, whom they call 'Aryans'. The MNO was one of the first organizations to advocate ending ethnic inequality by implementing structural changes such as reorganizing Nepal into a system of federal states, and eliminating the monarchy.

In the mid-1990s, the MNO began arguing that a real democracy would mean *loktantra* (power to the people), since *prajātantra* (the post-1990 political system) was a limited form of democracy, which gave power to people only as subjects (*prajā*) of the king (Hangen 2001). These ideas for transforming the country were extremely radical when the party founder, Gopal Gurung, first articulated them in the 1980s but became part of mainstream political discourse by 2006, largely due to the influence of the Maoists, rather than the MNO.

The party faced significant challenges in its quest to gain power for Mongols through the electoral system, and did not become a major player on the national level. The MNO won many seats in several village governments in Ilam district, yet never won a seat in parliament. Much newer than other parties, the MNO had few party workers with substantial experience or financial resources to contribute. MNO candidates could only run as 'independents' in elections: the Election Commission refused to register the MNO, following Nepal's 1990 constitution which prohibited political parties that refer to religious, ethnic or other communities in their party names and manifestos.[1] They perceived this rule as a restriction of democracy, especially as candidates who secretly represented political parties in the Panchayat era, when political parties were banned, could not list their party affiliations on the ballot. Furthermore, since village governments had little power to form or shape policy, the party could not implement its plans to make radical changes in the structure and policies of the state unless it won seats in parliament.

Although its form as an ethnic political party made it oppositional, the MNO worked within the democratic political framework. The party participated in local and parliamentary elections, and campaigned according to the rules. Though it was denied registration by the Election Commission, party leaders sought to rectify this by filing court cases.

The party's commitment to the electoral process, however, was not unconditional, as it threatened to use force to gain power if it was ultimately unsuccessful through elections. In party documents and speeches, activists and leaders declared that the revolution would begin 'within five years' if they did not achieve power, yet these deadlines were perpetually postponed. The symbolism of the MNO party flag depicts this dual approach to gaining power. The upper diagonal half of the rectangular flag shows a five-pointed star on a blue background, standing for peaceful methods of political action, while the lower diagonal half depicts a *khukurī*, a long curved knife used by Gurkha soldiers and by villagers, on a red background, symbolizing the threat of violence and bloodshed. MNO party songs also used images of violence that invoked martial masculinity to mobilize people, as discussed in Chapter 5. Such images glorified violence and aimed to prepare people to take up arms for the MNO.

Although the MNO won no seats in parliament, it made an impact in the rural areas where it mobilized support. The party stimulated public discussion about issues of ethnic equality. Many people who supported the MNO became passionately involved in politics for the first times in their lives. They came to think of themselves in a new way, as Mongols, and reinterpreted, questioned or changed their religion and other cultural practices. Their involvement in the party brought them to ask new questions, make new demands and change their view of their own relationship to the rest of society and the state. These cultural transformations formed part of the process of democratization.

Studying the MNO: ethnographic orientations

I began research on this project in the summer of 1993, and conducted most of the fieldwork between 1994 and 1997 in rural eastern Nepal. In five shorter trips to Nepal between 2000 and 2008, I followed up on changes in the MNO and the indigenous nationalities movement. Due to the Maoist conflict, I was not able to travel to eastern Nepal after 2000, but while in Kathmandu, I met with MNO activists from Ilam and other districts. Tracking the MNO over these years allowed me to understand the significance of the party in the context of the political transformations that have unfolded in Nepal.

My interest in ethnic politics in Nepal began with my observations of inequality between high-caste Hindus and other caste and ethnic groups during my earlier visits to the country in 1987 and 1990. While pursuing my graduate degree in anthropology, I read Lionel Caplan's classic book, *Land and Social Change in East Nepal*, which documents how Limbus in Ilam district lost land to high-caste Hindu settlers in the area, and their political responses to their increasing subjugation. When I visited Nepal in the summer 1993, I found that ethnic politics had resurfaced in the new multi-party democracy. Ethnic organizations in Kathmandu were sponsoring numerous seminars, meetings and cultural performances, and producing new publications. The Mongol National Organization differed from these organizations as it was a political party and because it was based in rural Ilam. I began investigating the MNO in order to learn more about politics in rural Nepal, as few scholars other than Caplan had written about this.

My fieldwork in rural eastern Nepal was multi-sited, enabling me to observe the MNO at several organizational levels. Part of my study was based in a village in Ilam district, for which I use the pseudonym Maidel. There, the MNO won more seats in the village government, called a Village Development Committee (VDC), than it did in any other village. I was drawn to this site in order to learn about how the MNO gained support there, how the party ran the village government, and the social and cultural effects of people's engagement with this party.

Maidel has a population of nearly 3,000 and covers an entire mountain, stretching from lowlands rice fields to alpine pastures at 12,000 feet. All VDCs are divided into nine wards, each with representation on the village government. These wards encompass and often cut across hamlets, or clusters of houses, which are usually occupied by people from a single ethnic group. Although I traveled throughout Maidel VDC, I was based in one ward that was the social and political center of the village. The majority of residents in this ward were from the Gurung ethnic group. My husband, Tika Gurung, accompanied me for over half of my time in the village and, although he is from a different part of Nepal, Gurungs in Maidel related to him as kin, and extended this fictive kinship to me. We lived in a Gurung household headed by the chairman of the VDC, an MNO member, providing me with a good vantage point on village politics.

In addition to participating in and observing village life, I collected interviews with over 100 party activists and supporters in Maidel. Because of the political nature of my research, I relied on party networks to find individuals to interview, rather than using a random sampling method. District-level activists first introduced me to village-level MNO leaders in Maidel, and these people in turn introduced me to others in the MNO. Following standard ethnographic practice, I use pseudonyms for all place names and individuals to protect the identity of those individuals who shared their stories with me and who I write about here. I use real names for two MNO leaders, Gopal Gurung and Kiran Akten, who wanted credit for their ideas and contributions to the party.

Much of my research took place outside of Maidel. I traveled throughout Ilam and Jhapa districts to study MNO activity beyond the village level, including the operations of the organization, party networks, and the creation and dissemination of the MNO's ideas. I interviewed key activists in the district network and attended party events such as mass-meetings, conferences and district-level meetings. I returned many times to the village homes of influential activists and frequented Ilam bazaar, the district headquarters, to attend district-level meetings and meet with MNO activists from all parts of Ilam. Finally, I studied the wider indigenous nationalities movement in Kathmandu by meeting with activists, collecting publications and attending public events.

Conducting research with members of a radical political party during a time of political transition was challenging because of the inherently political dimensions of the study of local politics, noted by other anthropologists as well (Aretxaga 1997; Pettigrew 1981). Both supporters of the MNO and of other political parties saw my research as a form of advocacy for the MNO. In the village of Maidel, some people from other political parties were not pleased when I told them I was studying the MNO. At their request, the local police interrogated me about my research shortly after I arrived. Rumors that the CIA or the Nepali government had hired me also circulated.

MNO supporters demanded assurance that my research would be devoted to the MNO rather than other parties, that I supported the MNO and its goals, and that I was not sent by either the Nepali or American government to undermine the party. After deciding that my presence was benign, leaders and prominent activists became enthusiastic about my research. At public gatherings they proclaimed that my research would benefit the MNO, as I would publicize their struggle to the world and help them gain international support for their cause. These party leaders encouraged everyone to assist me, emphasizing that helping me would help the MNO. However, many people in the party were slow to trust me. Given the restrictions on speaking freely about politics during the Panchayat era, which ended just a few years before I began my research, and the MNO's status as an unregistered party, this was not surprising.

While my access to this community was dependent upon my demonstrating a certain level of sympathy with the MNO's political project, I maintained a cautiously critical perspective on the party in my discussions with MNO members. In the later period of my fieldwork in particular, I shared my views on weaknesses in party organizing and inconsistencies between the party's practices and ideology with MNO leaders and activists. I explained how my view of race, among other topics, diverged from theirs. Although Gopal Gurung and some activists expressed their frustration that they could not convince me of the truth as they saw it, they still encouraged me to write about the party.

When Gopal Gurung read my dissertation, he had many critical comments, but his overall response was positive. He promptly printed up a leaflet to distribute throughout east Nepal, announcing that I had completed my 'Ph.D. on the MNO', and published a short book with the title *In Quest of Mongol Identity and Doctorate (PhD) on the MNO*, clearly referring to my work. In this book, he included a photo of me but wrote little about my ideas, instead reiterating many of the points from his earlier writings on the plight of Mongols. For Gopal Gurung, the fact that I wrote about his organization was potential political capital, enabling him to claim that his cause has attracted international attention.

As a woman, I experienced challenges in studying the male-dominated domain of formal politics in Nepal. Most MNO activists are men, and I was frequently the only woman at party meetings. Many men talked to me at length, helped me meet other MNO activists and supporters, and brought me to public events. However, because socializing is sex-segregated, my interactions with these men in groups were somewhat limited. I had access to men's public statements about politics, but I did not hear many of the huddled conversations that took place while men squatted in a circle and shared chewing tobacco. While I befriended many women, very few of them were interested in discussing the MNO's ideas in depth or participated in formal political activities. Fortunately, my husband Tika formed close bonds with men in the village, since he is Nepali and grew up in a village. Tika greatly assisted me in learning more about men's lives and activities.

Eastern Nepal: the MNO heartland in the 1990s

In the mid-1990s, when I conducted the initial and most intensive research on the MNO, the party's main sphere of influence and operation was eastern Nepal. While the party established district committees in eight of Nepal's 75 districts during those years, it was most active in two districts in east Nepal, Ilam and Jhapa (see the map in Figure I.1).[2] My research was centered in Ilam, where the MNO had the most support. Ilam forms part of the eastern border between Nepal and India. The district includes a small section of Tarai land in the south; but terraced hills, lush from Ilam's ubiquitous fog and rain, cover most of the territory. Some of these 'hills' reach heights of over 12,000 feet, and the snowy crest of Kanchenjunga, the third-highest mountain in the world, is visible from some hilltops on rare clear days. I also conducted research in Jhapa district, which lies

Figure I.1 Map of Nepal.

south of Ilam in the fertile plains, the Tarai, and shares a southern and eastern border with India.

The MNO's ability to mobilize support in eastern Nepal in the 1990s is related to the region's distinct social composition, political history and economy. Eastern Nepal is an extremely ethnically diverse region. In general, there has been a pattern of migration from the western to the eastern part of the country. Several ethnic groups, most notably Limbus and Rais, claim large parts of the east as their ancestral homeland; however, many other groups have migrated into the region, including Gurungs, Magars, Tamangs and low- and high-caste Hindus. The MNO gained the support of ethnic groups that historically occupied the area, as well as of the more recently migrated indigenous nationalities groups.

The economy of the eastern region is distinct as it is more market oriented than many other regions outside of the capital. Cash crops, including tea, dairy products, fruit, vegetables, cardamom, angora wool and a variety of grass used in making brooms, play an important role in agricultural production there. Nearly every household in the village in Ilam that was my main research site produced agricultural goods for the market, selling them to buyers from India or at the weekly markets (*hāṭ bazār*). The cash earned from this trade enabled many farmers to build brightly painted wooden homes, with glass windows and tin roofs, and to engage in innovative development projects such as cultivating silk, generating water-powered electricity and farming fish.

This market economy has a long history in the region, and may have roots in the British efforts to develop commercial agriculture in the eastern region of the Himalayas, as this area was closest to sea ports such as Calcutta on the Bay of

Bengal (English 1985: 71). Weekly markets existed throughout the region from the nineteenth century onwards (Stiller 1976), and many towns are named after the day of the week on which the market is held. The distinct, more lenient tax structures in the eastern hills of Nepal in the nineteenth century enabled farmers there to produce surplus agricultural products which they could trade (ibid.: 141–143). Since the 1960s, a network of roads in the area has accelerated this market-based economy by providing farmers with a means of transporting agricultural goods to markets.

Eastern Nepal is close to Darjeeling, a district and urban center in West Bengal, which lies just across the eastern border. For residents of east Nepal, the border is only an administrative marker. There is an open border between Nepal and India; citizens of these countries do not require visas or any form of documentation to move it. The border between Ilam and Darjeeling was only monitored along motorable roads, and was not clearly demarcated in many places. Many people in eastern Nepal have family members across the border, and move back and forth across it during their lives for marriage, family visits, work or education.

With this proximity to Darjeeling, people in eastern Nepal had access to education before most people in other parts of Nepal. While public secular education was virtually non-existent in Nepal until after 1950, the British began establishing secular schools in Darjeeling in 1846, and there were about 400 schools there in 1950–1951 (Magar 1994: 48). Residents of east Nepal who had the resources to do so could attend schools in these areas, and people in the region told me that this was a common practice. People from Darjeeling have also set up schools or taught in schools in Ilam and Jhapa. The MNO's founder and president, Gopal Gurung, was raised in Darjeeling and first came to Ilam district as a teacher.

In this social and economic context, many revolutionary political movements have emerged in east Nepal. The Limbus fought Prithvi Narayan Shah's army in the eighteenth century, eventually signing a treaty with the state, and continued to resist the authority of the Nepali state, as will be discussed in Chapter 1 (Caplan 1970). The region has been a stronghold for leftist politics since the mid-1950s. Communist organizations mobilized in the region after the fall of the Rana regime. In the 1970s, communists in Jhapa who were inspired by the Naxalites in India launched an armed insurgency known as the Jhapali movement (Hachhethu 2002a).

Ethnic political movements in neighboring Darjeeling and Sikkim were a source of inspiration to the MNO. In the 1980s in Darjeeling, Subash Ghising led the Gorkha National Liberation Front (GNLF), which demanded a separate state within India for Gorkhas, people of Nepali ancestry living in India. While Darjeeling remains within the state of West Bengal, GNLF achieved some autonomy for the area when the Darjeeling Gorkha Hill Council was established in 1988 (Magar 1994). In the Indian state of Sikkim, a political party called the Sikkim Democratic Front (SDF) emerged in 1993, and campaigned against high-caste Hindu political dominance there. Pawan Chamling, the leader of the SDF, was elected to the post of Chief Minister of Sikkim in 1994 (Kazi 1993). After assuming power in Sikkim, the SDF raised the social status of the ethnic groups in their population by officially recognizing Tamang, Gurung, Rai, Magar, Sherpa, Newar and Sunwar languages as 'state languages'. GNLF and SDF provided the MNO with models of what the party might accomplish some day in Nepal.

Thus, eastern Nepal offered a fertile ground for the development of new social and political movements like the MNO. Previous political movements, both in the region in Nepal and across the border, presented models of political organization and ideology. People were relatively economically secure, and could devote time to engaging in political activities. The area's border location provided additional cultural capital, most notably in the form of education. Although these economic, educational and political dimensions of eastern Nepal cannot completely explain why the MNO took root there, the confluence of these various factors created a space in which many people had the material and social resources and inclination to take part in political activities.

Theoretical orientations

Politics in the margins

In focusing on the MNO, this book explores democratization at the margins of the political system. The concept of margins, as I use it here, refers to people, space and discourse. First, it refers to the 'marginal populations' (Das and Poole 2004: 9) who are the focus of this book – the ethnic groups who have been historically under-represented in the state. While marginal in relation to the political center, many individuals in these ethnic groups hold considerable power and prestige within their own communities. Thus, the concept of marginality as it applies to populations is relative to a particular context.

Second, the concept of the margins refers to the political peripheries of the state. Social scientists have widely used the concept of the margins, in this sense, to refer to sites that are beyond state control and which the state views as 'wild' (ibid.: 7). In the context of Nepal, the margins of the state are largely congruent with the space defined as 'rural', referred to as the 'village' (*gāũ*). The village is a social category that is defined in opposition to more urban spaces, including small markets called 'bazaars', district headquarters, where the government offices for each district are located, and larger towns or cities (*sahar*). Nepalis view villages as distinct from these other spaces due to their relative lack of 'development' (*bikās*), a category which refers to material and economic features, such as roads and health care facilities, as well as characteristics of people, such as their degree of awareness or education (Pigg 1992). Implicit in this characterization of rural Nepal as lacking development is the idea that it is peripheral to the market economy. In fact, rural Nepal is increasingly dependent on the market economy. Agriculture remains a key component of the rural economy, but people must supplement farming with a variety of strategies to earn cash, including wage labor in cities or abroad.

Rural Nepal is also marked by its peripheral relationship to the highly central-ized state. Political power remained concentrated in the capital city after the introduction of a multi-party system in 1990; local governments have little autonomy from the center. From the state perspective, villages were assumed to be spaces of little political consequence, where political activity did not affect the center: villages were where political schemes formulated at the center were carried out, rather than generated.

The Maoist insurgency, rooted in rural Nepal, and the burgeoning studies of it disrupted any assumptions that villagers are apolitical or that politics in the village have no impact on the center. Studies of politics in rural Nepal are neces-sary for understanding how people outside the center experienced and partici-pated in the post-1990 political system, as several scholars have noted (Gellner 2002: 25; Hachhethu 2002b; Pfaff-Czarnecka 2004), and yet little scholarship on the topic exists, with some recent exceptions (Gellner and Hachhethu 2008). Most analyses of politics, and of democratization in particular, have been based on the happenings of the state at the political center, in the capital city.

As this study of rural activists in the MNO demonstrates, ordinary people outside of Kathmandu were politically active and engaged between 1990 and 2006, beyond participating in the Maoist insurgency. However, politically active villagers faced limitations in their efforts to create political changes due to the highly centralized yet weak state, among other factors. I ask what political strat-egies were possible for the MNO and what constraints the party faced in its efforts to create political and social change from a rural base.

Third, the idea of the margins refers to political discourses and practices that are not hegemonic: the discourse on ethnic inequality and the organizational form of the ethnic political party. Until 2006, the mainstream politicians and media did not consider the political discourse on ethnic inequality to be legiti-mate and largely ignored it. Ethnic parties were restricted by the 1990 constitu-tion, and viewed as threatening to national unity and democracy. As a small ethnic party based in rural eastern Nepal, the MNO has been a marginal political player at the national level.

By investigating the MNO, I aim to illuminate the margins of Nepal's polit-ical culture after 1990. Although most political analyses ignore minor parties like the MNO, such parties are relevant for studies of the boundaries of political cultures and how they change, as Herzog (1987) argues. Examining these parties can reveal what kinds of ideologies are excluded from the legitimate political culture and can increase 'our knowledge about potential change, about challenging groups and ideas, and about rejected alternatives' (p. 318). Had scholars and policy makers of Nepal paid more attention to minor parties, perhaps the Maoist insurgency, which was launched by a minor political party, would not have been so unexpected. Similarly, the demands for federalism and the abolition of the monarchy that were so central to the second people's move-ment of 2006, and appeared to some observers to have emerged only at that moment, were articulated by the MNO and other ethnic organizations much earlier.

Towards a cultural analysis of democracy

Democracy studies have primarily been conducted by political scientists, who have approached democracy as part of the realm of formal politics. In the past, political scientists emphasized the institutional dimensions of democracy, minimally defining it as a form of governance that employs the procedures and institutions associated with electoral politics (Schumpeter 1962 [1943]). However, most scholars today agree that, in addition to elections, democracies must uphold a set of political ideals and values that enables citizens to participate in the process of governance, including the guarantee of civil liberties, such as freedom of speech and free access to information, and the accountability of the state to citizens (Dahl 1971; Held 1996; Linz and Stepan 2001).

Many political scientists argue that democracy entails not just state institutions, laws and procedures but also the capacity for citizens to influence public policy through a variety of civic and political organizations (Linz and Stepan 2001; Schmitter and Karl 1996). Democracy, in this deeper sense, expands social justice by enabling a wider range of the population to take an active part in the political process. The existence of civil society, a form of associational activity that enables people to influence the state beyond their participation in elections, is also hailed as a necessary feature of democracies. A strong civil society can keep the authoritarian tendencies of the state in check, provide a space for people to engage in debates and discussions on issues of public concern, and instill democratic values such as tolerance and justice among citizens (Diamond 1996; Schmitter and Karl 1996).

Anthropologists have increasingly turned their attention to democracy, and have expanded the scope of inquiry in the field by examining it as a cultural phenomenon (Appadurai 2002; Caldeira and Holston 1999; Coles 2004; Frechette 2007; Goldman 2001; Greenhouse and Greenwood 1998; Gutmann 2002; Ignatowski 2004; Kaplan 2003; Paley 2001, 2002). Some ethnographers have investigated how democracy operates as a discourse that is interpreted through local cultural lenses and thus acquires diverse meanings in particular contexts (Frechette 2007; Gutmann 2002; Ignatowski 2004; Kaplan 2003; Paley 2002; Schaffer 1998). Differently positioned social and political actors may employ the idea of democracy to justify a variety of political projects. People may also use the discourse of democracy outside of the formal political realm as a way of talking about changing social values (Ignatowski 2004; Kaplan 2003). As a discourse, democracy acquires a range of inflections as political actors with disparate goals deploy and adopt it.

Anthropologists also focus on how democracy operates in particular cultural contexts, examining how people engage with the procedures and institutions associated with democratic governance and how it affects people's lives in unexpected and complicated ways (Caldeira and Holston 1999; Gutmann 2002; Paley 2001). Democracy as an ideal form of governance has never been fully achieved; rather, everywhere in the world democracy is 'disjunctive' (Caldeira and Holston 1999: 717). For Caldeira and Holston, democracy in practice in Brazil is disjunctive because there is a gap between the formal political institutions, which exhibit the normative characteristics of democracies, and people's experiences as citizens, as their civil rights to justice and liberty are not upheld. The particular forms of disjuncture that emerge in any democracy vary due to different cultural and historical contexts.

Through examining the mobilization of the MNO in eastern Nepal, this book sheds light on how people outside the political center perceived and experienced democracy and how they participated in creating the political and social changes entailed in democratization. I combine analyses of the discursive dimensions of democracy and the institutional features of democracy as they appear and operate on the ground, following several other anthropologists (Frechette 2007; Paley 2001). This approach entails examining how democracy operates both as an ideal and as a set of real institutions and policies, and how these two dimensions of democracy provide a framework for political action. Democracy as a discourse works in the realm of the imagination, shaping people's ideas of what kinds of politics are possible, what the political system and society should look like, and what kind of society a political movement should aim to create. In the realm of the practical, the institutions and procedures of democracy, such as elections and political parties, determine what kinds of political practice are possible in any particular moment, and influence the effects of those political practices. Structures and practices of the state also shape the character of society and the ability of people to exercise their rights as citizens. By investigating how the democratic procedures and government institutions work on the ground, we gain a more nuanced view of democratization that reveals the disjunctures between the formal and practical elements of the system.

In this book, I attend to the discursive dimensions of democracy, examining how the MNO interpreted the idea of democracy and used it to critique the post-1990 political system and to bring legitimacy to its own quest for power. To study the practice of democracy, I analyze the MNO's efforts to gain political power through political activities like elections and mass-meetings, and consider the party's efforts to create social change through its cultural productions. I show how MNO supporters in rural Nepal experienced democracy as disjunctive as there were gaps between the ideals and practices of democracy.

Ethnic parties and democracy

Ethnic parties, and ethnic politics more broadly, have often been viewed as being incompatible with democracy, even though they frequently emerge in new democracies. Political scientists and governments alike have often regarded ethnic parties as impeding democratization. These parties supposedly mobilize people on the basis of ascribed identities and divert people away from the concerns of the wider population. Horowitz (1985), for example, argues that ethnic parties encourage people to identify in narrow and exclusive ways rather than with the whole society. Political systems in which ethnic parties operate become less democratic because people vote, not as individuals who are concerned with the common good, but rather as groups concerned only with group needs. Because these categories are ascribed, politics take on a fixed character, reduced to a struggle between unchanging ethnic groups, rather than operating as democracies should, as competitions between fluid interest groups that coalesce around a variety of issues (pp. 296–298).

This negative view of ethnic parties and politics stems from the liberal foundations of the democratic ideal, which upholds the rights of individuals as paramount. In this ideal, all citizens are to be equal before the law, and citizens are to act in a universalist manner, shedding any particular group identities. Bringing particular identities into politics would undermine the state's capacity to serve the common good and bias it towards the special needs of certain groups. From this perspective, ethnic politics, and identity politics in general, appear to operate for the service of particular interest groups rather than for universal interests.

Political theorists critique this interpretation of identity politics, which is at the root of the negative view of ethnic parties and politics, in several ways (Gutmann 2003; Kymlicka 2001; Mohapatra 2002; Young 2000). They argue that group-based politics are necessary for achieving social justice because the state is typically not the neutral entity that it normatively should be. Societies are always composed of multiple social groups and the most powerful group often dominates the state. In this context, the ostensibly neutral stance of states towards groups and group rights can serve to legitimize the values of the dominant group. Thus it is necessary to recognize the interests and needs of identity groups in order to ensure that justice is achieved for all groups in society. Public policies that recognize social differences do not just serve particular interests of marginalized groups; rather, they can work to create a more just and democratic state for all citizens (Young 2000: 109–110). By demanding group rights, ethnic parties are calling for a new form of democracy that requires states to recognize and treat citizens as heterogeneous rather than as undifferentiated individuals, as Yashar argues for indigenous movements in Latin America (2005: 281–300).

The idea that ethnic parties threaten democracy because they lead to a fixed political competition between ethnic groups is mistaken. Voters who align themselves with ethnic parties are still making a choice. Not all people who could affiliate with an ethnic party do so; not all who are potential members of the community as the political party defines it identify themselves as such. The assumption that identity politics mobilize ascribed identities must also be examined more closely (Chandra 2004; Young 2000). Ethnic parties often claim that the identities of the people they represent are given at birth and have ancient roots; however, most social scientists would disagree. As anthropologists and other social scientists have argued for several decades, ethnic identities are not primordial or fixed but, rather, are constructed in particular social contexts. Ethnic identification is a highly fluid process. Power relations structure the formation and definition of ethnic identities, including relationships between different groups, and the relationships between ethnic groups and the state. New political contexts in which power relations are altered often bring about efforts to redefine ethnic identities. From this perspective, the identities that ethnic parties mobilize may be framed as primordial but they are in fact no more stable than identities that are mobilized through other political parties. Identities that are marked by primordial symbols may change and thus do not create the static cleavages and deadlocked political systems that theorists like Horowitz supposed would emerge from ethnic politics.

The identities that the MNO and other ethnic parties and organizations are mobilizing in Nepal are likewise not primordial; rather, these organizations are coalitions of numerous ethnic groups that are themselves internally diverse, and they have created new identities that encompass these groups. The MNO constructed a new collective identity by positing a single Mongol race that shares a common history. Although the Mongol category refers to the idea of a primordial racial unity, it actually brings together culturally diverse ethnic groups. Mongol is an ethnic category that emerged in a particular political history and context, and for particular political purposes; its use and meaning may change or fade over time as the political context changes.

Instead of an atavistic challenge to democracy, the creation of collective identities and the mobilization of these identities for political purposes can be a response to the institutions of democracy. Political parties must give voters a reason to align themselves with one particular party rather than another. Claiming that the party represents an identity in addition to a set of interests is a powerful way to do this. Ethnic parties seek to create a direct identification between individuals and a set of issues; they do not merely mobilize pre-existing identities. Furthermore, people can better represent their interests to elected officials and influence the process of policy making when they act as groups.

Ethnic movements, and ethnic parties can also be catalyzed by the idea of equality in the discourse of democracy. Chantal Mouffe (1988) argues that identity-based social movements arise within democracies because the discourse of democracy constructs political subjects as citizens who should all be equal. There is a disjuncture between this democratic discourse of equality and the ways in which other hegemonic discourses of gender, ethnicity or race construct some political subjects as subordinate to others. People begin to question these discourses and struggle for equality '...because they have been constructed as subjects in a democratic tradition that puts those values at the center of social life' (p. 95). As social cleavages are often constructed as ethnic differences, struggles against systems of subordination also take on an ethnic character.

In addition to responding to the institutions of and discourse on democracy, ethnic parties may also strengthen democratic institutions. Some political scientists argue that ethnic parties can play a positive role in the democratization process (Madrid 2005; Van Cott 2005: 228–232). Ethnic parties increase the political representation of marginalized groups. This has the subsequent effect of increasing the legitimacy of the democratic system from the perspective of the marginalized groups. Second, they increase marginalized groups' participation in elections. Third, these parties are more connected and responsive to their constituencies than traditional parties, and introduce more transparent means of conducting politics. Fourth, ethnic parties could reduce party system fragmentation and electoral volatility because marginalized groups will continue to support these parties, as they better address their interests.

These insights provide an important model for reinterpreting the role of ethnic parties in democratic systems. However, in making these arguments, political scientists focus on the performance of ethnic parties in elections, following the dominant mode of assessing political parties in their discipline. Van Cott (2005), for example, compares ethnic parties across Latin America and argues that certain legal and institutional conditions enable ethnic parties to form and become electorally viable.[3] Ethnographic studies of ethnic parties can reveal additional ways in which we can view the relationship between ethnic parties and democracies.

In this ethnographic study of the MNO, I take a more expansive view of what counts as politics than political science studies typically do. In addition to the activities and operations of the formal political realm – such as village government operations, elections, and political party meetings – cultural activities through which people try to influence the political system or change the balance of power are an important part of politics. Political participation means not just voting, as it does for many political scientists; it also includes other forms of political activity such as taking an active role in the party organization, or creating songs, skits or other cultural productions that advance political ideas. This broader view of the political realm results in a different picture of the significance of ethnic political parties, which is not limited to election results.

If the MNO and other ethnic parties in Nepal were assessed solely on their performance in elections, their significance could be overlooked. Most ethnic parties in Nepal have not fared well at the polls when compared with other political parties, and thus have received little scholarly attention – with a few exceptions (Lawoti 2005; Lecomte-Tilouine 2004).[4] Yet the MNO did more than participate in elections with lackluster results. Rather it presented challenges to the dominant discourse through speeches and writings, but also through cultural activities such as staging public boycotts of Dasain, the major national Hindu holiday. Even participation in elections had meaning beyond the outcome for the MNO. It was a form of contentious politics, a way of publicizing and critiquing the state's refusal to view ethnic parties as legitimate political players. The MNO tested the boundaries of the political system, pointing to ways in which the state was not meeting the ideal of democracy. The party constructed Mongol as a new political identity, bringing diverse groups of people together in order to create political and social changes. Through forging this identity, the party expanded political participation, leading people who did not think of themselves as political actors to become involved in politics.

My analysis of the MNO shows that, when viewed from an ethnographic perspective, ethnic parties share much in common with social movement organizations. The MNO's operation as both a political party and a social movement organization is not uncommon in Nepal. Most political parties 'evolved as movement organizations' (Hachhethu 2002b: 183) as they were not allowed to operate openly as parties during much of the country's history. Political parties spearheaded many major political changes, from the overthrow of the Rana family's autocratic rule in 1950, to the demands for a multi-party system in 1990. They continued to play this role through the 1990s and have led efforts to restore democracy after February 2005. Indeed, people in Nepal expect political parties to act as agents of social change (2005: 162).

Although political parties and social movement organizations are different in that the latter do not seek to gain direct political power, ethnic parties often engage in activities that are typically associated with social movement organizations. Like social movement organizations, ethnic parties aim to define, raise awareness about and mobilize support for a particular cluster of social issues, and engage a wide range of people in the political process of debating and working for social change. They engage in significant political activities beyond elections, such as expanding the participation of marginalized groups, broadening political discourse, and constructing new identities instigating changes in cultural practices. In these activities, ethnic parties may contribute to the process of democratization.

Organization of this book

In the chapters that follow, I examine the MNO as a way of understanding the rise of ethnic politics after 1990 and democratization in rural Nepal. Chapter 1 provides the historical context for understanding ethnic politics in Nepal. The chapter reviews Nepal's political history, then examines the complexities of ethnic diversity and the origins and scope of ethnic inequality. High-caste Hindu rulers gained dominance with the process of state building that began in the late eighteenth century. They pursued policies and constructed forms of nationalism that upheld ethnic inequality. During the Panchayat era (1962–1990), the state sought to assimilate the linguistically and culturally diverse groups in its territory into a homogeneous Hindu, Nepali language-speaking nation. Although the political changes of 1990 brought greater political and cultural freedom, ethnic inequality persisted, and subordinated groups mobilized to demand further changes in the polity.

Chapter 2 outlines the rise of the indigenous nationalities movement after 1990 and its major goals. The chapter compares the main types of organizations in the movement: indigenous peoples' organizations representing individual ethnic groups, the Nepal Federation of Indigenous Nationalities (NEFIN), a Kathmandu-based federation of over 50 of these organizations, and ethnic parties. Ethnic parties like the MNO have a relatively marginal place within the movement, and their participation in elections in the 1990s is reviewed here. The construction of a pan-ethnic identity for the diverse groups the movement sought to mobilize is one of the most significant outcomes of the movement. The chapter examines the meanings of the *ādivāsī janajāti* label that NEFIN advanced and the Mongol identity that the MNO forwarded.

Chapter 3 considers how the MNO, as a small, rural, low-budget and unregistered political party, operated as an organization in post-1990 Nepal. The chapter introduces the party's founder, Gopal Gurung, describing his life history and the core ideas in his most popular book. The chapter describes the party's organizational structure, and the various roles that people could hold in the party: supporter, activists or leader. Women were marginally involved in the party, although a women's wing existed for a few years. Through activities such as traveling, district assembly, and mass-meetings, people attempted to connect the different levels of the party and to build support for it. The structure of the party was both informal and centralized, which left village-level activists with little ability to initiate party activities.

Chapter 4 highlights the possibilities and limitations of political action in the margins in the 1990s by examining the operations of the MNO in the village. I trace the history of party mobilization in the Maidel, a village in east Nepal, where the party gained control of the local government. Elected officials from the MNO in the village government could do little to advance the MNO's goals of making radical changes in the state, and operated the village government much as representatives from other parties did. While village governments did not control resources or set local policies, they provided a space in which people could advance radical political ideas.

Support for the MNO in the village had multiple meanings. Some Panchayat era leaders joined the party to legitimize their participation in the new system; other people were attracted to the party's commitment to ending ethnic inequality, which resonated with people due to their negative interactions with the high-caste Hindus representing the state. Democratic practices were unevenly adopted in the village, as illustrated in local election campaigns and the relationships between factions and political parties. Although the MNO aimed to unite all Mongols as supporters of their party, different political party affiliations in the village led to conflicts between individuals in these ethnic groups.

Chapters 5 analyzes the MNO's efforts to create a unified Mongol identity through cultural productions: an MNO calendar that presented an alternative to the national *vikram sambat* calendar; a celebration of Tihar, a national Hindu holiday, that was reinterpreted as a Mongol holiday; MNO songs that defined Mongols as brave, masculine warriors who should fight for their rights in their own country; and an MNO cassette that celebrated the diversity of Mongols. In these cultural productions, the MNO challenged the dominant construction of the Nepali nation. The MNO also aimed to counter the focus on individual ethnic group identity advanced by the indigenous nationalities organizations, by creating a sense of cultural unity among Mongols that still allowed for the internal diversity of Mongols. As this project was fraught with complications, the MNO often resorted to defining Mongol identity by referring to the political party instead of defining a Mongol culture.

Chapter 6 continues this exploration of the MNO's involvement in cultural transformations at the village level by examining the history and multiple meanings of religious change among the Gurung community in Maidel. At the end of the Panchayat era, Gurungs in the village decided to quit Hinduism and become Buddhist, in an effort to reclaim what they saw as their ancestral religion. Local state authorities closed the local *gumbā* or Buddhist temple built by the Gurungs, insisting that they must register it. According to villagers, the authorities implied that by adopting Buddhism, the Gurungs were becoming involved in politics. After the MNO arrived in 1990, many people in Maidel connected this earlier religious movement with the goals of the MNO, as the MNO encouraged all Mongols to abandon Hinduism, defining Mongols as not Hindus. People interpreted the reaction of the local authorities to their *gumbā* as an example of the Hindu bias of the state. MNO activists in Maidel called for everyone to boycott Dasain, the major national Hindu holiday. Gurungs in Maidel followed the boycott, but MNO supporters and those who supported parties other than the MNO interpreted and implemented it in different ways.

The Conclusion examines the increased politicization of ethnic movements and the changing shape of the MNO. I analyze the participation of the MNO and other ethnic parties in the 2008 Constituent Assembly elections, and argue that the MNO's lack of support for ethnic territorial autonomy was a major factor in its failure to win seats in these elections. The MNO's participation in these elections must also be understood within the context of the changes that the party has undergone since the early 2000s. When the People's War reached Ilam in 2001, the Maoists severely disrupted the MNO's base areas in rural Ilam and Jhapa as they sought to eliminate political competition. After the second people's movement of 2006 and the end of the People's War, the party was reborn with the assistance of a 'sister organization' called the Mongol Mulbasi Youth Assembly. This organization, based in Kathmandu, mobilized support among students who had recently migrated to the city. Finally, the chapter examines how people in the MNO perceived and experienced democracy in the 1990s as disjunctive. The disjunctive dimensions of democracy may contribute to the growing use of violence in ethnic politics.

1 Democratization, ethnic diversity and inequality in Nepal

This chapter situates the emergence of the indigenous nationalities movement within the historical and political context of Nepal. In order to illuminate the significance of the 1990 political system for marginalized groups like the indigenous nationalities, I briefly review the major changes in political rule in the modern Nepali state. To contextualize the meanings of the identities that the indigenous nationalities movement has constructed, this chapter explains the complexity of ethnic diversity and ethnic categories in Nepal. Finally, this chapter explores the contours of ethnic inequality and the dominant construction of a Nepali nationalist identity that privileges high-caste Hindus. This background is essential for understanding how the indigenous nationalities movement has defined its issues and demands.

Political rule and democratization in Nepal

Authoritarian political systems have been in place for most of Nepal's history. From the late eighteenth century, when the Shah kings first consolidated the state, through the Rana family's 100 years of rule, which stretched into the mid-twentieth century, there was no popular participation in governance, as was true for South Asia in general. There were widespread restrictions on political activity during the Rana era. Thus, mobilization against the Rana regime during the first half of the twentieth century was instigated by Nepali elites, who were based in India and influenced by the nationalist movement there (Uprety 1992). Only after the Ranas were ousted from power in 1951 did people begin to formally participate in the political arena. Although the Shah monarchy returned to power, political parties were allowed to operate for the first time and the first general elections were held in 1959. Nepal's first democratically-elected government was formed by the Congress Party, which began to institute widespread changes such as land reform.

This brief period of relative political freedom ended in December 1960, when King Mahendra, who ascended to the throne in 1955, announced that Nepal was not ready for multi-party democracy. In 1962, the king unveiled the Panchayat constitution, which he claimed would provide Nepal with a unique and appropriate form of 'guided' democracy. This constitution remained in effect, with some minor amendments, until 1990. While the Panchayat system paid lip service to the idea of democracy, it operated as an authoritarian government, in which the king held supreme power, political parties were constitutionally outlawed and opposition to the system was highly controlled.

The system allowed for popular representation through committees, or Panchayats, modeled after an older South Asian system by the same name in which a group of village elders made decisions for the community. Elections were held to these Panchayats, which were formed at the village or town, district and national levels. Only the village and town Panchayats were directly elected. District Panchayat and most National Panchayat representatives were elected by, and drawn from, the members of the Panchayat in the level below them. Some members of the national Panchayat were nominated directly by the king, and 15 members were selected from among five 'class organizations'. These class organizations, representing peasants, youth, women, workers and ex-servicemen, were meant to replace political parties and ostensibly provided a vehicle for representing societal interests within the governance structure (Borgstrom 1980: 13–21; Rose and Fisher 1970; Shaha 1975; Whelpton 2005: 101).

Although the constitution guaranteed freedom of speech and expression, in practice such freedom was severely restricted by Panchayat era laws such as the Treason Act of 1961, which made it illegal to publicly criticize the king (Burghart 1996c). Writers who critiqued the Panchayat system were jailed, and their newspapers shut down. People voiced their opposition to the system only in hushed tones or in a veiled manner. In recalling the political culture of the Panchayat years, many Nepalis speak of their fear of repression and the lack of freedom of expression.

By 1979, dissatisfaction with the Panchayat system had grown to the point where the king decided to hold a referendum to determine whether people wanted to continue the system, with minor reforms, or establish a multi-party democracy. This was a moment of relative political freedom during the Panchayat era. Leading up to the referendum, political parties had the opportunity to operate openly for the time since the brief window between the fall of the Rana regime and the beginning of the Panchayat era. Many ethnic organizations engaged in activism during this time, as I discuss in Chapter 2. The results of the 1980 referendum showed that the majority of people, especially in the rural areas, wanted to continue the Panchayat system. The promised reforms to the system entailed an amendment to the 1962 Constitution, expanding the National Panchayat and allowing for 112 members to be directly elected, with the king still appointing 28 members. Questions remain concerning the transparency of the voting process in the referendum and there is evidence that the government used its power and resources to persuade people to vote in favor of the Panchayat system. However, the high rates of participation in the referendum and the considerable support for instituting a multi-party system suggested that further demands for political reform would not be long in coming (Whelpton 2005: 109).

Ten years later, the people's movement of 1990 brought about the restoration of a multi-party democracy, after 30 years of the autocratic Panchayat system.

The movement was launched by the Nepali Congress Party and a coalition of seven leftist parties called the United Leftist Front. They worked together to charter the Movement for the Restoration of Democracy, which sought the rein-stitution of a multi-party system and the dismantling of the Panchayat form of government (Whelpton 2005). There was extensive popular participation in the movement in the Kathmandu Valley, as students, human rights organizations and professional organizations staged protests (Adams 1998). Newars, in par-ticular, played a key role in public demonstrations in the cities of Kirtipur and Bhaktapur (Gellner 1997).

The multi-party system established in the constitution of 1990 was a constitu-tional monarchy, in which the king's power was greatly reduced. The 1990 con-stitution formally granted people the right to freely form political and social organizations and the right to the freedom of expression. With this unprece-dented level of political freedom, political parties and social organizations, including non-governmental organizations, proliferated. Whereas the media was monopolized by the government during the Panchayat era, there was a 'media boom' in the years after 1990, as newspapers and FM radio stations multiplied, offering perspectives from across the political spectrum (Onta 2002).

However, in many ways the transformations that were the goal of the 1990 people's movement never occurred. Perhaps the largest roadblock to democrat-ization was that the country never gained political stability. Between 1990 and 2006, three parliamentary elections and two local elections were held, and 12 governments were formed, largely due to disputes within and between the major parties. The Prime Minister's seat was occupied by a series of familiar faces from the high-caste Hindu political elite. The violence stemming from the Maoist insurgency that began in 1996 was the most serious challenge to political stability during this period. The Maoist People's Liberation Army eventually ousted government representatives from large parts of the countryside and estab-lished its own parallel state structures in several districts in western Nepal. In 2001, the infamous palace massacre of King Birendra and his immediate family by the Crown Prince Dipendra threw the country into further uncertainty.[1] King Gyanendra, the deceased king's brother, ascended to the throne. Claiming to seek to establish peace, King Gyanendra dissolved the parliament in 2002 and took complete control of the country in 2005. This act effectively suspended democratic politics until the 2006 people's movement reinstalled the parliament and curbed the king's power.

Second, the civil liberties granted in the 1990 constitution were not upheld. With the declaration of a state of emergency in 2001, in response to the intensifi-cation of the Maoist insurrection, the state severely curtailed civil liberties and the freedom of the press, and human rights abuses were widespread. During the People's War, people who were merely suspected of being Maoists were arrested and many people in state custody disappeared.

Democratic ideals of participation and accountability were also not achieved. State representatives, including elected officials and civil servants, were not accountable to the people. Many elected politicians sought autonomy from their voters (Pfaff-Czarnecka 2004: 173). They were not responsive to the demands and interests of their constituents and thus people were not able to influence the government.

In assessing these problems prior to 2006, some political scientists concluded that democratization in Nepal failed (Carothers 2002; Ganguly and Shoup 2005). Due to the many limitations of its political system, Carothers (2002) categorized Nepal as falling into a 'gray zone', somewhere between authoritarianism and democracy, along with many other countries that initiated democratic reforms in the 1990s (p. 9). Carothers characterized Nepal's political pattern as 'feckless pluralism', one of the main syndromes found in gray-zone countries. Such countries have 'significant amounts of political freedom, regular elections, and alternation of power between genuinely different political groupings' (p. 10). However, 'the whole class of political elites are profoundly cut off from the citizenry, rendering political life an ultimately hollow, unproductive exercise' (p. 11).

While democratization in Nepal was not without challenges, it would be inaccurate to characterize Nepali political life as hollow and unproductive. Like many studies of politics in Nepal, these works are state-centered, focusing on politics in the capital city and the activities of dominant political actors. Most significantly, these authors overlooked a crucial dimension of Nepali society that is relevant to democratization: the numerous social movements that have created substantial and positive political changes since 1990, including the Dalit, indigenous nationalities and women's movements. These movements laid the groundwork for the 2006 popular uprising and the wave of political reforms that took place in its wake.

Social movements like the indigenous nationalities movement were made possible by the granting of civil liberties in the post-1990 political system, the freedom of expression and of organization. This newfound freedom of expression was extremely significant to people, many who described the political changes of 1990 with the phrase, 'finally, we can speak'. Part of what people meant by this is that during the Panchayat era they feared that they would be thrown in jail for voicing any oppositional ideas. Yet some people did speak in oppositional terms then. With regards to ethnic politics, people were forming organizations and working to secure cultural and political rights from 1951, the end of the Rana era, onwards, as I discuss later. Yet if people could speak in the old political system, it was in muted tones, rather than publicly, and their voices could easily be ignored (Burghart 1996c; Kunreuther 2004). In the post-1990 period, their voices became more effective: people could now speak in public, and also gained the right to be heard. Social movements played important roles in defining the issues that were the center of public debates.

After 1990, marginalized groups were given the political space to organize and publicly articulate their views, but they did not gain formal representation within the state and remained excluded from other influential spheres, such as the mainstream media. Inspired by the discourse of democracy, which emphasized the expansion of popular political participation, but lacking access to formal politics, marginalized groups forged social movements as an alternative way to participate in politics and to articulate their demands.

Ethnic political activists, including those in the MNO, began speaking about the shape of the new political system, testing the new democracy by pushing at the places where it was least open. They talked about their expectations for how democracy should operate and what it should mean to live in a democracy. Ethnic political organizations like the MNO sought not just to secure rights and representation for a marginalized segment of the population, but also to transform the whole political system. For example, the MNO cited the government's refusal to grant it registration as an illustration of the limitations of the post-1990 system. Overall, the changes that activists in this movement have sought and created are necessary for the further democratization of Nepal: a redistribution and wider sharing of political power, and the right to the freedom of expression of political and cultural diversity. While Chapter 2 will explore the origins of and changes in this movement, the next section here provides background that is necessary to understand this movement, the scope of ethnic diversity and the transformation of categories of identity in Nepal.

Ethnic diversity

Ethnic diversity in Nepal is highly complex: there are multiple and overlapping categories of identity, and specific ethnic labels have shifted over time. Ethnicity, caste, religion, language and region are salient axes of identity. The 2001 census recorded data for 100 ethnic and caste groups and tabulated a total of 92 languages and at least seven religions (Gurung 2003). Regional divisions between the mountain region (*himāl*) in the north, the hill region (*pahāḍ*) across the center, and the plains (*tarai*) stretching along the south further fragment the population.

In contemporary Nepal, the most politically salient sociocultural groups are the high-caste Hindus from the hills, the low-caste Hindus (*dalit*), ethnic groups (indigenous nationalities, or *ādivāsī janajāti*) and the Madhesi (peoples from the Tarai region, including both ethnic and caste groups). None of these groups forms an overwhelming majority of the total population. As Table 1.1 illustrates, the high-caste hill Hindus comprise 30.89 percent of the population, Dalits 14.99 percent, indigenous nationalities 36.31 percent and Madhesis, including Dalits and indigenous nationalities from the Tarai region, 32.29 percent. All of these groups are composed of smaller groups. Gender and class, which have also been the basis of political mobilization, also cut across these categories. They differ from the other forms of identity listed here, however, because they are not perceived as being rooted in cultural differences.

Castes are groups who follow Hinduism and speak Nepali or other Indo-Aryan languages. They are hierarchically ranked on the basis of ritual purity and include Brahman, the highest-caste group; Chhetri, the second-highest group; and several low-caste groups such as Kami, Damai and Sarki. Low-caste groups (*Dalits*) have been mobilizing against caste discrimination.

Table 1.1 Population of major ethnic and caste groups, 2001

Group	Population	%
Caste hill Hindu elite (Bahuns and Chhetris)	7,023,220	30.89
Indigenous nationalities	8,271,975	36.31
Mountain	190,107	0.82
Hill	6,038,506	26.51
Inner Tarai	251,117	1.11
Tarai	1,786,986	7.85
Unidentified indigenous nationalities	5,259	0.02
Dalits	3,233,488	14.99
Hill Dalits	1,611,135	7.09
Madhesi Dalits	1,622,313	6.74
Unidentified Dalits	88,338	0.76
Madhesi*	3,778,136	16.59
Caste Madhesi	2,802,187	12.30
Muslims	971,056	4.27
Churaute Muslims	4,893	0.02
Others	265,721	1.16
Total	22,736,556	100.00

Source: Lawoti (2005: 99).

Note
* The Madhesi category includes all Muslims because most Muslims are from the Tarai. The total percentage of the Madhesi population is 32.29 when Madhesi who are also Dalits and indigenous nationalities from the Tarai and Inner Tarai are included.

All of these castes have homelands in both the hill and Tarai regions, and they are represented throughout the country. Regional origins are related to differences in political power among the highest castes. High castes from the Tarai region identify as Madhesis and are under-represented at the state level. Different terms are used to refer to members of the highest caste from these two regions: the term Brahman includes members of the highest caste from both the hill and Tarai regions, while Bahun refers to the highest-caste members specifically from the hill region.

Ethnic groups, currently known as indigenous nationalities (*ādivāsī janajāti*), have ancestral homelands in all three regions of Nepal. The official number of such groups stands at 59. These culturally and linguistically diverse groups include well-known peoples such as Gurungs, Sherpas and Magars. It is through their opposition to caste Hindus that these groups share a common identity. Many of these groups have historically spoken Tibeto-Burman languages rather than the Indo-European Nepali language that is the ancestral and current language of caste Hindus from the hills. Although these groups argue that they are not part of the Hindu caste system, the distinction between ethnic group and caste is often blurred in practice. The Newar ethnic group has its own internal caste system, for example. Furthermore, many of these groups have taken on characteristics of caste groups. In particular, many indigenous nationalities discriminate against low-caste Hindus by refusing to allow them in their homes or to share meals with them.

The ethnic groups that are organizing as indigenous nationalities are internally extremely diverse. As much variation exists within groups that share an ethnic label as exists between groups with different names. For example, the Tharu, Nepal's fourth-largest ethnic group according to the 2001 census, share neither a common culture nor a language; rather, many different groups of people across the Tarai began to see themselves as sharing a Tharu ethnic identity after some Tharu elites began a political movement to promote this idea in the mid-twentieth century (Guneratne 2002). Many Tharu share languages with other groups that are not labeled Tharu, such as those in eastern Nepal that speak Maithili (ibid.).

Ethnic labels lack historical depth and have often shifted over time. The appearance of a people as a coherent ethnic group reflects a group's particular historical relationship with the state more than its cultural distinctiveness (Holmberg 1989; Levine 1987). The state played a key role in the formation of ethnic identity by categorizing diverse groups of people under the same ethnic label and treating them as a single group, as is clear for the linguistically and culturally heterogeneous Rai ethnic group. During the state-building process, Shah kings applied the term 'Rai', which merely meant 'chief', to the headmen of linguistically disparate groups residing in eastern Nepal. Eventually, this term came to be used to refer to the people as well as their leaders, and the various groups came to be regarded as a single group (Gaenszle 1997: 355–356; Hofer 1979: 142).

The state also reclassified groups to reflect changes in their political importance. The internally diverse Tamangs, for example, became known as a singular ethnic group because the state used these people as a source of forced labor due to their location near the Kathmandu Valley. Before the 1930s the state had called these people 'Bhote' or 'Murmi'; it later reclassified them as Tamang to reflect their increasing economic importance (Holmberg 1989: 30). People also claimed new ethnic labels for themselves as their place in the political economy shifted. Tibetan-speaking peoples seeking higher status for themselves in the eyes of the state and in society often refer to themselves as 'Tamang' (Campbell 1997; Holmberg 1989; Levine 1987: 80).

With transformations in the state and the rise of identity politics since 1990, identities in Nepal are further in flux. Diversity has been increasing, as the changes in the census data between 1991 and 2001 indicate. Whereas the 1991 census collected data on 62 caste or ethnic groups, the 2001 census included data on 100 such groups (Gurung 2003: 3). The 2001 census data also revealed that linguistic diversity appears to be increasing, as 92 languages were recorded compared with only 31 in 1991 (p. 11). Although Nepali remained the dominant language, the percentage of speakers of other languages increased. Furthermore, many ethnic groups have increasingly identified themselves as members of non-Hindu religions over the last decade. For example, between 1991 and 2001 the population of Buddhists grew by 69.7 percent, while the population of ethnic groups that are characterized as Buddhist increased by only 24.9 percent (p. 24). These shifts reflect the political efforts of various sociocultural groups to renegotiate their identities and their place in the state.[2]

Since 1990, new collective identities for marginalized segments of society – indigenous nationalities, Madhesi and Dalits – have emerged. All of these categories are internally heterogeneous, and the Madhesi category partially overlaps with the other two categories. The next section examines the patterns of inequality that make these categories politically salient.

The emergence and persistence of ethnic inequality

Ethnic inequality has been a persistent and pervasive feature of the modern state, even though it was not widely discussed or acknowledged until the 1990s. The high-caste Hindus from the hill region constitute the dominant group in Nepal. They gained the upper hand in the political arena during the last half of the eighteenth century, when Prithvi Narayan Shah, the king of a principality called Gorkha, conquered and annexed the numerous small kingdoms that existed throughout Nepal. Since this 'unification' of the state, the Shahs, high-caste Hindus who claim to be descendants of royal clans from India, have reigned as Nepal's monarchy.[3]

The process of state building resulted in ethnic stratification as different groups of people were incorporated in the state on unequal terms. Many high-caste Hindus benefited from interactions with the emergent state and succeeded in sharing political power with the rulers. High-caste Hindus residing in Nepal's central hills were closely aligned with the state from the beginning and have continually held positions of power (Whelpton 1997: 41). The three main groups in this category are Chhetris, originally known as Khas people, living in the hill region since as early as the second millennium BC, as well as the Thakuri, who are members of the landed gentry, and Bahuns, both of whom supposedly emigrated from India around the twelfth century (Whelpton 2005: 8–10).[4]

Along with these high-caste Hindus, some members of the Newar ethnic group, the original inhabitants of the Kathmandu Valley, have also been an integral part of the 'ruling coalition' in Nepal (Gaige 1975: 160). They are classified as indigenous nationalities, yet they substantially differ from other groups in this category both socially and economically. Newars have an elaborate caste system and have maintained a complex urban society for centuries. After Prithvi Narayan Shah conquered the Kathmandu Valley in 1769, high-caste Newars became closely allied with the hill Hindu rulers and the monarchy, serving as bureaucrats in the palace. These Newars have continued to hold positions of importance in the political sphere, and their historical role as traders was enhanced by their relationship with the state (Gellner 1986).[5]

The process of state formation benefited high-caste Hindus, some Newars and some other ethnic groups. High-caste Hindus who supported the state's expansion efforts were rewarded with land grants, the state's primary way of building alliances and mobilizing human resources during this period.[6] The state secured the loyalty of many members of the Magar and Gurung ethnic groups who lived in territories near Gorkha, annexed early on in the state-building period, by giving them places in the army, accompanied by land grants. Some high-ranking Magars raised their status by becoming Chhetris in the nineteenth century (Gurung 1997: 502). However, state expansion created economic hardship for others. Peasants throughout Nepal were burdened with land taxes, compulsory labor obligations that supported the military complex, and occasional levies to meet the needs of the royal household (Regmi 1971: 64).

Among the peoples who came under the control of the state ruled by these high-caste Hindus from the hills were the many ethnic groups from the mountain and hill regions, and various peoples who lived in the Tarai, the southern plains region. Although some of these plains people were high-caste Hindus, histori-cally, they have had limited access to state resources and power (Gaige 1975). Low-caste Hindus from both the hills and the plains have also been excluded from state resources and power.

Some ethnic groups were enlisted to meet the bulk of the expanding state's need for labor. Magars and Gurungs were recruited into the army. Tamangs, residing in territories directly surrounding the Kathmandu Valley, the seat of state power, endured heavy taxation and compulsory labor requirements (Holm-berg *et al.* 1999; Regmi 1976: 18).

During the state-building process, many ethnic groups lost land to high-caste Hindus, as was the case for the Limbus of far-eastern Nepal in the nineteenth century. The state encouraged the immigration of high-caste Hindus to eastern Nepal, and instituted land tenure policies that favored these Hindu settlers. These settlers also acquired Limbu land by lending them money, eventually gaining titles to their lands (Caplan 1970).

The economic and political position of the indigenous nationalities has been significantly affected by their widespread recruitment by the British army since the nineteenth century and by the Indian army after India's independence. Of the hundreds of thousands of Nepali men who have been recruited into these armies, most have been Gurungs, Magars, Rais and Limbus, as the British regarded these peoples as forming a 'martial race' with superior innate fighting abilities. From 1914 to 1945, the high-caste Hindu rulers received payments from the British government in exchange for facilitating this recruitment process (Des Chene 1993: 68–73).[7] From then on, men in these ethnic groups actively sought employment in the British army in particular, as it has been one of the few avail-able ways for them to acquire wealth. Many, though not all, ex-soldiers increased their economic status (p. 77). Thus, families in Gurung and other ethnic com-munities continue to aspire to send their sons to the British army. Many former soldiers have channeled their wealth to gain influence in their communities, by taking leading roles in village politics and by promoting education (Caplan 1995: 45–50). Although some contemporary ethnic activists surmise that army employ-ment has made these people less willing to confront inequality and the lack of political opportunities in their home country (Gurung 1994), many former sol-diers have in fact been at the forefront of the indigenous nationalities movement.

High-caste Hindus from the hills have long held the majority of positions in the government and administration. In both the parliament in 1959 and the National Panchayat in 1969, high-caste Hindus from the hills held more than 50 percent of the seats (Gaige 1975: 164). Brahmans, Chhetris and Newars formed the overwhelming majority of officers in the national-level administration in 1854, 1950 and 1965 (p. 166), and comprised 92 percent of high officials in the bureaucracy in 1973 (Blaikie *et al.* 1980: 95).

This pattern of ethnic inequality persisted even after the democratic reforms of 1990. High-caste Hindus from the hills continued to dominate every sector of the government, and the leadership of most non-governmental sectors such as civil society and education. For example, this group comprised 60 percent of the upper and lower parliament combined (Lawoti 2005; Neupane 2000). Compared to the Panchayat years, the political exclusion of marginalized groups actually increased during the post-1990 political system: fewer indigenous nationalities were represented in the parliament, cabinet, administration and judiciary, and the 'near total exclusion' of Dalits in these sectors persisted (Lawoti 2005: 19). This trend is linked to the exclusionary set of institutions and policies that were implemented after 1990, including the unitary structure of the state and the first-past-the-post electoral system (p. 20). (Marginalized groups responded to their continued exclusion from the polity after 1990 by forming social movements.)

Discussions of ethnic inequality in Nepal concentrate on issues of the control of the state and access to state resources. However, ethnic inequalities are also reflected in a wide range of other socioeconomic indicators. As a recent study by the World Bank demonstrates, Brahmans and Chhetris as a whole, as well as Newars, have higher health indicators, longer life expectancy, higher rates of school attendance and lower levels of poverty than other sociocultural groups in Nepal (World Bank and DFID 2006: 18–29).

While there is a clear pattern of hill high-caste Hindu dominance, not all individuals from this group are privileged. Chhetris in the underdeveloped far-western region are more disadvantaged than those from other parts of the country, for example. Furthermore, hill high-caste Hindus do not have a mono-poly on political and economic power. For example, many Thakalis have been successful in business, and some Limbus and Sherpas have acquired considerable political power. Yet throughout Nepal's history, high-caste Hindus have dominated the apparatus of the state and have maintained a particular advantage in gaining access to state resources. Those visiting government offices or receiving services from the government will most likely interact with high-caste men from the hills. In this context, critiques of the state have taken the form of opposition to high-caste Hindus.

The discourse against high-caste Hindu dominance in post-1990 Nepal has focused in particular on the dominance of Bahuns, which is expressed in the term *bāhunbād* (Bahun-ism). This reflects the pervasive presence of Bahuns in the government, and creates a common enemy for the indigenous nationalities, Madhesi and Dalit movements. In articulating their opposition to Bahuns, these movements overlap with the anti-Brahman movements that unfolded in India, beginning in the early twentieth century (Dirks 2001). These political move-ments in Nepal thus draw upon broader, older themes in South Asian political discourse, even if indirectly.

Nationalism and ethnic inequality

The state's construction of nationalism reflects the dominance of hill high-caste Hindus, as it upholds their cultural values and practices as models for the nation. Official representations of the Nepali nation that promoted the idea of a homo-geneous nation began to shift after 1990, but did not go far enough to represent the Nepali nation as multicultural. Ethnic activists challenge the representation of the nation as homogeneous, yet are committed to the concept of the Nepali nation.

The creation of Nepal's first comprehensive legal code, the Muluki Ain of 1854, established the groundwork for ideas of the Nepali nation during the era of Rana rule in the mid-nineteenth century. This document classified the peoples who dwelled within the state territory and positioned them in a Hindu world order according to the principles of caste hierarchy (Hofer 1979). It ranked groups of people into five categories on the basis of their relative purity. At the top of the hierarchy were the high-caste Hindus, referred to as wearers of the sacred thread (*tāgādhārī*). Next were the *matwāli*, or alcohol drinkers, divided into unenslavable and enslavable groups. This *matwāli* category united diverse groups of peoples; today these people call themselves indigenous nationalities (*ādivāsī janajāti*) or Mongols. At the bottom were the impure but touchable castes, followed by untouchable caste groups with whom other groups could not share water. As the existence of the enslavable *matwāli* category attests, a group's ranking in the hierarchy of the Muluki Ain had political and economic significance. By subsuming all peoples within a caste hierarchy, the Rana state represented Nepali society as fundamentally Hindu. The adoption of caste as the basis of the country's legal system served to buttress and sustain high-caste Hindu dominance.

During the Panchayat era (1962–1990) the state solidified the idea of Nepal as a Hindu society and sought to create a culturally homogeneous population. The state promoted the Hindu religion, the Hindu monarchy and the Nepali lan-guage as signifiers of the national community. The Panchayat-era slogan 'One language, one form of dress, one country' (*Ek bhāsā, ek bhes, ek des*) reflects the state's efforts to create cultural uniformity.

The category 'Hindu' has a long history in Nepali political discourse, as both Prithvi Narayan Shah in the late eighteenth century, and the Ranas in the late nineteenth century used the concept to define the political community (Burghart 1996b). During the Panchayat era, the government actively worked to promote a Hindu identity among the people of Nepal, and thus to create a Hindu nation. Nepal was proclaimed a Hindu kingdom in 1962. The Hindu identity of the nation was performed through daily broadcasts of ritual music and sermons on Radio Nepal, and by government funding of Sanskrit schools. Hindu holidays became national holidays. National symbols promoted during the Panchayat era, such as the color red, the cow and the flag, referred to Hinduism and the Hindu monarchy.

Nation building was the primary objective of the education system after the end of the Rana regime. The education system worked to assimilate Nepal's diverse population into a unified nation by using the Nepali language as the sole medium of instruction. In 1956, the National Education Planning Commission recommended that only Nepali be used in schools, a plan explicitly intended to reduce the currency of the many other languages spoken in the country (Gaige 1975). Similarly, one of the main goals of the 1971 New Education System Plan was 'harmonizing diverse multi-lingual traditions into a single nationhood' (HMG 1971: 2).

State-published school textbooks, the backbone of the national education curriculum, delivered nationalist ideology to children. These books excluded the cultures, histories and languages of Nepal's ethnic groups, and privileged the experiences and knowledge of people from the Kathmandu valley (Ragsdale 1989). History textbooks presented a unifying national history, highlighting high-caste Hindu heroes while excluding narratives about noteworthy individuals from other communities (Onta 1996a). The Hindu bias of these books reflects the state's efforts to promote the Hindu identity of the nation and the fact that the authors of these textbooks were overwhelmingly high-caste Hindus and Newars (Tamang 1999).

Another means through which the state sought to depict a homogeneous Nepali nation was the census, taken first in 1911 and then every ten years thereafter. The census obscured the diversity of the population because even though the census schedules included questions about caste and ethnic identity, the state did not process or publish this data. From 1952–1954 until 1991, citizens were enumerated on the basis of linguistic and religious affiliation as well as caste and ethnicity, yet only the data on religion and language was made public (Gurung 2003: 1). The linguistic and religious data suggested that the nation was relatively culturally unified, and subsequent censuses conducted during the Panchayat years showed the number of Nepali speakers and Hindus as increasing. The census represented a majority of the population as Hindu; this was achieved in part by instructing census takers to categorize all members of many ethnic groups as Hindu. In 1952–1954, 88.9 percent of the population was Hindu, increasing to 89.5 percent by 1981 (Gurung 1998: 94–95). Furthermore, the 1952–1954 census showed that nearly half of the population, 48.7 percent, spoke Nepali as their mother tongue, increasing to 58.35 percent in 1981 (Sonntag 1995: 112).

This homogenizing form of nationalism and the unequal power relations that it upheld and concealed became central issues of public concern after the people's movement of 1990. Ethnic activists and marginalized groups began critiquing the state's vision of the nation during the Panchayat era. But with the restoration of a multi-party democracy, people had increased expectations that the representation of the nation would become more inclusive. During the crafting of the 1990 Constitution, fierce public debate raged over the shape that the nation should take under the new multi-party political system. The Constitution Recommendations Committee was formed in May 1990, and the majority of suggestions to the committee concerned issues of regional, linguistic, ethnic and religious identity (Hutt 1994: 35–36). These suggestions challenged the Panchayat model of a homogeneous nation, opposing the privileged status of Nepali in relation to other languages, the lack of religious freedom and the designation of Nepal as a Hindu kingdom.

Overall, non-dominant groups were unsatisfied with the 1990 constitution. Although it proclaimed that Nepal was a multi-ethnic, multilingual state, it did not completely abandon the older model of nationalism, as Nepal remained a 'Hindu kingdom'. Religious conversion was still banned, as an attempt to keep Nepali citizens from being wooed away to Christianity or other non-Hindu religions. Nepali retained its dominant status as the 'language of the nation of Nepal' and the language to be used in all official state business, although other languages were granted a modicum of recognition as 'national languages' (HMG 1990).

Organizing around issues raised in the drafting of the 1990 constitution helped identity-based movements to coalesce and gain visibility. Ending the dominance of the state by hill high-caste Hindus is the goal of the Madhesi movement, the Dalit movement and the indigenous nationalities movement. The next chapter examines the goals and organization of the indigenous nationalities movement.

2 The indigenous nationalities movement in post-1990 Nepal

Following the 1990s people's movement and the restoration of a multi-party political system, organizations representing regional, caste, linguistic, and ethnic identities moved to the forefront of the political landscape. The Mongol National Organization (MNO) emerged alongside numerous organizations that sought to gain political, economic and social power for Nepal's indigenous nationalities. This chapter describes the history and scope of Nepal's contemporary indigenous nationalities movement and locates the MNO within this movement. This movement created a collective identity for numerous, diverse ethnic groups in Nepal, a prerequisite for making political demands. It also spearheaded the post-1990 public debates over how the Nepali nation should be defined and how the state should represent and recognize differences within its population.

Origins of the indigenous nationalities movement

The indigenous nationalities movement emerged from several decades of low-key organizing. During the Rana and the Panchayat regimes, marginalized ethnic groups engaged in various forms of political action against the dominance of high-caste Hindus, ranging from rebellions to cultural revitalization organizations.

One clear case of opposition to high-caste Hindu dominance was the Limbu struggle against the state to retain their rights to their ancestral lands (*kipaṭ*) in eastern Nepal (Caplan 1970). The state was unable to vanquish the Limbus in the late eighteenth century and recognized Limbu political autonomy and rights to maintain direct ownership of their lands (Sagant 1996: 320–327). From the late nineteenth century onwards, Limbu leaders sporadically mobilized to stave off state proposals to terminate their rights to this land, until the 1960s (Caplan 1970: 184).

Ethnic conflicts rarely became violent. In the early 1950s, there were acts of violence in eastern Nepal against Brahmans (ibid.). In 1959, Tamangs in Dhanding and Nuwakot districts began rebelling against Brahman moneylenders and landowners, and accused them of taking Tamang lands through unfair practices. The Tamangs looted property, and beat many Brahmans. Hundreds of Brahmans filed a case in the court against the Tamangs to retrieve their looted assets, and to secure rights to their land. After government officials investigated the conflict in an attempt to resolve it, the movement became more violent (Devkota 2036 v.s.; Tamang 1987).

Prior to 1990, ethnic demands were often expressed through social organizations that focused on cultural preservation and revitalization. During the Rana era, these organizations emphasized cultural reforms because the state did not tolerate overtly political demands. However, these efforts had political undertones, and presented a subtle critique of the high-caste Hindu-dominated state. Newars in Kathmandu formed some of the earliest of these social organizations. Beginning in the 1920s and intensifying through the 1930s and 1940s, Newar intellectuals sought to promote their language through publications and by establishing Newari literary associations (Gellner 1986). Leaders openly criticized the state's renaming of the Gorkhali or Khas language as Nepali, claiming that only the Newari language should be known as Nepali, as historically it was called that name (ibid.). During this same time, some Newars began practicing Theravada Buddhism. The Rana rulers exiled Theravada monks from Nepal in the 1930s and 1940s, suggesting that the Nepali state felt threatened by this religious movement (Gellner and LeVine 2005; Leve 1999).

Many of the prominent social organizations in the post-1990 indigenous nationalities movement were formed between 1951 and 1960, when the Ranas lost power and Nepal first experimented with multi-party democracy.[1] These ethnic organizations promoted social cohesion and cultural preservation within single ethnic groups. Just before this period, in 1949, Tharu elites formed an organization called the *Tharu Kalyankarini Sabha* (Tharu Welfare Society) with the goal of reforming ritual practices and modernizing their community (Guneratne 2002; Krauskopff 2002). In 1954, Thakalis founded the *Thakali Samaj Sudhar Sangh* (Thakali Social Reform Organization), which managed and organized community events such as festivals and life-cycle rituals, operated rotating credit associations, and attempted to alter funeral and marriage practices so that they were less expensive (Fisher 2001; Manzardo and Sharma 1975). These organizations sought to uplift their own communities through reforming cultural practices instead of challenging the state.

However, some of these organizations had more political aims. In 1956, representatives of Gurung, Tharu, Limbu and Magar organizations met and established an organization called the *Pichadieko Bargiya Sangh* (Backward Class Organization). They formed a working committee with two representatives from each of these organizations, and each member organization sent representatives to the meetings of the other organizations. This umbrella organization eventually expanded to include twelve ethnic organizations, and was renamed the *Samyukta Janakalyan Sangh* (United People's Welfare Organization) (Gurung 2039 v.s.: 3). While this organization did not last, this style of cooperation between organizations representing single ethnic groups continued in the post-1990 movement.

During the Panchayat era, those organizations that were established during the 1950s continued to operate quietly, but overt forms of ethnic activism were curtailed. Ethnic political activity increased when a window of relative political freedom opened during 1979. Leading up to the referendum on the future of the Panchayat system, the state allowed political parties and organizations to be openly active. Although the freedom was short-lived, since the Panchayat system continued, many ethnic organizations formed during this time, several of which continued to work throughout the 1980s and after 1990.

In 1979, Gopal Gurung, the MNO president whose life and work will be discussed in the next chapter, and others held a conference in Pulchowk, Kathmandu to discuss the problems facing Mongols (Kurve 1979). The *Kirat Dharma Tatha Sahitya Utthan Sangh* (Society for the Promotion of Kirat Religion and Literature), initially based in Panchthar district, emerged during the flurry of organizing during the referendum, and sought to uplift the religion and languages of Rais and Limbus. The *Nepal Bhasa Manka Khalah*, a Newar organization focused on promoting the Newari language, was also formed in 1979, and brought together 115 small Newari literary clubs. Among this organization's demands were that Radio Nepal should permit programming in Newari and in other languages besides Nepali, that primary schooling should be available in the mother tongue of all communities, and that all people should have the right to speak and conduct business in court in their own languages (Gellner 1986: 134). During this year, Tamangs held their first country-wide conference (*New Light* 1979a) and a Tharu organization (*Tharu Kalyan Karini Pariwar*) held a large public meeting in Kathmandu (New Light 1979b).

An ethnic organization that many people associate with the Panchayat era is Seta Magurali, an acronym created by combining the first syllable of the names of six major ethnic groups in Nepal: Sherpas, Tamangs, Magars, Gurungs, Rais and Limbus. While many people referred to Seta Magurali, little concrete information about the origins of the organization or its activities exists. Some people suggested that Padma Sundar Lawoti, one of the few Limbu ministers in the Panchayat government, started the organization. Others claimed that the Panchayat government opened this organization to control ethnic organizing, and used Padma Sundar Lawoti to give it legitimacy. Other people insisted that this organization never really existed. Nonetheless, the name Seta Magurali captured people's imagination as it symbolized the origins of ethnic political organizing. Well into the 1990s, people still used the name 'Seta Magurali' when referring to ethnic political activism.

This brief history illustrates the continuity between the earlier forms of ethnic organizing and the post-1900 indigenous nationalities movement. The focus of these earlier organizations on promoting and preserving culture, language and religion, and on building coalitions across ethnic groups, continued in the post-1990 movement. The pre-1990 organizations were periodically involved in direct political action when the state became temporarily more open during the 1950s and then in 1979, and such political activities became more pronounced after 1990. The people's movement of 1990 ushered in a multi-party democracy, and catalyzed ethnic political activity. By organizing around issues raised in the drafting of the 1990 constitution, as discussed in the previous chapter, the indigenous nationalities movement coalesced. In response to these perceived shortfalls of the constitution, and in the space made available by the reforms of 1990, the indigenous nationalities movement developed into a prominent political force.

Central concerns of the post-1990 movement

The Mongol National Organization emerged as part of a social movement, widely referred to as the indigenous nationalities movement. Organizations in this movement represent numerous ethnic groups, most of whom have historically spoken Tibeto-Burman languages, including Rai, Limbu, Gurung, Magar, Sherpa and Tamang. The movement aims to increase social, economic and political power for these peoples, referred to collectively as Mongols or as indigenous nationalities (*ādivāsī janajāti*). Participants in this movement share the conviction that these communities have endured oppression by high-caste Hindus since the formation of the state in the late eighteenth century, and that they face the common problem of having 'fallen behind' them.

While the indigenous nationalities movement brings some voices to center stage, it eclipses others. In analyzing the social landscape, the MNO and other organizations pay little attention to the marginal position of low-caste Hindus and Madhesis, those from the Tarai region. Nor are they usually willing to accept low-caste Hindus or Madhesis as allies in their movement, or as members of the movement.

The diverse organizations in the indigenous nationalities movement make political demands and engage in cultural politics that support these demands. The central political demand of the movement has been to end the high-caste Hindu dominance of the state and create a more inclusive, representative and responsive state. Hindu dominance is most often referred to as *bāhunbād* (Brahmanism) because the Bāhun (or hill Brahman) caste is the most over-represented in the government. The movement demanded a new constitution, a federal system to enable ethnic autonomy, reservations for indigenous peoples in the government and other state-sponsored institutions, a secular state and the elimination of the Hindu monarchy. After the Maoist insurgency and the second people's movement of 2006, which restored democracy, the public at large embraced some of the indigenous nationalities movement's demands, leading to major changes. In 2008, Nepal eliminated the monarchy, established a secular state and committed to establishing a federal state structure; a constituent assembly began drafting a new constitution that will determine how the federal state will be structured and what rights will be given to marginalized groups.

Cultural politics includes activities through which indigenous nationalities define and promote the cultural practices of their own communities. Guiding these cultural activities is the belief that the indigenous nationalities should reject the culture of high-caste Hindus, which was imposed on them, and revive their own distinct histories, languages, religions and other cultural practices, including clothing, dances and festivals. Many participants in the indigenous nationalities movement have made dramatic changes to their cultural practices, quitting Hinduism and adopting Buddhism, for example. These cultural activities are intrinsically political because they challenge the state's previous strategy of assimilation and the status of high-caste Hindu culture as the national culture.

Efforts to preserve ethnic languages and to promote literacy or education in these languages have been a mainstay of movement activity. Ethnic activists have revived their languages through language classes, publications, cassettes of songs and films. The 1990 constitution guaranteed communities the right to primary education in their mother tongue, yet few funds or programs were provided to support this goal. Ethnic organizations demanded that the government create such programs, but they also began developing learning materials and holding their own classes.

Redefining the national identity of the state so that it reflects the cultural diversity of the population is a core focus of the movement. Indigenous nationalities groups proposed that Nepal should be a secular rather than a Hindu state, and national symbols such as the national language, dress, holidays, anthem, and calendar should not come only from the high-caste Hindu culture. The movement's most prominent effort to advance this issue was by advocating the boycott of Dasain, the country's major national Hindu festival, as discussed in Chapter 6. People began discussing this controversial initiative in numerous publications and conferences after 1990, and by the early 1990s many people had begun to boycott Dasain, at least in Kathmandu and eastern Nepal. In the call to boycott Dasain, the movement encouraged people to abandon a holiday that they had long celebrated (Hangen 2005).

Although the earlier phases of the movement focused on cultural politics, the movement has increasingly emphasized political demands. This shift occurred with the rise of the Maoist movement, when previously radical political ideas and strategies became more mainstream. While language (*bhāsā*), religion (*dharma*) and culture (*sanskriti*) were key phrases in the movement in 1990, the current emphasis is on the right to self-determination (*ātmanirnaya*) and ethnic autonomy (*jātiya swāyatta sāsan*). The centrality of the discourse of self-determination, the right of a group to determine its own future, stems from its currency in the international indigenous rights movement and in communist ideology. Self-determination is a broad term with multiple meanings; for the communist parties, self-determination can be granted only with the guidance of the party. In the indigenous nationalities movement, ethnic autonomy, or ethnic control over political and other aspects of life, is a corollary to the right to self-determination. Most indigenous nationalities activists see ethnic federalism as the best way to achieve ethnic autonomy.

Organizations within the indigenous nationalities movement

Organizations in the indigenous nationalities movement share common goals, yet engage in different forms of political action. The main types of organization are: social organizations representing single ethnic groups; federations of these organizations, both within and across ethnic groups; professional organizations (for journalists, for example); and political parties. Recently, mainstream political parties have also organized wings representing the indigenous nationalities. This section examines three types of organization: social organizations, now called Indigenous Peoples' Organizations (IPOs); the main federation of these organizations, the Nepal Federation of Indigenous Nationalities; and ethnic political parties.

The dominant organization in this social movement is the *Nepal Janajāti Ādivāsī Mahasangh* (Nepal Federation of Indigenous Nationalities, or NEFIN), composed of 54 member organizations that represent particular ethnic groups. NEFIN was *Pichadieko Bargiya Sangh* (Backward Class Organization) in 1956 (Gurung 2039 v.s.: 3) and the *Nepal Sarvajantiya Adhikar Manch* (Forum for the Rights of All Ethnic Peoples in Nepal) in 1986 (Fisher 1993: 12). When established in 1990, this organization was called the *Nepal Janajāti Mahasangh* (Nepal Federation of Nationalities, or NEFEN) and encompassed eight organizations. Originally, it aimed to coordinate the work of its member organizations, but it later developed into a body that articulates the goals of the movement, pressures political parties, society and international agencies to adopt these goals, and lobbies the government to make changes.

Sources of funding for NEFIN activities have expanded dramatically since the late 1990s. Originally the organization's modest expenditures were funded through donations of time and money from individuals. After 1997, however, government funding became available, and after 2000 NEFIN also began to accept funding from foreign development agencies (Tamang 2005: 14–15). The increasing visibility and legitimacy of this organization and its new sources of funding are reflected in the change in its official quarters: although it originally occupied a couple of rooms in a building by the dusty central bus station, it is now located in an elegant new multi-story house on the south side of the capital city.

Much of NEFIN's early work was devoted to establishing *janajāti* as a legitimate political identity and their concerns as legitimate and democratic (Tamang 2005). In the 1990s NEFIN raised public awareness about language rights, religious freedom and cultural revitalization by publishing pamphlets and held annual meetings and conferences in Kathmandu on topics such as 'Education in the Mother Tongue'.

In its first decade, NEFIN expressed its political demands primarily by operating as a pressure group, working to influence members of the various governments to accommodate the interests of indigenous nationalities. During the drafting of the 1990 constitution, for example, NEFIN made recommendations to the Constitution Commission, and later the organization spearheaded opposition to government initiatives to make Sanskrit language classes a compulsory part of the school curriculum. Since 1992, NEFIN has issued a declaration of its demands for policy reform at its annual general assembly. The demands included that the government declare Nepal a secular state, reform the constitution, ensure linguistic equality for all people, ratify international conventions related to indigenous peoples and minorities, introduce a federal system of governance, and develop an affirmative action program (ibid.: 20–21).

After 2002, NEFIN underwent a major shift and became increasingly engaged in overtly political activities. When the king asserted control of the government in 2002, NEFIN began to work with other civil society and political organizations to restore democracy. This new direction was largely due to the interests and approach of the general secretary of NEFIN from 2000 to 2006, Om Gurung. Gurung developed a new agenda to make NEFIN politically assertive. As Gurung told me, NEFIN argued that only democracy could protect and encourage the rights of indigenous nationalities, and that a true democracy would require the restructuring of the state and proportional representation in the state on the basis of ethnicity. Under Om Gurung's leadership, NEFIN pressurized political parties to adopt this agenda and worked with other organizations to restore democracy.

NEFIN also began to employ the strategies of political protest that were so ubiquitous in urban Nepal at this point. In 2004, NEFIN staged a street demonstration involving about 10,000 people to protest against the royal takeover of October 2002 (ibid.: 14). During the April 2006 people's movement for the restoration of democracy, NEFIN participated in many rallies and marches in defiance of the curfew. For example, NEFIN, in coordination with the Seven Party Alliance, contributed to a plan to hold demonstrations around the entire length of the ring road surrounding the capital by staging a 'democratic' cultural program and question–answer song match (*dohori*) (Stirr 2009). At the first meeting of the reinstated parliament, NEFIN protested outside Singha Durbar to demand a constituent assembly and a secular state (Sasaktikaran Sandesh 2006: 12). With these protests, the organization demonstrated its willingness to act as a political force. Taking part in the democracy movement was a way for NEFIN to have its agenda recognized and upheld in the new Nepal that emerged from this popular movement, Om Gurung told me.

In 2007, NEFIN signed a 20-point agreement with the interim government in which the latter promised to establish proportional representation on the basis of ethnicity in the Constituent Assembly, and at all levels of the state, among other things. This agreement signaled that the government considered NEFIN to represent indigenous nationalities throughout Nepal.

NEFIN is seeking to become more representative of the full range of indigenous nationalities. While each ethnic group can have only one representative organization in NEFIN, there are now multiple organizations for most ethnic groups. Since there is no clear process by which a particular organization is chosen to serve in NEFIN, controversies have occasionally erupted over which organization should represent an ethnic group in NEFIN. The number of indigenous nationalities that are represented in NEFIN has expanded. Regardless of its population size, each group is represented by only one organization in NEFIN. Smaller groups are thus over-represented in NEFIN, although in the past many NEFIN leaders have been from the larger indigenous nationalities, leading the smaller, more marginal indigenous nationalities to feel under-represented

(Onta 2006: 330). In 2007, NEFIN's executive committee included representation from smaller groups. However, few women are involved in the organization or in its member organizations.

NEFIN has operated mainly in Kathmandu, although most indigenous nationalities live in rural areas. The leaders of this organization are overwhelmingly urban intellectuals, well-educated, middle-aged men, many of whom have been involved in leftist politics and hold professional positions at colleges, law firms or development agencies. NEFIN tried to increase its activities outside the capital and established district coordination councils in 42 of Nepal's 75 districts by 2006; however, these remain far less active than the central organization.

Indigenous Peoples' Organizations (IPOs)

Organizations representing single ethnic groups first formed in the 1950s. Currently, several hundred such organizations exist, according to one estimate (Onta 2006: 320). Most of the indigenous nationalities have organizations that represent them, except for 11 of the most marginal of the 59 groups of indigenous nationalities (Tamang 2005: 16). These organizations originally called themselves social organizations (*sāmājik sansthā*) to emphasize their nonpolitical focus, but are now called Indigenous Peoples' Organizations, the standard international designation for such groups. This name change reflects the growing international influence in the movement.

These organizations focus on revitalizing the religions, languages and cultures of ethnic groups. In order to achieve these goals, they hold seminars, publish magazines and books and hold language classes. Cultural programs (*sanskritik kāryakram*), performances in which people perform dances, sing songs, and wear clothing that is meant to represent the identity of an ethnic group, have also been a mainstay of the IPOs. While these organizations prioritize cultural revitalization and the preservation of their ethnic group over political change, their cultural projects have clear political dimensions, challenging the state's past project of assimilating ethnic groups into the dominant national culture.

Most of the organizations are registered in the capital city and many of the larger organizations have village-level committees where the population of their ethnic group is the largest. The capacity of these organizations varies widely. While many of them lack paid staff, office space and telephones, seven organizations from the larger ethnic groups – the Limbus, Tamangs, Rais, Gurungs, Newars, Thakalis and Magars – have greater resources (ibid.: 17). Another potential shortcoming of these organizations is their infrequent use of voting to make decisions and select officers (Gellner and Karki 2008; Onta 2006: 324). These organizations prefer to make decisions by consensus to distinguish themselves from political parties and also because the leaders fear that voting will lead to divisions within their organizations (Gellner and Karki 2008). Yet this style of making decisions favors the more dominant voices in the organizations.

One of the most active and well-run organizations is the Limbu group, *Kirat Yakthung Chumlung* (KYC). Founded in 1989 with 68 members, the organization swelled to 12,000 members by 1995, and its activities also expanded. By 1998, KYC had chapters in 11 districts and 200 villages. By 2005, 15 people were employed by the organization (Tamang 2005: 18).

KYC was established as a 'nonpolitical, non-profit making social organiza- tion' (KYC 2049 v.s.: 1). According to the organization's charter, among its main objectives are promoting and preserving the Limbu language, script and culture and uplifting the Limbu community. In line with these goals, the organ- ization conducts research on these topics and works to 'enhance awareness among the Limbu community' (ibid.: 2049 v.s.: 3). From its inception, KYC ful- filled these objectives by organizing cultural programs with demonstrations of 'traditional' Limbu dances and songs and publishing a monthly Nepali- and Limbu-language newspaper and yearly calendar. KYC also supports the efforts of other indigenous nationalities by sending representatives to attend their cul- tural and discussion programs.

In 1993, KYC began a non-formal education program focused on revitalizing the Limbu language and educating Limbus. The organization developed text- books and trained teachers to teach the Limbu language and the Sirijanga script, in which it is written, to Limbus who did not speak or read it. KYC now con- ducts these classes in villages throughout far-eastern Nepal (KYC 2000 [2056 v.s.]). This project enacted the right of every community to preserve and promote its language, script and culture and the right to establish and operate schools to educate its children in their 'mother tongue', as guaranteed in Article 18 of the 1990 constitution (HMG 1990: 13–14).

KYC has also participated in political activities. Along with NEFIN and other organizations, KYC has lobbied the state to change its treatment of Limbu and other indigenous nationalities. When the new constitution was being drafted in 1990, KYC was also involved in efforts to have Nepal declared a secular state. Later, the organization worked with others to oppose government initiatives to make Sanskrit language classes compulsory. In 2008, the organization became involved in efforts to establish an autonomous region for Limbus, Limbuwan, in east Nepal.

Perhaps KYC has been so effective because of the relative cultural unity of the Limbus. Limbus have a clearly defined territory, a common language and script, and a strong sense of history, stemming from their long resistance to the Nepali state. The primary challenge for most of these organizations is to create a sense of unity within the group despite their internal cultural diversity. Publica- tions and seminars sponsored by these organizations address issues such as what religion Magars should follow if not Hinduism, and which of the many Rai lan- guages should serve as the Rai lingua franca. A sense of unity within these groups, even if it allows for some heterogeneity, would facilitate the develop- ment of state policies and institutions that support the cultures of indigenous nationalities, such as educational materials in ethnic languages.

Efforts to create shared identities while recognizing the differences that exist within ethnic groups have resulted in federations of these IPOs for at least two groups, Newars and Gurungs, also known as Tamus. The Gurung (Tamu)

National Council (*Rastriya Gurung (Tamu) Parishad*) was founded in 2000 to coordinate the dozens of Gurung organizations that had opened throughout the country and abroad. Its goals are to create uniformity within Tamu culture, facilitate mutually supporting relationships between Tamu organizations, and to enable these organizations to voice common issues together. One of its major activities is coordinating the celebration of the Gurung New Year (*Lhochhar*) in Kathmandu and Pokhara. In 2003, the group held its first national meeting, which 53 different Gurung organizations attended (Rastriya Gurung (Tamu) Parishad 2060 v.s. [2003]). However, not all Gurungs recognized this organization as the umbrella for all other Gurung organizations. Another Gurung organization, *Tamu Choj Dhi*, claimed that it already functions as the primary Gurung organization, as it has chapters throughout Nepal, and refused to join the council.

Since 2000 an increasing number of Nepali indigenous nationalities organizations have opened in places with many Nepali migrants, such as the USA, the UK, Japan, Hong Kong, the Gulf countries and Malaysia. In the USA, organizations for all of the largest ethnic groups exist, including the Tamu (Gurung) Society, the Newah Organization of America, and the Tamang Society of America. These organizations seek to promote and preserve these identities in the diaspora and provide ways for people to be involved in the indigenous nationalities movement in Nepal from a distance. They contribute funds to organizations in Nepal, issue declarations establishing their position on political issues affecting indigenous nationalities, and meet with representatives of organizations when in Nepal. These diasporic organizations are likely to play an increasingly important role in funding and shaping the indigenous nationalities movement.

As in most political sectors in Nepal, gender inequity has been persistent within the indigenous nationalities movement. The participation of women in all aspects of the movement is limited. NEFIN, however, has tried to increase the representation of women on its central committee. Because none of the other IPOs have established programs that specifically target gender inequity, indigenous nationalities women began establishing their own organizations in the 1990s. Most of the large indigenous nationalities groups now have women's organizations, and there are also several federations of these organizations. The National Indigenous Women's Federation–Nepal, for example, established in 2000, includes 13 member organizations, each representing a different ethnic group.[2] These organizations provide space for women, excluded from the main organizations, to be active in the indigenous nationalities movement. They address the problem of patriarchy within the indigenous nationalities movement, and the fact that it fails to represent women's issue as part of its main platform (Tamang 2006 2063 v.s.]).[3] Male activists have asserted that gender inequality is primarily a problem within the dominant Hindu society, existing within the indigenous nationalities only because of the Hinduization of these communities. They believe that resolving ethnic inequality will end any gender imbalances within ethnic communities.

Ethnic parties

Ethnic parties like the MNO represent an important yet marginal part of the indigenous nationalities movement. These parties view political power as the key to improving the status of the indigenous nationalities and assert that it is futile to try to gain power through mainstream political parties dominated by high-caste Hindus. These organizations offer one way for indigenous nationalities to obtain higher rates of participation in the formal political process and thus influence government policy and institutions. They aim to make the government more representative of the population and to increase the accountability and responsiveness of politicians, as the predominantly high-caste Hindu politicians have not been responsive to the demands and interests of people from other communities.

Marginalized groups, including the indigenous nationalities, have not been able to participate fully and make political demands in the mainstream political parties. High-caste individuals form the majority of the leadership of these parties, especially at the central levels (Hachhethu 2002a: 77–92). Excluded from mainstream parties, indigenous nationalities have turned to small parties to run for election. In the 1999 parliamentary elections, 80 percent of the indigenous nationalities candidates either ran as independents or were affiliated with small parties (World Bank and DFID 2006: 31–32).

Mainstream parties have a mixed record on ethnic issues. Immediately after 1990, these parties ignored ethnic grievances (Bhattachan 1995: 129–130), but gradually they began to address them in their party manifestos, policy documents and party wings. The Communist Party of Nepal (UML) opened the *Jātiya Mamila Bibhag* (Ethnic Issues Department) in 1998, while the Nepali Congress Party established an organization called the Nepal Indigenous Nationalities Association in 2001. Overall, however, these mainstream parties have done little to end ethnic inequality (Onta 2005: 45–46).

There are relatively few ethnic parties compared to IPOs and other types of party. Until 2006, only six ethnic parties existed, including the *Rastriya Janamukti Party* (RJP) and the Mongol National Organization (MNO). As of 2005, there were also 15 regional liberation fronts, such as the *Limbuwan Mukti Morcha* and the *Khambuwan Mukti Morcha* (Onta 2006: 322). These liberation fronts, which boycotted elections in the 1990s, argued that each ethnic group should control a region of the country. Initially they existed largely by virtue of their vocal leaders and the occasional pamphlets they produced. The Maoist party established some of these organizations, while others later aligned with the Maoists. Around the time of the 2008 elections to the Constituent Assembly, more ethnic parties opened, as will be discussed in the Conclusion.

These parties faced legal constraints that the IPOs did not encounter. Article 112(3) of the 1990 constitution barred the Election Commission from recognizing or registering any political party explicitly formed 'on the basis of religion, community, caste, tribe, or region' (HMG 1990). Although candidates from unregistered parties could run as independents, they were not assigned a single and permanent election symbol, as were candidates from other small parties.

Because voters place marks on these symbols on ballots in order to cast their votes, these symbols were crucial for creating a party identity and gaining votes. Supporters of ethnic parties viewed the Election Commission's refusal to register ethnic parties as proof of the state's Hindu bias. Ethnic parties were also hampered by their lack of access to mainstream media coverage. They were not mentioned on the radio, and rarely received coverage in major newspapers. The state's restrictions on ethnic political parties in the 1990 constitution suggest that lawmakers perceived these parties to pose a threat to the democratic system. The ban on ethnic parties remained in the Interim constitution of 2006, yet was not enforced in the elections to the Constituent Assembly in 2008.

The RJP and the MNO were the only ethnic parties to participate in elections in the 1990s, yet neither fared well. In order to assess the potential of ethnic parties to secure greater political representation for indigenous nationalities, it is important to determine why these parties performed poorly in these national elections. Here I examine the participation of these parties in elections in the 1990s, postponing a discussion of the 2008 Constituent Assembly elections for the Conclusion.

The RJP was one of the only ethnic political parties to secure registration from the Election Commission in the 1990s. It did so by broadening its explicitly ethnic agenda and claiming to represent all peoples who were oppressed. The party also eliminated the 'communal' term *janajāti* from its name, which was initially *Rastriya Janajāti Mukti Morcha*. Despite these changes, the RJP continued to focus primarily on indigenous nationalities issues, calling for a federal government, elections based on proportional representation, reservations for marginalized groups in the government and a secular state (Rastriya Janamukti Party 1994: 2–3). Most of the party's supporters and candidates were from the indigenous nationalities: of the 82 candidates that it put up for election in 1994, 80 were indigenous nationalities, one was *dalit* and one was Madhesi (p. 4). The party split in 1998 (Shreshta 2004: 24), and faced another crisis in 2002 when its founder and leader, Gore Bahadur Khopangi, accepted King Gyanendra's nomination to become a minister. This act discredited Khopangi's claim that he was working for political change and ethnic rights, and he was branded a royalist.[4]

The RJP never won a seat in parliament and did not secure the required 3 percent of votes cast necessary to achieve status as a national party in the 1990s. Its vote share did increase, however, between 1991 and 1999, as it ran an increasing number of candidates in each election (Lawoti 2005: 69). The RJP did not participate extensively in local elections in 1992 and 1997.

The MNO, a much smaller party than the RJP, participated in elections in east Nepal despite lacking registration from the Election Commission. In each of the three parliamentary elections held in 1991, 1994 and 1999, MNO candidates ran for election in the Ilam and Jhapa districts, yet the party did not win any seats, as illustrated in Table 2.1. The party was most successful in Ilam, where at least one candidate came in third place in every election, just behind two of the large national parties, the Nepali Communist Party (UML) and the Nepali Congress

Table 2.1 Votes for MNO candidates in nationwide elections in Ilam and Jhapa districts

District/constituency	1991		1994		1999		2008	
	# of votes	% of total votes	# of votes	%	# of votes	%	# of votes	%
Ilam 1	2,519	5.14	1,611	4.77	496	1.20	916	1.96
Ilam 2	6,019	12.77	2,396	7.49	693	1.71	779	1.76
Ilam 3	–	–	3,403	10.19	2,321	5.72	2377	5.54
Jhapa 1	–	–	–	–			868	1.81
Jhapa 2	–	–	383	0.91	361	0.66	232	0.47
Jhapa 3	–	–	525	1.37	1,098	2.08	–	–
Jhapa 4	–	–	–	–	–	–	103	0.19

Source: Election Commission, Nepal (1992, 1994, 1999) and interviews with MNO members. For 2008 results, see Election Commission, Nepal: www.election.gov.np/reports/CAResults/reportBody. php.

Note
The dashes indicate that the MNO ran no candidate in that constituency. There was no third constituency in Ilam in the 1991 elections. In Ilam district, the total number of constituencies was increased from two to three in 1994. Gopal Gurung ran in constituency two in 1991, and in constituency three in all later elections. MNO candidates were listed as independent candidates in the official election data until 2008. Thus, this election data from the 1990s was compiled based on the official election results from the Election Commission in combination with information from MNO leaders about candidates' names.

Party, and beating out another large party, the *Rastriya Prajātantra Party*. Between 1991 and 1999, however, the MNO received a decreasing number of votes.

This progressive decline may indicate that voters were increasingly discouraged by the fact that votes for candidates who did not win were wasted votes. As people became more familiar with how the electoral system worked in Nepal, they saw that MNO candidates did not have a realistic chance of winning parliamentary seats, especially when compared with national-level parties that had formed governments, held seats or at least obtained registration, like the RJP. This does not necessarily mean that people became less supportive of the MNO's ethnic political platform. Rather, they may have become more skeptical about the possibility of achieving these goals through elections.

In 1992 and 1997, the MNO achieved more success in village-level elections in Ilam district than it did in the national elections. As Table 2.2 illustrates, in 1992 MNO candidates were elected in 24 out of 47 village governments, called Village Development Committees (VDCs), and won the majority of the posts, including the chair and vice-chair seats, in two of these VDCs (*Nirbachan Aayog* (Election Commission) 2049 v.s. [1992]).[5] In 1997, however, MNO candidates were elected in only 19 VDCs, though they retained the majority in the two villages where they had previously established it (*Nirbachan Aayog* (Election Commission) 2054 v.s. [1997]). Overall, the proportion of votes cast for MNO candidates in local elections decreased between the 1992 and 1997 local elections: they won 13.47 percent of seats in 1992, but only 5.5 percent in 1997.

Table 2.2 Votes for MNO candidates in local elections in Ilam district

Year	# of VDCs where MNO won seats	Total # of seats MNO won	Total VDC Seats in Ilam district	% of total VDC seats MNO won
1992	24	57	423	13.47
1997	19	123	2,209	5.5

Source: Election Commission (1992, 1997) and interviews with MNO members.

Note
Election results for MNO candidates were ascertained by combining official data from the Election Commission with information about candidates' names from MNO leaders. The number of seats on each VDC was 11 in 1992; this was increased to 47 in 1997.

This decline reflects a nationwide trend in the 1997 local elections: across Nepal, the ruling Nepali Communist Party (United Marxist–Leninist) won more than 50 percent of the seats in VDCs (Hachhethu 2005: 166). In Ilam, too, the MNO lost seats to the Nepali Communist Party. The decline in the MNO's vote share may also be explained by people's increasing understanding of the limited role of village governments in the post-1990 political system, as I discuss in Chapter 4. Despite the government's support for the concept of decentralization, VDCs had little power or autonomy. The capacity of VDC elected officials to bring resources to the village depended on their networks with elected officials and bureaucrats at the district center, who were all members of the mainstream political parties. MNO candidates who were elected to the VDC were thus thwarted in their attempt to secure resources from the center because they did not win seats at the district or national level.

Many analysts interpret the failure of ethnic parties to gain seats in parliament as evidence that ethnic political parties are not viable in Nepal because voters do not support their platforms (Baral 2005: 46; De Sales 2002: 337–338; Hoftun *et al.* 1999). However, as Lawoti (2005) argues, the explosion of ethnic organizations after 1990 shows that ethnic issues were of concern to people, and there are many other reasons why ethnic parties did not fare well at the polls, such as the historical, internal and systemic challenges they faced when competing for votes (pp. 69–73).

The restrictions on registering with the Election Commission limited the MNO's ability to mobilize votes, as it was denied a consistent and common election symbol, access to media and government campaign funds. Nepal's electoral system in the 1990s also worked to the disadvantage of small parties like the MNO. Nepal employed a first-past-the-post (FPTP) electoral system, in which seats were allotted to the individuals who won the most votes, rather than a proportional electoral system, which would allot seats to parties according to the proportion of votes that they received (pp. 264–265).

The ethnic parties were also established much later than the major parties, which worked underground from 1962 to 1990 despite being banned. Thus, they lacked the funds and the experience of older parties. Furthermore, they had to compete with the established networks of other political parties, which had already gained loyal supporters. Finally, ethnic elites were reluctant to leave parties with district- and national-level networks to join these small new parties. As I discuss in the Conclusion, some factors that facilitated the viability of ethnic parties were implemented for the 2008 Constituent Assembly elections. The FPTP electoral system was replaced with a mixed electoral system and the constitutional constraints on the registration of ethnic parties were removed.

One identity-based party that achieved success in the national elections in the 1990s was the *Nepal Sadbhavana Party* (NSP), which seeks to end political discrimination against Madhesis, those who live in the Tarai region, in Nepal's southern plains. The NSP won six seats in parliament in 1991, three seats in 1994 and five seats in 1999 (p. 69). The NSP also formed part of several coalition governments between 1994 and 1999. Its inclusion in parliament furthered the aims of the movement as it 'helped the NSP to highlight Madhesi problems and demands' (op. cit.).

The NSP's greater success in elections than parties representing indigenous nationalities relates to several factors. The clearest distinction between the NSP and these other parties is that the NSP made an appeal to identity in very broad terms, on the basis of region rather than ethnic identity per se. By representing people in the densely populated Tarai region, on the basis of their identity as residents in that region, the NSP had a large pool of potential voters. Another important factor is that the NSP was able to register with the Election Commission, perhaps because its name, which means the Nepal Goodwill Party, contains no ethnic or regional references. Yet, as the case of the RJP indicates, registration alone does not guarantee electoral success. Differences between the Madhesi social movement, which has been organizing since the Panchayat years (Gaige 1975), and the indigenous nationalities movement may also be part of the answer. Madhesi politicians may have greater financial and social resources than their indigenous nationalities counterparts, and people in the more urban Tarai may have a higher degree of political consciousness than people in other regions. Other Madhesi political parties that emerged later also fared very well in the 2008 elections to the Constituent Assembly, as I discuss in the Conclusion.

Ethnic political parties are a more radical form of ethnic activism than IPOs because they aim to gain direct political power for indigenous nationalities. When compared with NEFIN and its member organizations, these political parties offered a broader-based form of political action. Because ethnic parties seek to have their representatives elected, the primary targets of their political activities are the voters, including those in rural Nepal. Since NEFIN's leaders are not elected by the population, the organization did not require the mobilization of rural society. Earlier in the movement, NEFIN and its organizations were largely based in the capital. Thus, in the 1990s, ethnic political parties were more oriented towards mass-mobilization and involved a broader segment of society than NEFIN.

By partaking in elections, the MNO demonstrated its support for the democratic system, showing that it was willing to work within the established, legal political framework to gain political power. Furthermore, the MNO abided by all of the government's rules for campaigning and elections, just as the mainstream, registered parties did. While the MNO was not successful in elections, save for in a few village governments in Ilam district, the significance of the MNO's participation in elections is not limited to the election results. Rather, the party's election activities were also a mode of expressing dissent in a public forum. By operating as a political party and participating in elections despite its lack of registration, the MNO rejected the authority of the state. In campaign speeches, MNO candidates called attention to the Election Commission's refusal to register the MNO, citing it as proof of the high-caste Hindu dominance of the state.

By participating in the elections, the MNO gained an arena in which they could publicize their political agenda. This symbolic dimension of participation in elections is also found in the political behavior of minor parties elsewhere in the world: minor parties participate in elections 'not so much for the purpose of winning, but rather as a means of being heard' and '...to draw attention to their grievances' (Herzog 1987: 321). Thus, the MNO acted not just as a political party but also as a social movement organization, by raising awareness about ethnic inequality in Nepal and mobilizing support for political changes.

The construction of collective identities

One major outcome of this movement was the construction of collective identities for diverse ethnic groups as 'indigenous nationalities' (*ādivāsī janajāti*), or as Mongol, as the MNO prefers. This was a crucial step toward mobilizing people to achieve political changes: since no single ethnic group is a majority in Nepal, groups must work in broad coalitions in order to be recognized by the state. These collective identities established this diverse group of peoples as an important collective political actor that could intervene in the political system. The right to assert these identities was made possible by the emergence of the democratic system. MNO supporters in particular believed that if they had called themselves Mongols in the Panchayat era, they would have been arrested.

The category *ādivāsī janajāti* is now recognized by both a wide sector of society and the government as a legitimate pan-ethnic identity. The creation of this identity has been a contested process, and debates continue about whether this should be the identity label for this group, and which peoples fall under this category. This section examines the contours and political consequences of these identity constructions.

The idea that Mongols or *ādivāsī janajātis* constitute a discrete section of Nepali society was established by the state in the 1854 legal code, the *Muluki Ain*, which corralled many of these groups together under the label *matwāli* (alcohol drinkers), as discussed in Chapter 1. The terms Mongol and *janajāti* build upon this earlier term, *matwāli*. While ethnic activists contested the derogatory connotations of this term, the community that they seek to mobilize is nearly coterminous with the group that was defined as *matwāli*. Peoples who were placed within this *matwāli* category adopted it as a label of self-reference.

Even though MNO activists and leaders rejected the word, villagers in the MNO's stronghold in Ilam often used the terms *matwāli* and Mongol interchangeably.

Both Mongols and *ādivāsī janajātis* are represented as peoples who have 'their own traditional religions, languages and cultures'. The emphasis on religion, language and culture reflects the importance that the Nepali state has given to these categories. In the census, the diversity of the population was recognized on the basis of language and religion until the 1991 census included the category ethnic group for the first time. Groups who make claims on the basis of difference cannot ignore these state-recognized categories. As Sonntag (1995) illustrates, the 1990 constitution's approval of education in 'mother languages' heightened the importance of language as a feature of group identity, and thus even groups without a clear common language mobilized to assert one.

Both Mongol and *ādivāsī janajāti* identities attempt to unite internally heterogeneous groups into a single overarching community by opposing them to high-caste Hindus. Both Mongol and *ādivāsī janajāti* categories are represented as 'not-Hindu', on the grounds that they are not part of the Hindu caste system, and did not historically practice Hinduism. This 'not-Hindu' categorization operates as a 'counternarrative of nationalism', to use Homi Bhabha's (1990) phrase. It rejects the pre-2006 definition of Nepal as a Hindu state, and counters the state's claim that the majority of Nepalis are Hindus.

Other labels for this pan-ethnic community circulated during the Panchayat era, when the state referred to these ethnic groups as 'backward castes' (*pichaḍieko jāti*) (Onta 2006: 308). The term *janajāti* first emerged as an ethnic label during the 1980 referendum, and then became more prominent in the late 1980s, when the indigenous nationalities movement was mobilizing more actively (ibid). Although the word *janajāti* was not new to the Nepali vocabulary, it previously held different meanings, and referred to either a tribe or the general public (Pragya-Pratishtan 2040 v.s.: 469). Its current use as a collective identity became familiar to people at the end of the Panchayat era, when it appeared in publications addressing ethnic political issues, such as the landmark book *Nepālmā Jana-jāti Samasyā* (*Nationalities Problems in Nepal*) (Tamang 1987).

In the 1990s, *janajāti* became the dominant name for these groups, largely through the efforts of NEFIN, initially called the *Nepal Janajati Mahasangh* (Nepal Federation of Nationalities), established in 1990. Activists in this organization selected the label *janajāti* to denote communities that are outside the fold of the Hindu caste system (Tamang 2005: 6), and that have 'their own distinct tradition and original linguistic and cultural traditions' (Nepal Janajati Mahasangh 2047 v.s.). However, since the various *janajāti* groups share no particular language, religion or culture, this aspect of the definition has the potential to fragment these groups.

Janajātis are also defined as Nepal's indigenous peoples (*ādivāsī*), the original inhabitants of Nepal, and, in particular, of specific regions of Nepal. This aspect of the definition became increasingly prominent, and the word for indigenous, *ādivāsī*, was added to the term *janajāti*. In 2004, *ādivāsī* was appended to the name of the *Nepal Janajāti Mahasangh*, which became the *Nepal Ādivāsī Janajāti Mahasangh*, or the Nepal Federation of Indigenous Nationalities (NEFIN).

Before 1990, the label *ādivāsī* (literally, 'first residents') was given primarily to small, semi-nomadic foraging groups such as the Chepang and the Raute. In India, the term *ādivāsī* was used as a name for tribal or indigenous groups. In the 1990s, when the concept of indigeneity became a prominent way of mobilizing support for ethnic political issues in the international arena, the term *ādivāsī* gained a new meaning in Nepal. Initiatives by the United Nations (UN) and other international organizations made the discourse of indigeneity a viable way for small groups of marginalized peoples to claim rights within states (Warren 1998: 6–9). When the United Nations declared an International Year for the World's Indigenous Peoples in 1993, ethnic groups in Nepal began to emphasize their identity as such. Members of Nepal's National Committee for the International Year for the World's Indigenous Peoples attended international conferences such as the United Nations' World Conference on Human Rights in Vienna, Austria, and held cultural programs to showcase the languages and other cultural practices of Nepal's indigenous peoples. Other organizations disseminated UN statements about indigenous peoples.[6]

These activities have intensified. Major annual celebrations are held on International Day of the World's Indigenous Peoples, August 9, in the biggest stadium in Kathmandu and elsewhere in Nepal. One prominent ethnic activist, Parsuram Tamang, served on the Council of the United Nations Permanent Forum on Indigenous Issues, and representatives of other ethnic organizations, including NEFIN, send delegates to the annual forum at the UN in New York. These activities enabled activists to contact donors, learn from other indigenous peoples around the world and gain global attention for their cause.

The concept of indigeneity is also a powerful tool for unifying a heterogeneous population by emphasizing their common historical relationship to the land of Nepal. The category of indigenous peoples excludes Hindu caste groups, which, indigenous nationalities argue, arrived from India. Caste Hindus are viewed as outsiders and as non-natives, a rhetorical move that also enables ethnic activists to portray the dominant group as colonizers. Indigenous nationalities are positioned as the bearers of the 'original' cultural forms of Nepal, and thus more authentically Nepali than caste Hindus.

The MNO also asserts that Mongols are the original inhabitants of Nepal and that caste Hindus came there as refugees from India. The MNO insists on using the term *mūlbāsi*, which can be translated as 'main residents', to express this idea of indigeneity, arguing that the term *ādivāsī* contains negative connotations of primitiveness. Some leaders of NEFIN, like Parsuram Tamang, argued that the term *mūlbāsi* (main residents) obscured the idea that the *janajātis* belonged to this land, as it suggests that there are other groups of people who could also be original residents of Nepal (Mukta Tamang, personal communication). Unlike NEFIN, the MNO has not engaged with the international indigenous peoples' movement.

The movement's representation of these ethnic groups as indigenous nationalities has been contentious. First, high-caste Hindus and some other people argue that everyone in Nepal is indigenous because the country was settled in waves of migration (Bhattachan 1995: 128). Second, there is some debate about whether all groups that fall under the category of *janajāti* are also indigenous; some ethnic groups in the mountain region arrived relatively recently (Tamang 2005: 7). There may be future efforts to distinguish between indigenous *janajāti* and non-indigenous *janajāti* (p. 9). Thus, depending on how it is interpreted, the concept of indigeneity may splinter the community. Third, the discourse of indigeneity may impede efforts to create coalitions of indigenous nationalities and other marginalized groups based on common political goals. Dalits and most Madhesis (other than Tarai dwellers who are also indigenous nationalities) are categorized as non-natives; they are positioned as outsiders who are less authentic and thus less deserving members of the nation.

In 2002, the government of Nepal established the National Foundation for the Development of Indigenous Nationalities (NFDIN). This was a major accomplishment for the indigenous nationalities movement, as the government conferred legitimacy on ethnic demands and adopted an official definition of *ādivāsī janajāti*. NFDIN listed 59 groups on its official schedule of indigenous nationalities and defined them as 'a tribe or community as mentioned in the schedule having its own mother language and traditional rites and customs, distinct cultural identity, distinct social structure and written or unwritten history' (National Foundation for Development of Indigenous Nationalities 2003: 7). Conflict over the boundaries of ethnic categories and over the precise number of ethnic groups within the country has since emerged. Sixteen of the groups listed on the NFDIN schedule were not reported on the 2001 census, and some argue that many of the groups on the NFDIN schedule are in fact subgroups rather than separate ethnic groups (Gurung 2003: 29). NFDIN's definition omitted part of the definition that indigenous nationalities had recommended, that *janajātis* were not part of the Hindu caste system (Onta 2006: 312), perhaps because it was too oppositional for the government. Furthermore, according to the NFDIN's definition, an ethnic group's inclusion in the *ādivāsī janajāti* category is dependent on it being listed on the official government list.

In an effort to recognize some of the differences between these ethnic groups, NEFIN classified the 59 groups on the official schedule into five categories, based on socioeconomic status: endangered, highly marginalized, marginalized, disadvantaged and advantaged (Tamang 2005: 8–9). Some see this as a necessary step toward creating programs and policies that address the particular needs of each community, while others see it as dividing the indigenous nationalities movement.

Arguments about whether or not a people constitutes a separate ethnic group will be difficult to resolve, as they depend more upon politics than upon objective cultural differences. Ethnic groups, as many social scientists have argued, do not emerge due to the existence of cultural differences; rather, cultural differences become salient and serve as markers of ethnic groups in particular political and economic circumstances (Eriksen 1993). Both the government and ethnic activists seek to represent ethnic groups as bounded entities with an objective existence, but the internal diversity and fluidity of these groups complicates this image. Although some of the ethnic labels have long histories, these ethnic groups are not static, and the meanings of ethnic identity have changed over time, as discussed in Chapter 1.

While *ādivāsī janajāti* is the dominant way of framing a collective identity, the MNO asserts a different identity, Mongol, for the same group of peoples. The MNO explicitly rejects the term *ādivāsī janajāti*, vociferously arguing that it means 'nomads' or 'gypsies', contrary to the widely accepted definition of the term. By defining this group as Mongol rather than *janajāti*, the MNO asserts a racial, rather than cultural, identity for this group.

The MNO argues that Nepal is a country composed of two distinct racial groups: Mongols, who make up 80 percent of the population, and Aryans, the name it uses to refer to caste Hindus, who make up 20 percent. In speeches and publications, the MNO claims that Mongols are one of the three races of humans, along with 'Negros' and 'Aryans'. In his book *Hidden Facts in Nepalese Politics*, which was widely read and very influential, as we will see in Chapters 3 and 4, Gopal Gurung writes, 'the Mongol people are not from Mongolia ... out of three lineages of human kind, one was the Mongol race, and the other two were the Negroid and the Aryans. And our fighting is with the black Aryans' (1994: 106). MNO supporters and leaders assert that Mongols and Aryans can be distinguished from one another on the basis of physical traits: Mongols have flat noses, sparse male facial hair and stocky bodies, while Aryans have pointy noses, abundant male facial hair and taller, thinner bodies.

The terms 'Mongol' and 'Aryan' are derived from eighteenth- and nineteenth-century colonial categorizations of South Asians. 'Mongol' emerged as a racial term in the late eighteenth century, the dawn of the ethnological era, when the veritable father of race science, Johann Friedrich Blumenbach, identified five principal human races, one of which he labeled the 'Mongolian' race. From that point forth until the 1960s, the term Mongol (or other permutations of the word including Mongoloid or Mongolian) was used in anthropological studies of race to describe a distinct division of humans defined by a set of physical characteristics (Boas 1938; Cole 1965; Prichard 1848; Tylor 1893). The term Aryan was initially a linguistic label, used by philologists to describe the Indo-European family of languages, but later became a race label referring to all the peoples who spoke these related languages (Trautmann 1997: 13). The MNO revived and elaborated upon parts of this colonial race discourse in order to suit a new political movement.

The terms Mongol and Aryan first circulated in Nepal through social science writings. In the late nineteenth and early twentieth centuries, scholars such as the colonial administrator Brian Hodgson (1874), whose writings on Nepal have had enduring influence, and James Cowles Prichard (1973 [1813]) first applied these ethnological categories to Nepal's population. With the emergence of a public education system in the 1950s, race theory became widely known. Social science college textbooks published in India and Nepal presented Nepal's population as composed of Aryans and Mongols, and were probably responsible for introducing many educated Nepalis to these terms (Chatterji 1974 [1951]; Sharma 2039 v.s.). Nepalis who were in grade school in the 1970s and 1980s recall learning these terms in their social studies classes, and contemporary grade school textbooks reiterate these terms.[7] The terms Aryan and Mongol were also used in ethnological writings by Nepalis and foreigners (Bista 1967; Chatterji 1974 [1951]; Landon 1976 [1928]; Levi 1905).

Many people, particularly in rural areas, were not familiar with these terms until the MNO began to organize after 1990.[8] Despite the pervasive use of racial terms in social science literature in Nepal, Aryan and Mongol were not part of the vernacular vocabulary of identity there. Race has not been a hegemonic means of classifying people in Nepal. Most significantly, the Nepali state has not used race terms as categories for the basis of legislation and administration. Nepal's population was never categorized into races in the census, nor do any of its constitutions make any reference to the racial composition of the population. For example, the 1990 constitution does not say that Nepal is a 'multiracial' state, as well as a 'multi-ethnic and multilingual' state. Thus, it appears that the MNO has resurrected these categories from the margins of discourse about difference in Nepal.

By employing the term Mongol, the MNO maintained some dimensions of the state's categorization of ethnic difference in the Muluki Ain along the lines of *jāt* – caste. The ethnic groups who were encompassed in the *matwāli* caste ranking overlap considerably with those whom the MNO calls Mongols. Like race, *jāt* defined difference in hereditary and exclusive terms. The category Mongol seemed plausible to people as a category of identification because ideas about identity as linked to biology were present in Nepal through the discourse of *jāt*. While some continuity between the framework of caste and race is evident, the MNO perceived its assertion of Mongol identity as a clear and total rejection of caste categories, which upheld the political dominance of Hindus. However, the state moved away from categorizing its citizens in terms of *jāt*; in the 1990 constitution and the 1991 census, people were categorized on the basis of language, culture and religion. The MNO's assertion of a racial identity represents a rejection of this cultural definition of ethnic difference, as well as of the state's older definition of ethnic groups as castes.

Social scientists have observed many cases in the world in which peoples who were classified by a dominant group as a race reappropriated the meanings of the racial labels, and used them to mobilize people for political action (Hall 1985; Sharp 1996). By contrast, the MNO embraced a racial framework, although the dominant group did not impose it upon these groups of people. The 'scientific' race discourse was about hierarchy, about asserting the superiority of white colonizers in relation to the people they were colonizing. The MNO deletes references to this hierarchy, and the location of the Mongol race within it, altering the meanings of the term Mongol. Rather, the MNO highlights the global applicability of race. This aspect of race was also present in the concept from its ethnological beginnings, as race was a way of trying to assign the world's population to a limited number of groups. Yet ethnologists never imagined that these global racial categories could provide the basis of claims to belonging to a transnational community.

By calling themselves Mongols, these numerous, small, marginalized ethnic groups unite themselves with a global community of Mongols that extends throughout Asia. As Kiran Akten explained to me,

> scientists have divided people in the world into three races (*varna*). One is white, one is red and one is black. Among the red group, there are [people in] China, Japan, Thailand, Burma, Naga, and Assam, Korea and Nepal's Rais, Limbus, Tamangs, Magars, Gurungs, Meches, Koches, Dhimal, Tharu, Thakali, all of these people are called Mongols. When we talk of the world's Mongols, we are recognized as Mongols. According to the world's history, according to other religious texts, according to the different books of other countries, this red group of people is known to be called Mongols.... Mongol has a meaning that is known by the world. For example maybe you had heard the word Mongol in America.

Race discourse offers a way for the representatives of these small ethnic groups in a peripheral part of the world to repackage themselves as belonging to one of the 'three races' of the world. By connecting Nepal's ethnic minorities to larger transnational communities, the MNO seeks to position their cause on a global political stage. In writings and speeches, MNO activists also draw parallels between ethnic inequality in Nepal and racial divisions under apartheid in South Africa, and compare Gopal Gurung to Nelson Mandela. The appeal of the term Mongol for people in the MNO is that they believe that 'it has a meaning that is known by the world'. The MNO hopes that using a name with a perceived international presence will enable them to capture international attention and legitimacy. The MNO's use of race illustrates the influence of transnational discourses of identity on this movement, and shows that these rural political actors were trying to position their movement in an international political context. In this way, the discourse of race is similar to that of indigeneity in that both derive their utility from being global identity categories.

The MNO promotes a racial definition of identity to argue that a culturally heterogeneous group is biologically united. Race also provides the MNO with an authoritative social scientific discourse that they use to discredit the classification of their community by the state, which does not use race as an official category in the census or legal codes. In MNO discourse, race appears as a scientific, modern and universal way of categorizing difference, in contrast to the parochial South Asian-specific framework of caste. By adopting the term 'Mongol', the MNO rejects the state's categorization of their community. Finally, the MNO uses race, which is a global framework for understanding human diversity, to bring international attention to their political cause. With the term 'Mongol', the MNO redefines fragmented and obscure ethnic groups as a united and globally recognizable race. The MNO argued that Mongols elsewhere in the world would be sympathetic to their plight. However, the MNO's appeal to its fellow Mongols may go unheeded, as outside Nepal the term generally refers to citizens of Mongolia rather than to a race.

Some MNO activists and supporters have adopted race as a form of self-identification. When describing how they became involved in the party, many individuals told me, 'I looked at my own face in the mirror, and I saw that I am Mongol.' This phrase is based on a popular Nepali adage, 'look at your own face in the mirror before talking' (*āphno anuhār aināma herera kurā garnu*), which means one should recognize one's own faults before criticizing others. People in the MNO use the first part of the adage in a more literal manner, to mean that by looking in the mirror, one should recognize one's own identity, rather than one's own faults, as it is inscribed in one's own facial features. Just as in its use in the standard adage, the mirror in the MNO phrase is used as a metaphor for truth. The phrase is used to express the embodied nature of Mongol identity for those who are willing to confront the truth.

Regardless of whether the MNO is successful in the future, its discursive work to create race as a form of self-identification in Nepal may have a lasting impact. The strengthening of racial identities may increase animosity between marginalized and dominant groups.

Indigenous nationalities or Mongols?

NEFIN and the MNO are both working for the same heterogeneous group of peoples, yet they refer to this population in divergent ways, as '*ādivāsī janajāti*', and as 'Mongol'. The emergence of both Mongol and *ādivāsī janajāti* as ways of constructing this community suggests that difference is created, at least partially, through political contexts. People identify in multiple and fluid ways, but it is the work of identity politics to represent identities as if they were concrete things that can be possessed by groups and by individuals belonging to groups. The emergence of different ethnonyms for this community is related to the different political strategies of the organizations that use and forward these names. Because the representation of difference is part of the process of political mobilization for organizations operating within the framework of identity politics, the constructions of difference that they articulate reflect their political strategies and claims.

The term *ādivāsī janajāti* represents these groups as nationalities, not a single nation. This framework makes sense for NEFIN as a federation of organizations that each represents a different ethnic group that is supposedly culturally distinct from all other groups. Furthermore, it is not crucial for NEFIN to insist that *ādivāsī janajātis* are an essentially unified group, as this organization is not trying to secure direct political power. The term *ādivāsī janajāti* is framed largely within the categories of difference that the state recognizes and uses: language, culture and religion. NEFIN's representation of this community as *ādivāsī janajāti* meshed with this organization's initial strategy working as a pressure group to make changes within the existing structure.

The MNO's insistence on using the term Mongol, rather than *ādivāsī janajāti*, reflects its more confrontational relationship with the state. The MNO asserts that the unity of Mongols, and their difference from caste Hindus, is embodied and thus inescapable. In the face of cultural heterogeneity, race suggests an absolute form of unity. Mongols are not just a collection of parallel groups who all have similar languages and cultures – they are a race, one people and one lineage (*vaṁsa*). In addition to using the word *varna* to refer to race, activists in the MNO use the phrase 'Mongol *vaṁsa*', or lineage, emphasizing that Mongols are a group of kin. They also refer to Mongol identity as residing in the blood, and implore fellow Mongols to 'recognize their own blood' (*āphno ragat chinnu*). This representation of essential unity is useful for the MNO, because their strategies of gaining power by winning votes or by staging an insurrection require unity.

The racial identity that the MNO uses de-emphasizes language, religion and other cultural forms as markers of identity. In asserting race as the primary dimension of identity, the MNO held out biology as a form of authenticity that could appeal to those individuals who did not speak their ancestral languages or live in their ancestral homelands. Even those individuals who lacked cultural authenticity could be legitimate participants in the movement for ethnic rights as the MNO presented it. By using Mongol rather than *ādivāsī janajāti*, the MNO could thus attract some individuals who might not feel that they were able to participate in the NEFIN organizations and other IPOs. As we shall see in Chapters 3 and 4, however, the MNO attracted people from a wide range of ethnic groups in east Nepal, including Limbus and Rais who spoke their ancestral languages and lived in their ancestral homelands, as well as Gurungs and Magars who did not.

As noted earlier, race has not been an official category in the Nepali state's classifications of its population. The fact that the state has not used race as a means of marking difference may in fact be part of the appeal of this racial categorization for the MNO. By employing the term Mongol, the MNO rejects state-assigned categories of identification on the basis of caste, language, culture and religion. The MNO represents its claims in a format that the Nepali state restricted until 2008 – the 'communal' (*sampradāyak*) political party – and likewise defines this community in terms that avoid the state's current definition of them as linguistic or religious minority groups.

The MNO vociferously argues that *ādivāsī janajāti* actually means nomads or gypsies, although this is not the way in which the term is popularly understood in Nepal today. The MNO's objections to the term *ādivāsī janajāti* symbolize its rejection of NEFIN's political strategy. In the MNO's manifesto, Gopal Gurung writes that: 'The actual meaning of the word is that *janajātis* are not citizens of any country because they do not have any country.' For the MNO, just as nomads are described as those who do not have their own country or state, and do not hold state power, those activists who use the term *ādivāsī janajāti* do not seek direct state power. The terms Mongol and *ādivāsī janajāti* connote different relationships between the organizations that use them and the state.

Conclusion

The emergence of both *ādivāsī janajāti* and Mongol as ways of framing the same heterogeneous group of people demonstrates that there is nothing pre-determined about the way that an identity will be formed for a group of people. A particular history and set of cultural practices do not inevitably produce a certain identity; rather, there is always an element of human agency and creativity involved in the construction of identities.

Constructions of this community as both *ādivāsī janajāti* and Mongol reflect the structuring forces of historical and contemporary dominant, frameworks of identity, both national and transnational. The terms '*ādivāsī janajāti*' and 'Mongol' originated outside Nepal and held weight in Nepal because of their connections to global discourses of race and indigeneity. Activists in the movement were drawn to this transnational discourse because they saw themselves as speaking to an international audience, and realized that gaining international support for their cause may help them advance their claims within Nepal. Representations of 'Mongols' and '*janajātis*' are also shaped by historical, state-sponsored categorizations of peoplehood. The considerable overlap in how NEFIN represents *ādivāsī janajātis* and the MNO represents Mongols reflects these shared historical influences.

Some readers may contest my inclusion of the MNO under the banner of the indigenous nationalities movement. However, while Gopal Gurung and some other MNO leaders emphasized the distinctions between the MNO and NEFIN, and between the Mongol and *ādivāsī janajāti* categories, most people I met in Ilam viewed these organizations as accomplishing the same general goals in different ways, and the categories as overlapping, if not interchangeable. Many people were drawn to the MNO after they took part in NEFIN organizations and other IPOs; others were first involved in the MNO and later became involved in these other organizations. As we will see in Chapter 5, the MNO leadership increasingly tried to draw boundaries between its party and these other organizations. Yet the shared conceptual space of these organizations underscores their co-participation in a social movement.

3 Between political party and social movement

People and political activities in the MNO

Fluttering high on a bamboo pole, the red and blue party flag of the Mongol National Organization marked the location of the Mongol National Organization's Village Assembly office in Sukrabare's ramshackle bazaar. On the front of the two-story wooden building hung a faded MNO signboard, announcing the party's main slogan, 'We Mongols are not Hindus'. Below it was a larger sign, painted in bright blue letters, for the farm supply store on the ground floor of the building: 'Pigs, goats and bulls castrated here.'

Kiran Akten, the MNO's general secretary, brought me to see this office on my first visit to his home in Sukrabare, yet during my numerous visits to this village, no MNO meetings were held there. Instead, the MNO usually held informal gatherings at Kiran's breezy bamboo frame house, which sat high on pillars at the edge of the jungle. In my travels through Ilam district, I encountered many such 'offices', shops or homes in high-visibility locations that boasted MNO signboards and flags, yet contained no staff or phones, no pamphlets or files, and were rarely used as meeting spaces.

By inquiring inside a building displaying an office sign, people could meet individuals who could offer them some information about the party. Beyond serving as visible contact points for people interested in learning about the MNO, the existence and placement of these offices indicates the efforts of party activists to give the small, unregistered party a presence in the public domain. While it was impossible for the MNO to achieve its goals of gaining control of the state and instituting major state-level structural and policy changes that would benefit Mongols, its actions were effective in other ways. The MNO built support for ethnic politics in rural Nepal by disseminating a discourse about ethnic inequality. In considering the MNO's activities, it is important to recognize that political action that does not accomplish its stated goals may still have other meanings and unintended effects (Melucci 1988).

These party offices also encapsulate the contrast between the ideal of how a political party should operate as a bureaucratic organization and the MNO's informal operations in practice. In this chapter, I show that in its own way, the MNO communicated a set of ideas to people and constructed a political community along new lines. I focus here on the operations of the party in Ilam district and at the regional (eastern Nepal) level, and examine the challenges of communication and coordination between the levels of the party. I aim here to describe what it meant to try to organize, operate and participate in a small scale, low budget, political party in rural Nepal in the 1990s.

The first part of the chapter describes how Gopal Gurung founded the MNO, his present role in the party and the basic structure of the MNO. I then examine the main roles that people play in the party, including the role of women and debates about the place of gender politics within the MNO. Next, I examine how party activities expanded support for the MNO and created a political community. Through participating in party activities, people in the party gained a sense of being Mongol, as being part of a lived political community.

Founder-President, Gopal Gurung

Even if people in Nepal know nothing else about the Mongol National Organization, most are familiar with Gopal Gurung (see Figure 3.1). Now elderly, and diabetic, he spends most of his days at his home on the outskirts of the southern part of Kathmandu. In the 1990s, a narrow mud path led through lush rice fields towards his modest one-story home, marked by the MNO's red and blue flag and a sign stating 'Mongol *ṭol*' (neighborhood). Here, he received visitors, worked on his latest book and kept up correspondence with party activists and international human rights agencies in a bright front room appointed with a couch and sitting chairs upholstered with white flowered sheets. Linoleum covered the floor and enlarged photographs, showing his round face and portly body nearly drowning in marigold garlands as he is welcomed at mass-meetings, hung on the walls. One shelf was filled with bottles of imported liquor, a chicken-shaped clock and other tokens from his travels overseas. On another shelf were his books, including Sun Tzu's *The Art of War*, *Marx and Engels Through the Eyes of their Contemporaries*, *The United Nations' Resolutions*, *Inside Sikkim: Against the Tide* and others works of political theory, history, and literature in Nepali and English. As these books suggest, he is well educated, and earned a Master's degree in Political Science at Tribhuvan University in Kathmandu in 1979.

I frequently visited him here at his home whenever I was in Kathmandu, and our interactions were initially somewhat formal. He often spoke to me as though delivering polished speeches rather than in a conversational style and he seemed to present himself to me as he wished to be presented to the world beyond Nepal. One steamy, rainy August day in 1996, I arrived and found him sitting cross-legged on his couch, his round stomach protruding beneath a sleeveless under-shirt, rather than his usual 'bush shirt', and working on his latest book *Nepāl ra Bharātmā Bāhunbād* (*Brahmanism in Nepal and India*). Seeing him surrounded by open books and papers spilling out of his worn leather briefcase reminded me of my own writing habits, and when I told him this, he laughed. As the tape-recorder rolled, he began to talk, in Nepali heavily peppered with English, about his life and how he became a political leader. My recounting of his life story here is culled from the long, scattered, informal narrative he shared with me that day.

Figure 3.1 Gopal Gurung.

Born in 1935, and raised in a village in Darjeeling, Gopal Gurung's involvement in politics came out of his childhood exposure to political activities, and his
experiences as a teacher, writer and journalist. He first encountered politics through
his father, Tej Bahadur Gurung, who became politically active upon retiring from
the British army, like many ex-servicemen. In the 1940s, his father was involved
in the All-India Gorkhali League, an organization that worked for the rights of
Nepalis in India and in a Gurung organization; later he became involved in the
Communist Party of India. Gopal Gurung recalled learning much about politics by
listening to his father give speeches to laborers on the Darjeeling tea plantations,
by listening to meetings of communist activists in his home, and by watching his
father organize a huge strike in Darjeeling. Though Gopal Gurung insisted that he
has never supported the Communist Party, he admits that this early exposure to the
party has influenced him: 'My father was a communist at first, although he was not
well educated. But it influenced me a bit. But it was natural that it would influence
me because my family was not an aristocratic family.... I experienced more
sorrow than happiness. When people see trouble, people think about communism.'
His family background and his exposure to communism, he explained, led him to
'take the side of the poor' throughout his life. His interest in nationalism and ethnicity was influenced by his father's involvement in the Gurung organization and in
the All-India Gorkhali League in India. Many Nepali social movements have been
launched from Darjeeling, as Nepalis did not always have the freedom to pursue
oppositional movements in Nepal (Onta 1996b; Uprety 1992).

Gopal Gurung came to Nepal and began teaching in 1952 in Ilam district, at
the age of 17. There were few schools in Nepal at that time and he founded a
small elementary school, holding classes in an old goat pen. He laughed as he
recounted his first teaching position: 'I was young at that time,... I used to wear
half pants. But compared to those who hadn't studied at all, I was educated. I

opened the school in the goat pen, and taught there. I was the founder of that school as well. Now finally, it has become a high school.'

Later, he served as assistant headmaster and headmaster of two schools in Jhapa district and, in 1964, he taught school for one year in the British army camp in the town of Dharan, where hopeful soldiers tried to join the army, and soldiers in the Gorkha regiments of the British army trained before heading overseas. Schoolteachers frequently become involved in politics in Nepal because their respected status and far-reaching influence in rural communities gives them an excellent base of supporters. But it was also observing the condition of the people coming down from the hills to join the army that made him decide to become involved in politics:

> After leaving teaching, I wanted to give something new to the people. When I was teaching at the British army camp, I used to think about these things. I was a writer and a poet also.... People came down from the hills, from Panchthar, and Ilam, to join the British army. When their families came they stayed in an inn, a shelter for travelers at the camp. It was very dirty.... The people there had little kerosene lamps, and they carried large baskets, and came carrying huge walking sticks. And then they cooked in old, old pots and ate *ḍhĩḍo* (a thick porridge of cornmeal or other grain flour and water). My teacher's quarters were right next to that inn and whenever I went to my quarters, I would see them. I saw that these people had an instinct and I wondered, why? Our people have been fighting in wars for 200 years. For 200 years, they have been joining the army. Even so, why are these people in this condition? I thought about this a lot.

He lost this teaching job the next year, but seeing the condition of these people inspired him to conduct a 'life study' of the people in the villages of eastern Nepal:

> In 1964, I walked alone from Biratnagar [a city in Morang district]. I had only an umbrella, a bag and a coat. From there I walked to Jhapa [district], and from Jhapa I went to Ilam [district], through [the town of] Sanischare. From Panchthar [district], to [the town of] Dhankuta, and from Dhankuta to Dharan, there wasn't even a road there. I returned to Biratnagar from there. It took me four and a half months.... At that time I was quite young, 27 or 28 years old.

He recounted that, through this tour of eastern Nepal, he renewed contacts with many former students, and met many people who later would become supporters of the MNO.

Through his writings, Gopal Gurung gained prominence and began to formulate his political ideas.[1] In 1960, while teaching in eastern Nepal, he began to work as a journalist, writing articles on a freelance basis for newspapers. He moved to Kathmandu and continued working as a journalist while attending Tribhuvan University. He began publishing and serving as the editor-in-chief of a Nepali language newspaper, called *New Light*, from Kathmandu in 1967. This newspaper played a leading role in disseminating his ideas about ethnic inequality in Nepal and was published until 1988. The circulation of *New Light* reached 3,000 copies, with distribution in many parts of eastern Nepal as well as in Kathmandu. From 1972 onwards, Gopal Gurung began writing in *New Light* about ethnic discrimination and the plight of the 'martial races' in Nepal, as he then called them, using the English words. Since the All-India Gorkha League, which his father was involved in, also used this label (Magar 1994: 62), it is possible that Gopal Gurung first encountered the term 'martial races' as a youth in Darjeeling. In 1979, a brief period of relative political freedom in the Panchayat era, he and others held a conference in Pulchowk, Kathmandu to discuss the problems facing Mongols (Kurve 1979).

In 1985, he published a book titled *Nepāli Rājnītimā Adekhā Sachāi* (*Hidden Facts in Nepalese Politics*), which spread his ideas and his name to more people than he had reached through *New Light*. The book, which Prayag Raj Sharma aptly calls 'the first blueprint for ethnic resentment', (Sharma 1997: 486), played a major role in creating support for the MNO, and for the ethnic political movement in general.

The slim blue paperback of about 100 pages contains neither chapters nor section headings but rather strings together editorials that he published between 1984 and 1985 in *New Light*. Gopal Gurung published three Nepali-language editions of the book and a fourth edition in English in 1994, called *Hidden Facts in Nepalese Politics*. Over 4,000 copies of the first three editions of the book were sold. However, even though the book had been banned, a larger number of people probably read it, as copies circulated throughout eastern Nepal. People who got hold of a copy read it furtively, fearing that they would be arrested if they were discovered reading such controversial material, before passing the book along to their friends. A single tattered copy made the rounds through the village of Maidel in the late 1980s, just prior to the end of the Panchayat regime.

With its polemic tone and blunt presentation of the oppression of Mongols, the book made a strong impression on those people who read it. MNO activists frequently draw upon the examples given in the book when giving speeches, and when trying to convince others to join the MNO, thus publicizing the 'hidden facts' to those who cannot read. Throughout Ilam and Jhapa, MNO supporters told me in interviews that reading *Adekhā Sachāi* (*Hidden Facts*), as they referred to the book, played a large role in their decision to join the MNO. As the book is composed of many short segments, it is not necessary to read it all the way through, or in sequence, in order to follow the main ideas. This structure, and its relatively straightforward style, may have increased the book's appeal to those villagers with lower reading skills, and to those people who had to read the book in secret.

The 'Nepalese politics' of the title refers not just to the workings of the Nepali state, but encompasses the entire sphere of power relations in Nepal.[2] Throughout the book, Gurung brings 'hidden facts' in this sphere into light to demonstrate 'the exploitation, suppression, and deprivation' of Mongols (Gurung

1994: 8), and also to argue for the necessity for Mongols to gain political power. He argues that it is the hidden nature of these facts that illustrates the Mongols' lack of political power in Nepal: 'If our Mongol race had political power, these events and so many other hidden facts like it would have been included in the history and our Mongol people would be better off not only economically [and] educationally but also in every other respect' (p. 49). For Gurung, then, the book represents an effort to rewrite the history of Nepal from the perspective of Mongols.

The 'hidden facts' which Gurung seeks to expose are clustered around several themes. One major theme in the book is the discrimination that Mongols face because of the high-caste Hindu domination of the Nepali state. Here, Gurung describes the lack of religious freedom in Nepal as a Hindu state, the lack of government jobs for Mongols, the high-caste Hindu bias of mainstream political parties, and the formulation of nationalism in the Panchayat era Nepali state as excluding Mongol identities, and as affiliating Nepal's identity with that of India.

One passage from the book that exemplifies this theme is the story of an incident in which high-caste Hindus killed Ratnakumar Bantawa Rai, a political activist in the Communist Party (p. 44). While the official story holds that Rai was killed by the police for his activities in the Communist Party, Gurung reports that 'the leftist Bahun leaders conspired against Bantawa and trapped him to be shot dead' because 'he had many times raised the issue of racial discrimination in their group discussion in the Jhapa Communist Party and had hinted that the Bahuns were exploiting the Rais and Limbus and Hindus were cheating the villagers by all means' (op. cit.). For Gurung, this event is significant because 'our Mongol race lost a promising leader' (op. cit.). This story was often included in MNO speeches.

A second prominent theme is the plight of the Gurkha soldiers, composed largely of Mongols, who join the British army and receive what appears to be a large salary, in the context of village Nepal, for risking their lives in foreign conflicts. Gurung presents this history of foreign army employment as detrimental to Mongols, as it has channeled Mongols away from involvement in their own country, and has been a form of exploitation of Mongols as they are relatively underpaid for their services. Yet he also holds up the Gurkhas' world-famous bravery and martial skills as a model that Mongols should emulate in fighting for their own rights in their own land:

> For two centuries we Gorkhas were fighting and dying like sacrificed animals in foreign lands and in return we neither achieved any rights of freedom nor could earn any amount of wealth or wisdom for coming generations. In such a dilemma of desperation, shouldn't we take our chance and fight for our own sake as the only resort? In order to check such boiling questions the rulers will have to share all freedoms and rights with the downtrodden Mongol people when there is time.
>
> (Gurung 1994: 42)

These ideas are echoed in many MNO songs, as we shall see in Chapter 5.

A third theme in the book concerns how the Hindu religion has oppressed Mongols: the caste system discriminates against Mongols, and Hindu myths contain negative representations of Mongols. By following the Hindu religion, Mongols were blinded to their subjugated position:

the Bahun priests gradually hypnotized our fore fathers [...] with the fanciful stories of the Hindu religion and made them worship the Hindu gods and goddesses. They inculcated a confused tradition and culture, which created complexes [on] both sides. Our fore fathers never raised their heads of reverence [*sic*] and taught us to follow in their steps, never questioning the Hindu priests and rulers as well. Not only in schools, but in colleges and universities also, our children had to study literature, history and everything written by the Hindu authors. So even literate people are today not ready to accept this new dimension of thought and waste their valuable lives in the service of their Hindu masters, forgetting their own identity, dignity and entity. The source of our thinking process is so much distorted that we can't think for ourselves. The slave mentality still strongly holds us.

(Gurung 1994: 83–84)

Passages such as this directly attacked the high-caste Hindu power wielders in Nepal. Because of this radical book, Gopal Gurung was arrested in 1988 under the State Offense Act and sentenced to three years in jail. The State Offense Act made it illegal for anyone to damage the image of or attack the royal family, or disturb the peace of the country in any way. This Act was broadly interpreted and frequently invoked to arrest people during the Panchayat era for a variety of activities that criticized the authoritarian Panchayat state.[3]

When the multi-party system was re-established in 1990, Gurung was released, having spent one year and eight months in jail.[4] While in jail, he decided to found the Mongol National Organization on January 1, 1989, although no party activities took place until 1990. People in eastern Nepal heard that he had founded the MNO and began forming party committees as soon as the multi-party system was announced, without waiting for direction from Gopal Gurung. As he recalled, 'After I opened the party in jail, people opened and formed committees on their own. They took their own initiative. Because they were acquainted with me from my book, and from my earlier newspaper. They knew my line.'

Gopal Gurung's assertion that people in east Nepal took the lead in forming party committees is supported by the fact that, when people first began to hold mass-meetings to raise support for the party, they were calling the party a slightly different name, the Mongol Kirat Party.

This suggests that the support for the MNO in eastern Nepal emerged not just from the distinctive economic and political features of the area, but also from the fact that he had already established a network of people in this area who knew him and supported his ideas. Many people whom he met while he worked as a teacher in Ilam and Jhapa and as a journalist in eastern Nepal went on to support the MNO. While traveling around all of the districts of eastern Nepal in 1964 to conduct what he described as his 'geographical study, a life study of the people', he strengthened contacts with people in rural eastern Nepal who knew him from his articles and poems. Conducting business for his newspaper also regularly brought him to eastern Nepal, and his writings were distributed throughout the region.

MNO structure

As the party president and founder, Gopal Gurung is at the top of the organizational hierarchy of the MNO. While the MNO had few supporters in Kathmandu in the 1990s, living there has enabled him to be in regular contact with journalists, politicians and other ethnic political activists. He has made efforts to internationalize the MNO's cause by contacting journalists in India, Nepalis posted overseas with the British army, human rights organizations like Amnesty International, and by meeting with foreign scholars, including me. From his location in Kathmandu, he has taken on projects that directly confront the state. He filed a case against the Election Commission for refusing to register the MNO. The case was heard at the Supreme Court and was finally rejected.[5] He also wrote a letter to King Birendra in which he requested him to step down from his throne, since the monarchy had outlived its appropriateness for Nepal. The king would be appointed as Nepal's first president, but once his first term ended, he would then run for re-election for president, Gopal Gurung suggested.

As he lives in Kathmandu, Gopal Gurung was somewhat removed from the daily workings of the party in eastern Nepal in the 1990s. Communication between him and the activists in eastern Nepal was irregular, even though he wrote them letters, called those few activists who had access to telephones and made occasional visits to eastern Nepal. Most of his visits to eastern Nepal were during elections, or for special programs like mass-meetings or party conferences. On several occasions, he spent several weeks in Ilam and Jhapa, walking from village to village 'to listen to what activists want and think', as he told me.

Gopal Gurung wielded what Weber (1946: 246) has called 'charismatic authority'. Many people within the party perceived their allegiance to the MNO as allegiance to him, and credited him with having 'opened their eyes' to the real plight of Mongols. Most people in the party viewed him with the utmost respect. Many people wrote devotional songs to him and had garland-draped pictures of him in their homes. His photographs appeared as a central feature in many party publications. People considered him to be the ultimate authority, and tried to consult with him before making any major decisions regarding the party. Such charismatic figures are often at the center of small social movements (Wallace 1969).

In the 1990s, the MNO was in the midst of the process of 'the routinization of charisma', in which authority becomes invested in lasting institutions rather than in individuals (Weber 1946: 262). While Gopal Gurung initially asserted that he would remain the life-long president, he later decided that the party should hold elections for this post at its first national conference in 1998. At this conference it was decided that elections for president would be held at the national conference, held every five years. Not surprisingly, Gopal Gurung ran unopposed and won unanimously, and it is unlikely that he would be voted out of the position. However, holding these elections legitimized his position by transforming it into an acquired position, rather than one that he as an individual embodies.

After the president, the next level in the party was the rather clandestine Central Assembly, the inner circle of party leaders who made major decisions concerning the party. Central Assembly members were chosen by Gopal Gurung for their devotion to the organization, rather than for their political experience, further supporting the idea that charismatic authority is at work in the MNO. No one would tell me, or most others in the MNO, the names and number of people on this committee, when it met or what it did. Party members asserted that it was necessary to keep this information secret, as they believed that the Nepali state might take action against MNO leaders at some point in the future.

After Gopal Gurung, Kiran Akten was perhaps the most important figure in the MNO in terms of generating ideas that guide the party. Kiran Akten was head of the Central Assembly and held the post of general secretary of the party for a few years in the 1990s. Kiran was a farmer in his early thirties who had spent a few years in the Indian army, like many MNO supporters. Like Gopal Gurung, Kiran was also a charismatic leader. With elegant and expressive facial features and a penchant for flashy outfits like white suits, Kiran was a magnetic personality and was renowned throughout Ilam and Jhapa districts for his powerful, emotional speeches and songs. As one elderly Gurung lady told me, echoing the voices of many villagers, 'When Kiran Akten gives a speech, everyone's eyes fill with tears.' Many people in the MNO said that it was listening to Kiran's words that brought them into the party. People in the MNO referred to him as an intellectual, and assumed that he was well educated, although he attended school only through fifth grade. Kiran was a 'local intellectual'; such people, 'may lack formal credentials but they are recognized communally as producers of authoritative knowledge and interpreters of social reality' (Warren 1998: 25–26).

The district assemblies and village assemblies formed the final two layers of party organization. The MNO constitution did not specify the composition of these committees, nor elaborate upon their functions. The Ilam district assembly was composed of a chair, a vice chair, a secretary and a number of members. Village assemblies existed in every village (VDC) where the MNO had a group of supporters. On the MNO village assembly in Maidel, where I did much of my research, there were representatives from each of the nine wards in the village, and a committee chair, a vice chair and a secretary.[6] One member of each village assembly served as a representative to the district assembly, and was supposed to coordinate activities and channel information between these two levels.

Participation in the MNO: leaders, activists and supporters

People used the labels 'leader' (*netā*), 'activist' (*kāryakartā*) and 'supporter' (*sahayogī*) to describe the different roles that individuals could play in the party. Supporters were all of the people who voted for the MNO, showed up at large party events, and contributed small amounts of money for party events like the MNO's First Annual Conference. Supporters often described themselves to me with the phrase 'I am just an ordinary supporter', emphasizing that they saw themselves as being marginally involved in party activities. While the party distributed membership cards when first mobilizing, there were no required annual membership fees and the MNO kept no comprehensive list of people who were supporters.

The activist category included everyone who worked for the party as suggested by the literal meaning of the word *kāryakartā*: 'one who does work'. Activists received no monetary compensation for their involvement in the party, unlike some full-time activists in the major political parties. They covered most of their own expenses to conduct party work, although wealthier members of the party often provided food for everyone at large gatherings. Activists engaged in different forms of work for the party, depending upon whether they operated at the district and regional (eastern Nepal) level, or at the village level. Party work ranged from creating and disseminating the party's songs or plays to campaigning in village elections. The district/regional-level activists were the most respected and influential activists within the party, and were known by all MNO supporters.

Kavita Rai, one of the leading women activists in the MNO, and reportedly a member of the Central Assembly at one time, joined the party just after it formed. She matched Nepali ideals of feminine beauty with waist-length, shining black hair and fair skin. Though she was in her thirties, she was unmarried and was one of the most outspoken, opinionated women I have met in Nepal. Wearing pastel-colored nylon saris and carrying a handbag, she traveled extensively throughout Ilam and Jhapa districts giving speeches at mass-meetings. Kavita compared district-level activists like herself to teachers, as they the disseminate the ideas of the MNO:

> The work of our party is to teach our people everything, from foot to head, from A to Z (*ka* to *gya*): we have to teach them what our language is, what our rights are, whose children we are, whose country this is, what we have to do, what people's duties are, and what Mongols' identity is. And the activists in our party are the teachers.... They are just like teachers, going from village to village and telling people what our party's goal is, what our party's ideas are; that's our work.

Because Kavita acted as a teacher in her capacity as a district-level activist, villagers regarded her as an educated person, even though she had only studied for a few years of grade school. She attended district-level meetings and also participated in party activities in her home village of Sukrabare. When she was not helping her family run their liquor and snacks stall out of their one-room thatched-roof home during the weekly market, she trained younger women to give MNO speeches.

Activists like Khom Bahadur Gurung from Maidel who worked exclusively at the village level were not as involved in the dissemination of party ideas as district-level activists were. The primary work of village-level activists was mobilizing party support during elections. Like the majority of village-level activists, Khom Bahadur was a young man in his mid-thirties who had completed some high school education, and sported baseball caps and jeans. During the local election of 1997, he contributed cash earned from his popular dry goods store to provide almost all of the campaign funds required for two MNO candidates to run for village development committee chair and vice chair. He also accompanied these candidates for days at a time on their travels throughout the distant wards of Maidel, participated in village-level party meetings where the campaign strategies were planned, and tried to convince voters to support the MNO.

The difference between the activist and leader categories varied, depending on the context and the perspective of the person making the distinction. From Gopal Gurung's point of view, all of the people who work in the party are activists rather than leaders. Other individuals were considered to be leaders in the village, yet were only activists at the district/regional level. For example, Maidel villagers thought of Nar Bahadur Gurung as a party leader, as he was instrumental in mobilizing support for the party there, but his activities at the district and regional level were limited, and district-level leaders and activists thought of him as a village activist.

There were about a dozen people in Ilam who almost everyone in the party, aside from Gopal Gurung and Kiran Akten, called leaders. These leaders took a creative role in forming and disseminating party ideas, but also made decisions about the organizational side of the party, such as when meetings would be held, and whether identity cards should be issued to party members, to distinguish those Mongols who 'just have Mongol faces' from those Mongols who are in the MNO. These leaders were from several different ethnic groups, and had enough resources to be able to devote substantial time to the party.

One such leader was Mukta Rai, the chairman of the MNO Ilam district assembly and a former policeman, with a rotund figure, a friendly round face and perpetually ruddy cheeks. He had moved to Ilam district from his home district of Solu Khumbu after he joined the police force. During the late Panchayat years, he was posted to the area near Maidel, and married a local woman. After 1990, he began campaigning for the MNO, giving speeches at mass-meetings in the area. Soon thereafter, he lost his police job because of his involvement in the party. He lived in a small bazaar town on a windswept ridge across the valley from Maidel, where he and his wife managed to support themselves and their two children by selling tea, alcohol and snacks in their smoky three-room home. For weeks at a time, either alone or with Kiran and other activists, Mukta walked through the hills on party business wearing a tweed sports coat, twill trousers and leather dress shoes.

Women's participation in the MNO

Men made up the overwhelming majority of activists and leaders in the MNO. Only a handful of women were activists at the district level, or were involved in the official decision-making branches of the party. The few women who were more involved in party activities usually were more independent than most women in Nepal, and shared a few characteristics with politically prominent Nepali women in general. Tawa Lama (1995) points out that most of the women who were elected as Members of Parliament in the first elections after the 1990 people's movement were older than 40, more educated than most women, or unmarried, either single or the widow of a prominent politician. Similarly, I found that politically active women in the MNO were either older women with daughters-in-law to carry out the most time-consuming household and agricultural tasks, unmarried or divorced women living at their natal homes, or upper-level high school students and thus relatively well-educated for the village. Kavita Rai's relative independence, as an unmarried woman in her thirties, facilitated her participation in politics.

Men in MNO leadership positions assumed that women would not be involved in the central work of the party, but rather would do party work that specifically related to women. Activists who were women were always marked as 'women activists' and were given party positions that were labeled 'women's posts', while men were simply called 'activists' and held unmarked positions.

A women's wing of the MNO operated for several years right after the party formed.[7] A signboard for the MNO women's wing that I spotted in the back room of someone's house showed the silhouette of a fist with bangles, a ubiquitous symbol of femininity, against the horizontal blue and red background of the MNO flag. Women told me that the women's wing had initially been quite active, but had faded by the mid-1990s. When Radhika, the chair of this wing, stepped down from her post because of personal problems, a new woman was appointed chair but she did not hold any subsequent meetings. The male leadership of the party described the women's wing as a way for women to be involved in the party, and for women to recruit other women to vote for the party. Similarly, Radhika stated that the goal of the women's wing was to increase women's participation in the MNO. No one suggested this organization would address issues of gender inequality as they pertained to 'Mongol' women.

While only a few women were activists and leaders, many women were involved in the party as 'ordinary supporters'. Most of these women supporters were reluctant to be interviewed about the party and insisted that they 'didn't know enough' to answer my questions. Yet these same women fervently discussed politics among themselves. While few women were involved in making decisions about who would run for election as MNO candidates, they knew the political affiliations of every individual in the village. Before the local elections, women passionately discussed who would vote for which party, who had left or joined the MNO, and how various candidates might do in the election. Thus, women probably influenced the outcome of elections, though it was difficult to document this.

Male leaders and activists in the MNO viewed women's rights as holding little relevance to the main goals of the party. Elsewhere in the world, as well, leaders in nationalist and ethnic political movements often regard issues of women's equality as secondary to the all-encompassing issues of securing rights for the nation (Radhakrishnana 1992). Early on in my stay in Maidel, I heard a conversation in a tea shop that reflected the general view of gender politics that most male MNO activists held. Mina, a daughter-in-law in the household, was busy making tea to serve to a group of men in the MNO who had gathered there on the way home from their fields. The Communist Party (UML) had gained control of the government in national elections a few months earlier and the party was instituting populist programs to secure people's favor. Nar Bahadur began complaining that the Communist Party was giving too much attention to issues of 'women's liberation' (*nārī mukti*). A second man grumbled, 'Yes, they say things should be equal between men and women!' 'Women are going to plough!' cried another man, as the other men laughed. 'Chop trees and dig up rocks!' chimed in a third man.

Nar Bahadur commented, 'I really liked one thing that Kiran Akten said about women's liberation – that the Hindus, the Bahun-Chhetris, need it, not us. Under Hinduism, a woman can't eat until her husband has eaten and then she has to eat off of his dirty plate,' he asserted. 'If a 20-year-old woman's husband dies, she can never remarry. It's not like that in our Mongol society! We don't need women's liberation!' The others nodded in agreement, smiling and murmuring, 'That's right.' Unwilling to let this be the last word on that topic, I ventured, 'What you said is fine but there are other ways in which Mongol women may also need women's liberation. Look at the few women involved in politics, in the MNO. Look at the number of women who have little education!' Nar Bahadur and others responded that these problems were the result of the negative influence of Hindu society. One man told me, 'Once the new generation gets away from the ideas of Hindu society, Mongol women won't need women's liberation!'

Throughout this conversation I was acutely aware of Mina hunched in the shadows by the hearth preparing tea, peeling potatoes for dinner, holding her baby and refraining, as usual, from joining the conversation of guests in the house. When I asked her for her opinion about the conversation, she just laughed and said, 'Who knows!' Another more outspoken daughter-in-law in that household often complained about her heavy workload and lack of freedom, and she might have chimed in had she not been out gathering firewood.

Kiran and other men in the MNO asserted that the party did not need to address women's liberation because Mongol women were already free. I frequently heard the argument that Mongol women are free by comparison with Hindu women, and if there are instances in which Mongol women appear not to be free, it is because of the influence of Hindu society. This representation of Mongol women as free was part of a wider discourse that describes women of 'tribal' or 'ethnic' groups in Nepal as sexually free and independent, in opposition to Hindu women, particularly those of high castes, described as sexually and socially controlled.[8] Women who wished to organize for women's rights within the boundaries of the MNO had an uphill battle, as men in the party viewed women's rights as irrelevant to their cause.

Kavita Rai was more critical in her interpretation of gender relations among Mongols. Like Kiran and Nar Bahadur, she asserted that Mongol women were much freer than Hindu women and blamed the influence of Hinduism for the oppression that Mongol women do experience. Unlike these men, however, Kavita felt that the movement for women's rights in Nepal was necessary and applicable to Mongol women. Kavita regularly read feminist magazines published in Kathmandu and recounted that in her campaigning for the MNO she urged Mongol women to fight for their rights. She refuted the notion that Mongol women were in a better position than Hindu women, as they were more likely than Hindu women to be uneducated. She also discussed some social problems that Hindu and Mongol women shared, such as the lack of rights to their parent's property. Fighting to secure these rights was a major goal for the women's movement in the 1990s, and Kavita praised Mira Dhungana, a woman lawyer, for bringing a case to the Supreme Court to try to change these laws. Overlooking the fact that this lawyer is a high-caste woman, Kavita described her as a model that all women should follow to gain their rights: 'Mira Dhungana fought alone not just for her individual rights but for the rights of all women in the future.' Kavita allowed gender politics to take precedence over ethnic politics in this case.

This debate over the place of women's rights within the MNO's struggle for Mongol rights highlights the awkward relationship between gender politics and ethnic or national politics that other scholars have noted. Women are expected to postpone political claims regarding gender and to subordinate these to the nationalist cause (Aretxaga 1997). Yet women's participation in nationalist politics substantially shaped these movements, bringing feminist concerns to the forefront of these movements (Aretxaga 1997; Jayawardena 1986). Kavita and the few other women who passionately talked about the need for women's rights were not able to bring these issues to the forefront of the MNO.

Party activities

In this section I examine three forms of political activity in the MNO: traveling, assembly meetings and mass-meetings. Through these activities, individuals in the MNO planned and coordinated other activities, taught people about MNO ideas, and connected with other individuals in the party, thus creating and sustaining a political community. All of these activities consisted of face-to-face interactions between people at different levels of the party. Written communiqués from the upper levels of the party to the lower levels were irregular and infrequent. Activists at the village level frequently bemoaned the MNO's paucity of written materials, which were limited to the MNO manifesto, Gopal Gurung's books and a handful of pamphlets that activists periodically produced. Thus, personal interactions were the main form of communication within the party, and orchestrating these interactions inevitably required traveling.

> *Traveling*
> Walking uphill and downhill, across ridges and resting places,
> We've arrived to meet brothers, to spill the miseries of Mongols,
> Oh, sisters, to spill the miseries of Mongols.
> The only present we've brought is the sorrows of Mongols,
> Just the sound of the breath of life and hot blood,
> Just the message of rising up.
> Uphill and downhill.

Kiran Akten wrote this song while on a month-long journey through the hills, and sang it while strumming his guitar one chilly, moonlit night for me and a small group of activists who were accompanying him on another trip. As this song expresses, traveling was a ubiquitous and arduous feature of life for MNO activists, as it was required for all party activities. Activists who could afford tickets traveled by rickety, overcrowded buses as far as possible, though breakdowns, inexplicable delays and the circuitous route of the winding roads often meant that bus travel saved little time over walking. Most activists walked uphill and downhill through the mountains to their destinations on the steep, narrow trails that are the main highways of rural Nepal. Cliff-hugging paths were made more treacherous in the rainy season, which seemed to be much of the year in Ilam, when green moss would cover already slippery clay. A false step could send a traveler plunging off the side of a mountain. I preferred to follow flatter, wider paths where they existed, even if they made for a longer trip, but the activists I walked with, like most people in rural Nepal, could walk more quickly on hilly routes than on relatively flat terrain. With the notoriously unreliable and slow postal system, and scarcity of telephones, traveling by these means was the only way for activists to plan party events, publicize the MNO's ideas and meet one another.[9]

Traveling deserves to be examined not just as a means for conducting other party activities, but also as a meaningful political activity in its own right. In her description of Meratus politics in Indonesia, Anna Tsing (1993) argues that we should pay attention to travel practices as ways of forming particular types of knowledge and communities. Her observation that 'Meratus politics are a politics of traveling' describes politics in Nepal equally well, especially at the rural level (p. 127). Of particular relevance is her insight that 'effective traveling and visiting become central practices of leadership and community-building' (ibid.). Traveling in east Nepal, however, was not an activity that was available to everyone as it was time-consuming and required access to at least some cash to occasionally pay for bus fares or food. Furthermore, travel was particularly difficult for women.

The importance of traveling to political practice constrains women's participation in the MNO, as well as in politics throughout Nepal, because women are less free to travel than men. Anna Tsing (ibid.) points out that Meratus women could not travel and participate in politics because they were burdened by household tasks (p. 128). In Nepal, women in the MNO faced additional obstacles to travel because their families saw frequent travel as inappropriate for them, as society would regard them as uncontrolled and thus immoral.

Leaders and district- or regional-level activists in the MNO like Kiran constantly received MNO visitors at their homes, and frequently traveled themselves. On my first visit of several days to Kiran's home in the southern Ilam village of Sukrabare, four MNO activists from other parts of Ilam district came to visit him and stayed at his house. One visitor came to tell Kiran about disputes within the party, another to recount other party news, a third came to invite him to perform at cultural programs, and the last visitor hoped to arrange a mass-meeting. As I learned from my many later visits to Sukrabare, and from Kiran's wife, this was not unusual. As his wife complained to me, while restoking the fire to cook dinner the second time that night to feed late-arrived activists from northern Ilam, 'It's so much work. People from the party are constantly coming. This is the problem with being married to someone in politics!' Furthermore, Kiran was often gone on party-related journeys, and much of the household work fell to her. Kiran's family was not well off and these additional visitors strained their food resources.

One of the visitors, named Dilli Ram Khawas, arrived long after we had finished eating dinner one night. Dilli Ram hunched over as he walked, dragging his shoeless feet and leaning on a cane; his thinning hair was matted and oily and his cropped army pants and jersey were shiny with ground-in dirt. A small drab green canvas backpack with an umbrella strapped to it hung from his shoulders. Kiran introduced him as one of the MNO's most faithful activists and explained that, during the Panchayat years, Dilli Ram had been imprisoned and tortured for his involvement in the then-outlawed Congress Party. Beatings and electrocution had disabled him to the extent that he could not wear shoes, change his own clothing or bathe himself; the limited range of motion in his arms made it challenging for him to feed himself, and electrocution to his tongue made it difficult for him to speak clearly. Despite these limitations, and perhaps because of them since he could not do farm work, he spent most of his time traveling between villages to visit MNO supporters and activists.

Kiran described Dilli Ram as a 'great friend of the MNO' and insisted that I accompany him on his travels through Ilam, as he would be able to introduce me to many MNO supporters in the villages. I agreed but with some hesitation, since I had trouble understanding Dilli Ram's speech, and was squeamish about the lice that occasionally scurried across his chest. During the two weeks that I trailed along with Dilli Ram, we walked everywhere, even to those villages that were located on motorable roads, because it was impossible for him to climb onto buses. I struggled to keep up with him on the slippery wet clay trails, clomping along in my expensive hiking boots and lugging my large backpack full of clothes and equipment. MNO supporters and activists in the villages we visited received him warmly and gave us food and lodging for a few nights. People from all around the village gathered at the houses where we stayed to listen to Dilli Ram recount news about the state of party support and about the activities of party activists in the other villages he had visited. Dilli Ram carried nothing but pamphlets in his small backpack on his travels, and handed out frayed copies to the people who came to meet with him at every village. With the assistance of another activist, from time to time he wrote and published these pamphlets as a way to spread news about mass-meetings and election results in distant villages. This pamphlet, called *Mongol Vaṁsaharuko Susamachar* (*Mongols' Good News*) was one of the only efforts in the MNO to regularly and formally communicate party news to supporters. Both the pamphlets and his stories of individuals in places he had visited created a sense of community for people in the party.

District and regional activists like Dilli Ram traveled frequently, and thus created and sustained bonds between people in the MNO. Through these itinerant individuals, people in disparate villages gained a sense of the MNO as operating as a whole. Yet Dilli Ram's visits throughout the Ilam and Jhapa districts carried a different set of meanings for people than Kiran's visits. Because the party was instantiated through these personal interactions, it came to be embodied in particular individuals. Villagers were happy to see Dilli Ram, as he brought news of the party and reminded people that the party existed. Yet he was considered to be a 'peon of the party', in the words of one district assembly member. By contrast, when Kiran visited such villages people were honored, as he represented the official presence of the party. Kiran often traveled for the purpose of attending a party event, but even if nothing was planned, people would arrange some kind of meeting once he arrived. For example, once when Kiran came to Maidel to meet with Nar Bahadur, a village-level activist, Nar Bahadur called party supporters to come to listen to Kiran speak one night. About 50 MNO supporters and activists crowded into a cavernous, kerosene lamp-lit room at an MNO activist's home, and listened while Kiran spoke for hours about the MNO's ideas. Thus Kiran and Dilli Ram invoked the party in very different ways for people.

Assembly meetings

MNO village assemblies, in Maidel as well as in other villages I visited, rarely held formal meetings or other public party events. However, people who were members of the village-level committees met regularly in the course of village life and frequently discussed issues such as the state of party support, and the problem of the party's lack of registration with the Election Commission. Some MNO activists in Maidel regretted this lack of formality, and wished that the MNO could be as organized as its rival party, the popular and highly regimented Nepali Communist Party (Unified Marxist–Leninist), which held weekly party meetings in the village.

The district assembly held meetings on a monthly basis in an aging guest house owned by an ex-British soldier and MNO activist in Ilam bazaar, the district center. The guesthouse displayed a faded MNO office signboard. On the second floor of the guest house was a dingy room, largely empty save for a few piles of locked tin trunks, a scattered assortment of benches, wobbly chairs and a small table or two, that became a functioning party office when district-wide meetings were held. Initially these meetings were held on the fifteenth of every Nepali month, but when this became a widely known fact, members of the assembly decided to change the date of the meeting every month, for the sake of party security. To inform members about the meeting date, the assembly secretary was supposed to send out notices by mail, telephone where possible or word of mouth. These somewhat unreliable forms of communication made it difficult for assembly members to receive news of the meeting time. Furthermore, as many district assembly members lived in villages far from the district center, people regularly walked five or more hours to attend these meetings, or traveled on buses for at least as long.

Given these circumstances, it was not surprising that these monthly meetings were sparsely attended. Many times, I arrived at the appointed meeting time and found only two or three men, puffing on cigarettes and chatting as they sat in the smoky, dimly lit room. We often waited for hours for other members, occasionally making short forays out into the bazaar to buy tea or snacks. Villagers who had traveled from distant districts to attend the meetings expressed anxiety about these delays, as they hoped to catch buses or begin walking so that they could reach their homes before dark. On several occasions, the quorum required for the committee to hold votes, 50 percent of the members of the assembly, was not reached, and the meeting was postponed. When the meetings were held, the specific agenda was often unclear, and it seemed as if little was accomplished in the way of party business. The lack of clear direction at these district meetings may also have led people in distant villages to decide that matters at home were more pressing than the meetings.

While these meetings may not have been successful in terms of contributing to the MNO's operations as a formal organization, they provided a forum for activists from distant areas of the district to meet, and to discuss ideas related to the MNO's mission of achieving equality for Mongols. Once, while we waited for others to arrive, an elderly Rai man from northern Ilam discussed the government's language policy with a young Limbu man from the western part of the district, and they compared their own efforts to teach their children Rai and Limbu languages. When the formal meeting was disbanded due to insufficient attendance to reach the quorum, we went to a local tea shop for drinks and snacks and talked for hours about the problems of Mongols. These meetings thus established and strengthened contact between MNO supporters who lived far from each other and might not have met otherwise.

One reason behind the informality of the village assemblies and district assemblies was that there was often little communication and coordination between the levels of the party. Activists at the village level in particular sought more guidance from the district and central assemblies. Nar Bahadur Gurung, an activist from Maidel, talked about how the village assembly was left to its own devices: 'The district assembly has not been able to formulate viable programs and circulate them. We have to prepare our own programs. We create our own pamphlets and other materials for election and other daily activities of the party.... We don't have connections between us and the district or central committees. When we call them, then they come, otherwise they will not come here on their own.' He said that he wanted to hold more village assembly meetings, particularly because people liked to attend meetings, but beyond generally raising people's awareness about the plight of Mongols, he wasn't sure what programs he should be pursuing to advance the party. One Gurung man, a former Indian army employee who was on the village assembly in Maidel, compared MNO supporters to leeches that wave around in the air after being alerted to the presence of a food source, waiting for something to latch onto. They were interested in participating, but not sure where to direct their efforts or energy.

The lack of coordination between the district and regional levels of the party was evident at a meeting where leaders and activists from both Ilam and Jhapa district gathered to plan the MNO's first national conference, the party's biggest goal for that year. Ganesh Man Limbu, an ex-British soldier and elderly leader from Jhapa district, arrived at the meeting and proudly presented stacks of pamphlets, printed on flimsy magenta paper, announcing the date and location of the MNO's first national conference. Ganesh Man had made a substantial contribution towards making the conference a reality by paying for the printing of these pamphlets. Yet those members who were present insisted that the date of the national conference had not been finalized and that they would probably not be able to raise enough money to hold it on the date specified on the pamphlet. The pamphlets had to be tossed away, and Ganesh Man was understandably annoyed.

In an effort to create closer links between the village and district levels of the party, the MNO decided to hold training sessions, or 'classes', for village-level activists. To conduct these classes, Kiran Akten and Mukta Rai, chairman of the MNO's Ilam district assembly, traveled from village to village for an entire month. I joined them for a few days and observed a class at the home of the chairman of the MNO's village assembly. Twenty-seven activists, all middle-aged or older men who were farmers or retired soldiers, sat in a circle on straw mats, while Kiran sat on a wooden chair (see Figure 3.2). Kiran asked the men to consider the meaning of an MNO slogan: 'We Mongols are not Hindu, we are not castes (*jāt jāti*)' (*Hāmī Mongol Hindu hoinan, jāt jāti hoinan*). Kiran explained that the words *jāt* and *jāti* only apply to Hindus. Mongols are not Hindu and do not follow a caste system, he elaborated, instructing people to use the word *sāmudāya* (community) instead. Kiran then posed common questions that MNO activists might receive from fellow villagers, such as 'What is the MNO's main goal?' and dictated the proper answers that they should give. Kiran's teaching style thus followed the dominant mode of Nepali education, heavy on rote memorization and dictation. Many years later, Kiran published a

Figure 3.2 Kiran Akten holds a political class for activists.

palm-sized booklet with the title *Mongol National Political Class Book*, so that they could have a quick reference source on the MNO's basic ideas. This class thus encouraged village-level activists to convey information provided to them by the district level of the party, rather than to initiate party activities or develop new party ideas at the village level.

MNO activists in the village and district assemblies expected that the party should function as a centralized and formal organization, and were frustrated when it did not. The MNO attempted to resolve these organizational problems after I completed my research in east Nepal. At the MNO's first national conference, held in Ilam bazaar in June 1998, the party issued a constitution, devoted almost entirely to organizational issues. This constitution outlined the roles and responsibilities of people at each level of the party, described how each level should function and provided guidelines for how new village and district assemblies should be established. Along with the party's decision to hold elections for the post of party president, the MNO's focus on organizational issues suggests that the party was trying to replace authority vested in charismatic leaders with authority that emerges from a bureaucratic form of organization.

Mass-meetings

Mass-meetings (*āmsabhā*) are important venues for political parties to contact potential supporters, given the limited circulation of print and electronic media in rural Nepal. At MNO mass-meetings, groups of activists gave speeches and sang songs to a crowd of people. Mass-meetings were usually held in a large, open public space such as a schoolyard, spacious pasture on a hilltop or cross-roads so that passers-by would overhear the speeches and hopefully stay to listen. Activists organized mass-meetings to draw new people into the party or to shore-up flagging support for the party. Most mass-meetings were held prior to national elections, when it was most important to publicize the MNO's ideas to large groups of people.

At mass-meetings MNO ideas were communicated through both songs and speeches. When local groups of activists planned mass-meetings, they invited individuals renowned for their oratory skills, such as Kiran Akten and Kavita Rai, to come to their villages. Mass-meetings provided entertainment for many villagers, who regarded them as festive occasions and attended in their best outfits.

During the early 1990s, the party held mass-meetings in almost every village where it had some supporters. According to Dilli Ram Khawas, who claimed to have participated in nearly every mass-meeting the MNO had ever staged, the party held as many as 20 mass-meetings in a single year, and any-where from 100 to 1,500 people attended them. Many supporters told me that it was by attending a mass-meeting in their village that they had first heard of the MNO.

MNO mass-meetings were often planned with only a week or so's notice, making it difficult for me to attend more than a few of them. Just after local elections had been called in 1997, Kiran invited me to accompany him to a mass-meeting in a predominantly Limbu hamlet in Anandanagar, a village in Jhapa district. We set out from his home the next morning, taking a series of bumpy bus rides, and walking for an hour in the glare of noon-day sun, through fluorescent green rice fields, before arriving at the site.

Preparations for the mass-meeting were well underway in a schoolyard. A line of six MNO flags on bamboo poles flapped in the wind in front of a small platform of school tables. On the platform, a school desk held a cassette player, a microphone and a car battery that powered the audio equipment; 15 or so MNO activists perched on tiny school benches under the shade of a plastic tarp. About 100 people were scattered across the treeless yard, taking shelter from the harsh sun under large umbrellas. MNO songs in Limbu and Nepali blared from a pair of loudspeakers attached to a bamboo pole. A black cloth sign lettered in silver paint announced both in Limbu (in Sirijanga script) and in Nepali (in Roman script, rather than in the usual Devanagari):

Yalambar year = 5058
Mulbāsi must have the right to study their own language!

We are the *mulbāsi* of this country. This country doesn't have to register our organization; the United Nations will register it! We won't request this country to give us registration. Long live the *mulbāsi* of this country!

Catering to the largely Limbu population in this village, the sign highlighted Limbu identity by using the Limbu script and referring to the Limbu calendar by announcing the 'Yalambar year'. Equally, the sign asserted an indigenous identity, using the term *mulbāsi*, and reminded people of international support, via the United Nations, for indigenous peoples and their political efforts. The sign proposed that the authority of the UN could replace that of the Nepali state in granting the MNO party registration.

An hour or so after the official starting time, the program began. During the first hour, the MNO party secretary of the village called activists up to the platform to receive badges, pieces of brightly colored construction paper pasted together and inscribed with felt-tip pen, naming their role in the party; I was presented with a 'chief guest' badge. Most Nepali public functions feature these badges. A group of young village girls and a teenage boy with a guitar sang the Welcome Song, with lyrics consisting of a single word: *swāgatam* (welcome). Following the song were two 'welcome speeches' by party officials from the village. The first man began his remarks in Nepali, but soon shifted into Limbu, as both he and the majority of those in attendance were Limbu. Four activists, whom the Anandanagar village party activists had called from nearby towns and villages, then gave longer speeches. The activists were men from various ethnic groups, Newar, Dhimal, Rai and Limbu. Through the scratchy microphone, the speakers delivered their speeches in the urgent, dramatic tones used in political oration throughout Nepal, over the din of children playing and adults chatting while they fanned themselves in the mid-day heat. Between the speeches, a young Rai man who professed to having been influenced by Kiran Akten's songs stepped up on stage with his guitar and performed a song he wrote called 'Rise Up Mongol Youths'.

Kiran Akten was the final speaker of the day, and while the previous speakers had talked for no more than 20 minutes each, he held forth for over an hour. Cows heading home from the pastures in the late afternoon passed by the crowd and kicked up dust on the field's edges. A young woman listened as her goats grazed in the grassy space beyond the yard. A few passers-by on bicycles pulled up and then, after a few minutes, disembarked to sit and listen to Kiran. While Kiran spoke, the chatter that had continued throughout the program ceased, as everyone listened with rapt attention. Kiran's presentation was far more theatrical than the other speeches. When speaking in a melodic, soothing tone, he moved his arms in graceful, sweeping gestures. At other moments, such as while addressing the general concern about the MNO's lack of registration from the Election Commission, his face turned red as his voice raged, while he shook his fist in the air: 'Did the British give the first party in India registration?' he thundered. 'You go abroad to Hong Kong and Malaysia and risk your lives, but here you talk about registration. Whoever talks to me about registration, I'll spit at them!!' he hollered. He wove songs with words like 'whatever others call us, we are Mongols' into the course of his speech, spellbinding the crowd with his rich, clear voice. Kiran ended his dramatic speech by encouraging all those present to be ready to fight for Mongols: 'The Mongol Liberation Army has begun training! Youths be ready! *Jaya* Mongol!'

After the program, much of the crowd drifted homewards, but activists clustered by the platform and eagerly began asking Kiran and the other speakers about points that they made in their speeches, or about other MNO-related issues. I followed Kiran and a group of about ten young men and a few women to the home of Mohan Sereng, a young Limbu man who had organized a Mongol youth group in the area. In the last light of day, the group rested on Mohan's porch and talked about the relationship between politics and religion. A young activist from Anandanagar asked Kiran: 'People ask me which religion Mongols should follow. What do I tell them?' Kiran replied, 'The MNO says that we should follow whatever religion we want, other than Hindu dharma. My personal belief is that we should follow the religion that suits our identity.' He continued, explaining that politics is bigger than religion: 'If Hindus in Nepal didn't have political power, they wouldn't be able to put their devotional songs on the radio.' And so the talk continued late into the night, interrupted only when we ate the evening meal of rice and chicken that Mohan's sisters and wife prepared for us.

As was often the case, though the formal program lasted for about three hours, interactions between activists who gathered for the meeting continued long after the program was officially over. Mass-meetings were thus simultaneously a way for the MNO to communicate its ideas to the wider public and to stimulate discussions about party ideas. These meetings provided a forum for people to connect with charismatic leaders like Kiran.

Mass-meetings, held largely at the time of elections, were one of the few contexts in which the MNO could attempt to capture public attention. Larger political parties also voice their positions through media coverage and through public political protest. Public protests, such as transportation strikes (*chakka jam*), and business strikes (*bandh*), became central to political culture in Nepal during the 1990s. These public protests demonstrated the strength of the political parties or organizations sponsoring them to the extent that they were able to coerce the public into obeying their will, for example by not using vehicles during transportation strikes (Lakier 2007). The MNO has only participated in one such protest. On February 8, 2006, the MNO called a *bandh* in Kakharbhitta, a bazaar town in Jhapa district on the eastern border with India, to protest the municipal elections called by the king and to call for establishing a republic. This was also an unusual form of action for the MNO because they were coordinating with other larger political parties, all of which were also boycotting these elections, which were perceived as the king's attempt to legitimize his direct rule.

There are several reasons why the MNO rarely engaged in public protests. First, the MNO's support base in the 1990s was almost entirely in villages. Kakharbhitta, the site of the 2006 *bandh*, is one of the only bazaar towns in which it had any support in the 1990s. Public protests are a way of trying to control public space in order to claim and demonstrate political strength, and they are predicated on the existence of public, commercial space. A *bandh* would have no tangible effects in most villages in Ilam, which had no motorable roads and a limited commercial space, with a few tea and dry goods shops and itinerant vendors, that was open for business once a week. It takes extensive support in areas with public space to enforce one of these protests. Parties or organizations threaten people with violence in order to force them to comply with their protests. The MNO did not have the necessary strength in these bazaar towns to enforce these forms of protest.

Second, without media to publicize the events, the effects of the protest would be limited. Media coverage of these public protests is key in order for the political party to gain public recognition as a powerful organization with the capacity to demand support. There is negligible coverage of rural events in print media or on radio stations, and a very limited circulation of print media in rural Nepal. Mainstream media paid little attention to ethnic political issues in the 1990s. The types of political activities the MNO could carry out were thus constrained by its rural basis and its lack of access to public space.

Conclusion

Although the MNO officially had a formal, regimented structure, the operations of the party were in practice informal and highly fluid. Decision making was ostensibly centralized, yet in practice was erratic and loosely orchestrated, largely because communication between levels of the party was sporadic. While the MNO had the structure of a bureaucratic organization, its was propelled by charismatic leaders. People in the organization expected the MNO to operate on the basis of bureaucratic organization and authority, and interpreted the party's lack of conformity to these ideals as a sign of weakness. Some people in the village characterized the MNO as being more like an organization (*sangaṭhan*) than a 'real party'. Thus, these people saw the MNO as an entity that blurred the lines between social movements and political parties. This interpretation was probably related to the MNO's loose organization and its lack of power at the district and national levels, even while it participated in elections and had seats in some village governments.

People expected the MNO to be a centralized organization, like other political parties. There were few instances in which people at the village level initiated party programs, aside from the occasional mass-meeting or assembly meeting, without the guidance of an upper-level activist. People's expectations that the MNO would operate as a centralized, hierarchical organization were rooted in their historical experiences of politics in Nepal as highly centralized forms of power. The Nepali state has been highly centralized since its inception, and the political center retained much of the decision-making power in the country even after 1990. A few people expressed fear that if they were to plan things on their own, Gopal Gurung might be angry and kick them out of the party. Indeed, Gopal Gurung removed several district-level activists from the party, on grounds that were not fully disclosed to me. Thus, while some activists wanted to be more engaged in party activities, they could not, as they had neither directions nor authority from the upper-level leaders to initiate activities.

The MNO's organizational challenges point to several characteristics of the political system in the years following the institution of multi-party politics in

1990. First, political freedom was very recently and unevenly established. The idea of political freedom is central to the concept of democracy in general and MNO supporters espoused the ability to freely speak and meet as one of the more tangible effects of the political transition. Yet people did not trust that the state would uphold the right to political freedom if they challenged the notion of what was considered to be proper forms of political expression. MNO supporters were aware of the dominant view of ethnic politics as threatening to the state that continued into the 1990s and recalled the state's willingness to use coercion to curb political expression during the Panchayat era. Even though there were no incidents in which the state acted to curtail the activities of the MNO, people in the MNO felt vulnerable in carrying out their political activities, as they worked for an unregistered, ethnic political party. They responded by maintaining secrecy around the central committee and by changing the district-level meeting times to prevent possible retribution from the state.

Second, the MNO's organizational problems demonstrate the challenges that political actors face in engaging in politics at the rural level and outside of the framework of major political parties. Major political parties offered institutional and financial support for their rural activists. Without a strong center, and without a model of how to run a decentralized organization, the MNO struggled to coordinate its activities in rural Nepal. They lacked funds to produce publications and to strengthen the organization. Due to the highly centralized nature of the Nepali state, it was difficult for the MNO to influence or change the political system by operating at the village level, as I explore further in the next chapter.

Although the MNO did not operate as people in Nepal imagined that a political party should work, it did make changes in the lives of the people who participated in it. Although the MNO was not able to achieve its stated party goals of gaining state power, it introduced a new discourse of ethnic equality to village Nepal, and led people to transform their identities, thinking of themselves as Mongols. In these ways, the party acted as a social movement organization.

Figure 3.3 MNO activists pose with flags.

4 Democratization and local politics

An MNO village government

Every Monday, when the weekly market was held, the chairman of the Maidel village government or Village Development Committee (VDC), who everyone called Baje (grandfather), spent most of the day sitting on his verandah. There, Baje and the Bahun man from the neighboring village, appointed as the VDC secretary by the district government, attended to the requests and resolved the disputes of the dozen or so villagers who came to see them. A smoke-blackened wooden cabinet containing files, official stationary for Maidel VDC and a stamp and ink pad to imprint all official documents stood against the back wall of the porch. Across the front of Baje's house and barn, MNO slogans were boldly painted with red clay: 'There should be ethnic equality, there must be a secular state!' (*Jātiya samānta hune parchha, dharma nirapeksha muluk bharne parchha*); 'For the total elimination of the present ethnic inequalities in this country, let's vote for the rooster [the MNO's election symbol]!' (*Deś mā bhaeko vidhyamān jātiya asantulanko purna antyako lāgi, bhāle chinha mā matdan garau.*) On the walls of the front porch, MNO pamphlets announced: 'We want a president, not a king' (*Rājā hoinan, rāstrapati chāhanchha*); above the pamphlets hung the treasured family photo of Baje receiving an award from the king during the Panchayat regime, for his contributions to the development of the country.

This scene from 1997 encapsulates the contradiction between the MNO's radical ideas and its operations in the village. Baje had run for election to the post of VDC chairman as an MNO candidate, claiming to uphold the party's slogans of calling to end ethnic inequality by changing the structure and policies of the state. Yet, in his work on the VDC, Baje carried on the business of the village government just as representatives to VDCs from other parties did. MNO elected representatives to the Maidel VDC could not actually further their party's plans for transforming the state; rather, they upheld the local presence of the state.

This chapter examines the contradictions between political ideals and practices that the MNO contended with during the 1990s. Such contradictions are characteristic of the process of democratization, in which the discourse of democracy creates new political expectations, yet political and social structures do not allow for these to be fulfilled. After the institution of democracy in 1990, people had high expectations for their ability to create dramatic social change through participation in the political system via political parties. Yet political actors in the village were faced with a highly centralized state structure that gave little power to village governments. Furthermore, while the MNO sought to mobilize people by convincing them to support its program of ending ethnic inequality by bringing Mongols to power, local political practices and social structures constrained the ability of voters to choose parties on the basis of ideas. A discourse of political affiliation as concerning party ideals existed side by side with practices of personalized politics.

In this chapter, I examine the history of MNO mobilization and examine contradictions between the MNO's stated goals and ideas and its operations in this village. I address the possibilities and limitations of political participation in the new multi-party system. While the post-1990 system promised to bring about new modes of political participation, there was considerable continuity between the Panchayat system and the multi-party system at the level of village politics.

The village of Maidel was one of three villages in the northeast corner of Ilam district where the Mongol National Organization had considerable electoral success, considering its status as an unregistered ethnic political party. In local elections in 1991 and 1997, MNO candidates won the majority of seats in two village governments, or (VDCs), and gained many seats in a third VDC. The MNO's success in Maidel VDC did not change the social structure or distribution of power within the village. Yet, the party introduced people to a new discourse of ethnic rights. This party's challenge to high-caste Hindu dominance resonated with people in Maidel due to their experiences with state institutions.

A sketch of Maidel

The village of Maidel is a political unit, one of 48 VDCs in Ilam district. Sprawling across two enormous hills, covering about 1,700 hectares (34,000 *ropanī*) of land, the VDC encompasses a tremendous variety of ecological zones, stretching from semi-tropical forest and lowland rice terraces at the edge of the Mai Khola river, to highland yak pastures and a 12,000-foot peak at the border with Darjeeling. Frequent rains and persistent fog throughout the year make it a strikingly verdant, though gloomy, area.

Like many villages in Ilam, much of Maidel appeared prosperous. Maidel's sprawling homes of painted wood, glass paneled bay windows and gleaming tin roofs reflect the strong orientation towards a market economy in the area. Nearly every household sold dairy products or engaged in some form of cash cropping or production for the market. Cardamom (*alaichi*), butter (*ghiu*), broom grass (*amliso*) and vegetables were some of the most prominent commodities produced here and throughout Ilam district, marketed in cities in neighboring West Bengal.

Maidel is about a four-to-five-hour walk from Ilam bazaar, the district center, where district government offices and the largest market in the district are located. People in Maidel referred to themselves as living in a remote corner of the district because there was no road that connected the village to the district center until 1997. In 1997, villagers dug a road connecting Maidel to roads leading to Ilam bazaar, and ancient Land Rover jeeps, said to be first owned by British colonizers in India, began reaching Maidel several times a week. Funds for the road came from the Nepali Communist Party (UML) government's Build Your Village Yourself program, an effort at decentralization that allocated 300,000 rupees (about $5,450, at the time) to each VDC to use as it saw fit. These jeeps were used to transport cash crops from Maidel to Ilam bazaar, goods for Maidel's few stores from Ilam bazaar, and as many passengers as possible.

Within Maidel's population of approximately 3,400, there was a total of 524 households, and a wide range of ethnic groups. Ethnic groups that the MNO call Mongols – Gurungs (192 households), Rais (150), Limbus (82), Sherpas (43) and Magars (22), one Tamang and one Bhote household – made up the majority of the households. Hindu caste groups were a minority in Maidel, with 20 high-caste households (Bahuns and Chhetris) and 13 low-caste households (Kamis and Damais).

Men from the largest ethnic groups, Gurung, Limbu and Rai, dominated local politics in Maidel. They were the most active participants in all political parties in the village, the dominant MNO and Communist Party and the less popular Congress Party. Men from these ethnic groups held most of the elected positions, and were the most active members of various development committees, such as the forest management users group. No low-caste or high-caste Hindus were on the village government.

Low-caste Hindus interacted regularly with the other groups within the village as they worked as tailors, blacksmiths and day laborers. However, they were not allowed inside the homes of other ethnic groups, and often perched on the threshold of the door during these visits. Many low-caste Hindus, and some Rais, had converted to Christianity and attended weekly services at a church in ward seven, run by a pastor who had moved to Maidel from Darjeeling.

The 20 households of high-caste Hindus were on the margins of Maidel, residentially, as well as socially and politically. Most high-caste Hindus in Maidel lived in a hamlet contained on a small knoll on the way to a neighboring village that has a large population of high-caste Hindus. They held no elected positions, few local posts, and interacted infrequently with the 'Mongol' ethnic groups. I rarely saw Gurungs and high-caste Hindus visit each other socially. The relationship between the high-caste Hindus and the other ethnic groups within the village was not tense; it simply was not very extensive.

Like all VDCs, Maidel is divided into nine wards, each of which has political representation on the village government. Most of these political units circumscribe more than one residential cluster, or hamlet, that is predominantly the home to people of one ethnic group. Almost all of the population of ward four was Gurung, with the exception of a few houses of Damais, or low-caste tailors. Ward four was the power center of the village, because the village government leaders for at least the past 50 years came from one Gurung family, Baje's family, who lived here.

I lived with my husband Tika in ward four, in Baje's house, which villagers called the 'big house' (*thulo ghar*); although it was no larger or fancier than most others, it was considered '*thulo*' because of the political prominence of the family.[1] While the aging, weathered house had once been home to over ten people, there were only six members of the household when I lived there: Baje, a reserved, elderly man with white hair and unusual blue eyes; his portly, out-spoken wife who I called Aama (mother); their clever, ambitious son, Nar Bahadur, who was about the same age as Tika and me; Bhauju, Nar Bahadur's quiet, hardworking wife with high-cheekbones and large brown eyes; and their two children, a young girl in grade school and a baby boy. During most of the Panchayat era, and into the present multi-party system, Baje served as head of the village for 30 some years until his death in 1997. Baje's father had been the headman (*thari mukhiyā*) during the Rana era, and Baje's son, Nar Bahadur, was elected to be the next VDC chairman in the 1997 local elections, held about a month after Baje's death, just before I ended my fieldwork. A short stroll up the hill from the 'big house' was the crumbling VDC office building, the official site for the business of the village government to take place; however, most meetings were held, and all files were kept, on the spacious verandah of the 'big house'.

Ward four was also the social and economic center of the village because the small bazaar with its shops and occasional post office was located there. This location was probably due to Baje's influence, since he was instrumental in initi-ating the local weekly market in the 1960s. When the VDC decided to place a new health post in ward four, individuals living in other wards protested that ward four was becoming a 'municipality' (*nagar pālikā*). The VDC reconsidered its plans and placed the new health post in neighboring ward five, a short dis-tance from the bazaar.

The bazaar consisted of ten houses, arranged in a rough rectangle around a large courtyard-like space. Many people living there set up small stores on the first floor of their homes where they sold a limited variety of dry goods like Puja brand laundry soap, incense, Tiger brand batteries, glucose or arrowroot biscuits, low-grade tea leaves, salt and sugar. Sita Aama, one of the most active women in the MNO in the village, ran a tea shop out of her home here, which served as one of the main places of congregation in the area. The weekly market, held every Monday morning in the open space in the middle of the cluster of houses, was one of the social highlights of village life. On market day, merchants from Maidel and neighboring villages sold vegetables, tobacco, glass bangles and cheap ready-made clothing under bamboo shelters or at small wooden stalls. People came from all corners of the village to stock up on supplies, receive mail and socialize: older people ate greasy rice flour donuts (*sel roṭī*) with tiny dishes of spicy curry and got drunk on millet beer (*jā̃ḍ*) and spirits (*raksī*) in smoky tea shops, while young men in jogging suits and baseball caps played on the carom board for hours.[2]

In the middle of the bazaar, on a bamboo pole more than twice as high as the tallest building in the bazaar, flew an MNO flag. The blue and red flag domi-nated the bazaar, and was visible from all the homes and trails on the upper hillside that wrapped around the bazaar on three sides. Baje's son, Nar Bahadur, and his friends were the most active in mobilizing support for the MNO in Maidel and they raised this flag the very day they established the party there. This flag symbolized the MNO's conquering of the local political arena. However, the party had little support in the village at the time, just after the people's revolution of 1990, and it was a risky act, but Nar Bahadur was eager to establish himself as a political leader.

How the MNO came to Maidel

Nar Bahadur told us the story of how the MNO was established in Maidel one chilly, rainy evening after we'd eaten dinner and everyone else in the family had gone to sleep. Tika and I sat by the fire and listened quietly as Nar Bahadur talked in a hushed, serious voice:

> During the Panchayat system, all the young people including my neighbors and friends were communists. The village of Maidel was entirely communist. One time, they planned to beat up my father and three other men in the village. These communist guys used to have meetings and they didn't speak to us. Only Harka Bahadur and I were not part of any party, so they called us *maṇḍale* (thugs who worked to support Panchayat leaders). The whole village was talking about us. I had some good friends who told me that the communists were planning to do something bad to the two of us. My friend also told me that the communists had decided that they will never accept us in the Communist Party even if we went to them. At that time I was thinking, if the communists do anything to me, I will do something to them too. This happened after the people's movement of 1990.
>
> A few years earlier, I had met Mukta Rai and we had a good friendship. He had told me, 'Don't join any party until I say something to you.' I listened to him. One day at this critical time, I received a letter from Mukta. He had invited me to attend the Mongol meeting at Alubari bazaar and he asked me to bring people. So I talked to Communist and Congress friends here and said, 'You people are in the Communist and Congress Parties. In a democratic system, you should also listen to others' ideas. So let's go to Alubari bazaar on Friday.' These people accepted my request, so about 50 of us went from Maidel. When they heard Kiran Akten speaking at the meeting, they couldn't criticize him, they had to praise him. Nobody criticized him.... After the meeting, I bought tea and snacks for all the Maidel people and then we walked back to Maidel. On the way back we talked about different aspects of the Mongol party. Nobody criticized it, and only one guy didn't change his mind. It all happened on Friday.
>
> On Monday we decided to put up a party flag in Maidel bazaar. We bought cloth and had the flag made by the tailor. We put up the flag at Maidel on the same day, the day of the bazaar. When we did this, Communists and Congress people in Maidel and the next village over were talking

about me saying, 'Nar Bahadur has brought an ethnic party here. We should do something about this!' At home, my father and mother were upset. They were worried that something might happen to me and told me not to do it...

At last, Harka Bahadur and I wrote a letter to all the people in Maidel calling them to attend a meeting at the VDC office and they all came. Then we talked about different aspects of the MNO. At the end people said, 'if that is true, then we will join your party. What do we need to do to be a member of your party?'... When Kiran Akten and Gopal Gurung came here, there was a long queue to get membership. Kiran Akten strung the membership cards together like a garland of flowers and showed it to everyone. Then the election came and the MNO won the local elections. Only then was I relieved; otherwise I was always running around.

The political tension in Maidel in the aftermath of the 1990 revolution that ended the authoritarian Panchayat system comes through in Nar Bahadur's narrative. As he noted, the Communist Party of Nepal (Unified Marxist–Leninist, or UML) was the strongest political party in Maidel as it had long been working underground throughout eastern Nepal and in this village. The UML held no public meetings, protests, or campaigns until after the Panchayat era ended, but many young men in the village had already pledged their support to this party and had been involved in its clandestine activities. The Congress Party established itself much later, and gained only a small following in the village. Nar Bahadur did not mention a third large political party, the *Rastriya Prajatantra Party* (*RaPraPa*), which was seen as the party for those who had supported the Panchayat regime, and was unpopular immediately after 1990; the *RaPraPa* had no members in Maidel and won no parliamentary seats from Ilam district.

Baje and other Panchayat era leaders and their families were unable to align themselves with the Communist and Congress Parties that had worked to overthrow the Panchayat system, and abstained from participating in local politics for several months after the revolution. Their lack of political allegiance further subjected them to the scorn of fellow villagers, who branded them *mandales*. In the months after the spring of 1990, when the multi-party system was established, there was considerable backlash against individuals who had served as village leaders in the Panchayat regime. Communist Party supporters began to openly criticize and occasionally physically attack ex-'*panchas*', as they were called. Nar Bahadur alluded to the ostracism and threats he and his family experienced at this time. Baje's wife, Aama, recounted that threats of violence from fellow villagers appeared so menacing that the family relocated their sleeping quarters from a window-lined room to a more secure inner room. The lives and political careers of Baje, the Panchayat era village chair (*pradhān panch*), and his family were endangered.

The MNO arrived in the area at this critical time, and offered the possibility of political salvation for Nar Bahadur. Notably, Baje's family and its allies were most active in building support for the MNO in Maidel. The MNO offered Nar Bahadur and other ex-Panchas a new political identity: it allowed them to defend themselves from allegations that they were stooges who had upheld an unpopular political system, and to re-package themselves as advocates of social change and as legitimate political actors in the new multi-party system. Nar Bahadur's recollection of telling his friends that they should listen to other ideas in a democratic system suggests that, for him, engaging with the MNO was emblematic of the political possibilities of democracy. In villages other than Maidel, too, Panchayat era political elites became MNO supporters. Gopal Gurung acknowledged that many such people 'joined the MNO to save their lives', fearing that the communists would kill them.

Affiliation with the MNO also helped the family maintain its political lineage, as Baje's son, Nar Bahadur, won the position of chairman in the second local elections, in May 1997. By supporting the MNO, this Gurung family in Maidel that had provided the headman in the village for three generations, throughout a series of political restructurings in Nepal, was able to maintain its power. While the MNO speaks of radical social change, at the village level, local elites were able to maintain their positions of power within the village by joining the MNO.

Nar Bahadur described how his father, Baje, initially disapproved of his involvement with the party. Baje told me that he hadn't been afraid of the party, but neither had he been particularly eager to run as an MNO candidate. However, Baje felt obliged to support the MNO because it was the party that his son and many others had chosen to support. In other conversations I had with Nar Bahadur, he noted that only after he and his peers had convinced a number of influential people in the village to join the party was he able to convince Baje to run for village chairman again, as an MNO candidate. This suggests that only once the MNO appeared as a viable political force in the village was Baje willing to support it.

Like many other seasoned politicians who were recruited to run as MNO candidates in local elections, Baje never acted as an MNO activist. He attended no party meetings, nor did he ever make public speeches supporting the MNO. This did not prevent MNO activists from claiming Baje as an MNO hero after he died in 1997. Perhaps Baje had latched onto the MNO primarily to save his political career, but the MNO leaders ultimately claimed him as a great Mongol leader.

On the day of Baje's funeral, hundreds of people from Maidel and the surrounding villages gathered in the courtyard of Baje's house to join in the funeral procession (*malāmi*) up the hill to the cremation site, tucked away in the bamboo forest. Among the crowds were numerous MNO activists, carrying MNO flags. Seeing this, Nar Bahadur requested these activists not to carry the flags, explaining that it would be awkward because people from other political parties had also come to be in the funeral procession. The activists obeyed Nar Bahadur's wishes, but decided to organize another event that would explicitly be for the MNO to honor Baje.

About a week after Baje's cremation and a few weeks prior to the local elections, MNO leaders from Maidel and surrounding villages held a memorial service (*sokh sabhā*) on the day of the busy weekly market in the center of the bazaar. MNO activists had asked Nar Bahadur for permission to hold their memorial service at the *thulo ghar*, Baje's home, but Nar Bahadur refused, because, even after Baje's death, the house was the de facto VDC office, and VDC work would continue there as it did every Monday. Nar Bahadur's close friend, Harka Bahadur, hung an MNO flag and a loudspeaker from the roof of Nar Bahadur's family's tea shop, closed because of Baje's death, and lined up a few school benches for seating. A rickety table served as the podium, and held a microphone and a picture of Baje draped with a flower garland. It had been pouring rain, but the storm let up enough so that there was a good turn out: about 40 MNO activists from Maidel and the surrounding villages attended, perching on the narrow school benches. As it was bazaar day, people of all political persuasions, who were getting weekly supplies, playing carom board or getting drunk, hovered about as the program began.

Harka Bahadur welcomed everyone and spoke briefly about Baje's prizes and achievements, then listed the program's speakers. Next, Chatur Man Sauden, an MNO district committee member, carried a large MNO flag on a bamboo pole and led the crowd up the steep path to the cremation site, high on the hill. I followed about 50 people through the thick bamboo forest for the 15-minute walk. When the procession arrived at the stone cremation pyres in the clearing in the forest, Chatur Man, the MNO district chairman Mukta Rai, and a few other activists planted the MNO flag near the Buddhist prayer flags *lungtā*) that the Gurung lamas had placed there during the cremation. A few people in the crowd quietly protested, and suggested that the MNO flag should be placed farther away from the *lungtās*, but they were ignored. Following Mukta Rai's instruction, we all gathered around the place where Baje had been cremated, threw flowers we'd carried with us into the pyre and closed our eyes, pressing our palms into a namaste for a minute of silence in his memory.

After we plodded down to the bazaar, a series of seven speeches by MNO party officials began. Harka Bahadur introduced each speaker by noting each man's post in the party. Most of the speakers celebrated Baje's political life and career not by directly linking his life with the MNO but by recounting his achievements, and noting that he'd been not just a village or district leader, but a leader for the whole nation of Nepal. Only Mukta Rai, the chairman of the MNO's Ilam district committee, explicitly brought up MNO ideas, and described Baje as a model for all MNO supporters: 'Even though he has gone and left this world, we should never quit our own principles (*siddhānta*). We should work in the way that he worked. We need to work with unity. When the election time comes we should remember him when it comes time to fill the seat of the president. He has gone and left this VDC in the hands of you activists. You should remember that he raised a voice for Mongol liberation.'

MNO leaders insisted that the program that day was a memorial service (*sok sabhā*) with the aim of remembering Baje's life, rather than a mass-meeting (*āmsabhā*) for promoting the MNO. Yet the party's presence dominated all aspects of the memorial service, even if most speakers did not talk about the MNO platform or campaign for the upcoming elections. Although only Mukta Rai described Baje as an exemplary MNO activist, the program as a whole served to represent him as an MNO hero. An MNO flag hung behind the podium, and all who spoke at the program were MNO party officials or MNO elected VDC members, and Harka Bahadur introduced them as such. They ended their speeches with the party salute of '*Jaya* Mongol!'

With local elections coming, and with Baje's son running for the post of VDC chairman, this ceremony was a chance for activists to remind people that this great leader was elected as an MNO candidate. By focusing on Baje's achievements, such as the many years he had held office, and his award from the king, MNO activists sought to boost the MNO's prestige by associating him with their party. By placing the party flag at his cremation site, the party officials sought to remember Baje as, foremost, an MNO member. Forgotten was Baje's role in upholding the unpopular Panchayat regime and the fact that he had never publicly advocated MNO ideas. The MNO may have helped Baje to gain legitimacy as a political actor in the multi-party system, but Baje, in life and in death, also helped the MNO to become a legitimate political force in the village.

The MNO in practice in the village

A central contradiction characterized the MNO's operations in the village: MNO candidates who were elected to the village-level government (VDC) participated in running an arm of the state, while simultaneously representing a party that was refused registration by the Election Commission and aimed to overhaul the state. Despite the radical ideas of the party, MNO elected representatives to the VDC ran the village government much the same as representatives elected from other parties in other villages did.

To understand this paradox, it is necessary to examine the structural location of village governments within Nepal's previous political systems. Village governments have historically had limited financial and administrative autonomy, as the district-level government has continued to control the delegation of funds from the central government to the village level, and to make decisions about administration at the village level. The central government gave funds to the district governments to use in development projects in various villages within the district. The government employees who were posted in the villages – the postal worker, many of the schoolteachers, the school headmaster, health care workers, the secretary of the VDC and the policemen – were all appointed by the district-level government.

Village governments have been closely linked with higher levels of the state. They were initially established by central state authorities in the late eighteenth century, who appointed individuals living in villages as headmen called *thari mukhiyā* to serve as 'vehicles of government' in the villages (Caplan 1975: 150). Headmen were responsible for collecting land taxes from villagers in the area and for delivering the revenue raised from that area to district tax offices; they were also granted the right to perform minor judicial functions within the village (Caplan 1975: 150; Sagant 1996). Headmen usually maintained these posts for life, and were succeeded by their sons (Caplan 1975: 152). In the Panchayat system, village government representatives were elected to their posts rather than appointed by the center. However, the elected representatives in Maidel, and in surrounding villages, were often descendants of those who had been appointed as headmen, or had themselves been appointed headmen in earlier political systems. This pattern of inheritance of political posts also existed in other parts of Nepal during the Panchayat system; and elections were often skipped in favor of appointments to these positions (Hachhethu 2008).

In Nepal's multi-party system, the role of the headman changed surprisingly little. Throughout three political systems, Baje's title shifted from *thari mukhiyā*, to *pradhān panch* in the Panchayat era, to VDC chairman (*gāũ vikās samiti adhyaksha*) in the multi-party era. One Monday afternoon, as we snacked on boiled potatoes during a lull between his meetings with villagers, I asked Baje about how his work as a village leader was different during these different political systems. He responded, '...It really wasn't that different. When I was a *thari mukhiyā* it was just like this is. People would come and say "this injustice has occurred, someone did something to me, you must look into this" – it wasn't that different. It was just about the same, the work as a *thari mukhiyā* and the work in the Panchayat era was just about the same.' As Baje recounted, the roles and responsibilities of village leaders remained remarkably constant throughout dramatic changes in Nepal's political system. Village chairmen and representatives continued to serve as mediators between the state and the local, facilitating central government projects at the local level by collecting land taxes, implementing development projects, registering life-cycle events and adjudicating minor disputes between villagers.

MNO candidates who held seats at the village level derived their authority from central state authorities and carried out work that supported the projects of the central government. Given these constraints, as elected members of VDCs, MNO candidates could do little to advance the extensive changes that their party called for at the central level of the government. Projects carried out by the MNO-run VDC did not promote MNO ideology or a Mongol identity; rather, these MNO representatives acted just as representatives from other parties did. Instead of engineers of social change, MNO representatives on the village government became administrators in the local work of the state.

One of the few substantial changes that occurred after the MNO gained control of the Maidel VDC is that the village chairman's ties with district-level officials were weakened. In order for villages to secure state resources that were channeled through the district, village chairmen needed close relationships with district officials. Throughout the Panchayat era, Baje succeeded in gaining the favor of the chief district officer (CDO) and other district officials, enabling him to secure resources for Maidel, such as elusive government-distributed rice and a drinking water project. The king had even awarded him a medal for his excellent service to the country. However, as Baje recounted, the district-level officials, mostly high-caste Hindus, were 'shocked' when he joined the MNO. The CDO of Ilam district pleaded with him to join the mainstream Congress Party, offering him a seat on the Congress Party district committee, and 50 *man* (about 4,100 pounds) of rice. But Baje refused the CDO's invitation, and told him that the people of Maidel had requested him to be the VDC president for the 'Mongol party'.

Perhaps the MNO appeared to Baje to be the only avenue for him to maintain power at the village level, since there was little support for the Congress Party in Maidel. By joining the MNO, however, he sacrificed his close connections with the district government. Consequently, the village did not receive funds that were channeled through the district for many projects that the VDC proposed. By aligning himself with the MNO's ideology and its critical stance towards central state policies and high-caste Hindus, Baje saved his political career yet became less effective in his role as village chair.

Personalized politics in a multi-party era: local elections in Maidel

Early one drizzly morning right before the local elections in 1997, Aama called me to come down from my room for the morning meal. In the smoky kitchen, I found Bala Ram Gurung, an MNO supporter from ward five, and Aama in a heated discussion about the elections. As Aama served us brass plates heaped with *gundruk* (dried, fermented greens), potatoes, rice and *ghyu* (clarified butter), Bala Ram reported on the political situation in ward five: 'People are saying that since both Nar Bahadur and Bhim Bahadur are fighting for the village chairman seat, the election is a fight between brothers.' Aama's son Nar Bahadur and Bhim Bahadur, who was running for chairman as the Communist Party (UML) candidate, were closely related cousins. Aama, always opinionated, protested in her gravelly voice, 'Ah, people don't understand. They're in different parties! You have to fight for your own principles (*siddhānta*). This is a fight between two parties. In Panchayat times, five or six people would run for the same position but they'd all be in the same system. There were no parties. Now you have to fight for your own ideas and ideology.' 'Right, right,' Bala Ram agreed, between mouthfuls of rice. Having brought up the topic of MNO ideas, Aama continued, 'I don't know why our people have to follow the Communist Party. It's a Bahun party. Soon they'll learn. It seems to me that Aryans and Mongols will have to split apart at some point!' Bala Ram shook his head in agreement with Aama and added, 'Yes, those people should look at their own faces in the mirror, and understand what their own identity is!'

In their conversation, Aama and Bala Ram referenced the ideals of democracy discourse: people should determine their political affiliation and vote by considering the ideas of that party. Furthermore, they suggested that people from Mongol ethnic groups should support the MNO and its ideas; to do otherwise would be a betrayal of their Mongol identity. Thus they interpreted ethnic political parties as compatible with the democratic ideal of political choice based on ideology, rather than one based on loyalty to individuals. Yet they recognized that many people who did not 'understand' would vote for individuals rather than parties.

In many ways, party politics in Maidel intersected with a personalized politics, in which personal connections were the underlying force behind political affiliation. This became particularly clear during the weeks prior to the local elections in 1997. In these village-level elections, parties did not strive to represent a particular set of goals and ideals. Rather, candidates who campaigned in these elections emphasized renewing and building personal connections with their fellow villagers rather than communicating party ideas to them (see Figure 4.1).

In the three weeks prior to the election, Maidel was transformed. Wherever people gathered in the village, they talked of nothing but the election: women and men speculated over who would win, gossiped about who had switched party allegiance, and berated candidates from the opposing parties. Party flags were everywhere, and the red and blue MNO flags were flying from almost every house in Maidel. Simple election posters on thin news stock paper that the MNO village committee had printed up in Ilam bazaar were pasted on the front wall of every MNO supporter's home. The posters featured a simple plea to vote for two candidates: 'For the development of Maidel vote for Nar Bahadur Gurung for Chair; Min Bahadur Sauden for Vice Chair.' The candidates' names were printed in huge, bold letters, while the words 'Mongol National Organization' were printed in very small script at the bottom of the poster. The poster offered no explanation of the MNO's platform nor any of the party slogans such as those I saw on national election posters. By referring to development in general terms rather than a party platform, and emphasizing individual candidates over their party affiliation, the MNO's local election campaign maintained continuity with Panchayat era elections (Hachhethu 2008).

Nar Bahadur humbly denied that he was interested in running for president right up until the elections were called and, even once he was running, he insisted that he had only acquiesced to running at the insistence of his friends

Figure 4.1 An MNO supporter examines a local election ballot.

and fellow villagers. Throughout the campaign, Nar Bahadur sported a shiny blue polyester tracksuit jacket, a pair of army green pants and a pair of hiking boots, and carried a small camouflage backpack containing a few notebooks and papers. With this outfit, his elf-like features and youthful demeanor, he appeared like a trekking guide rather than a candidate to be the next leader of the village. His running mate, Min Bahadur Sauden, a wealthy cardamom farmer and trader, was much older than him and dressed in more typical village attire for a man of his age: a Nepali cap (*topi*), muffler and a suit jacket over a tunic and trousers. In the weeks prior to the election, Nar Bahadur was hardly ever at home, and when he was, Min Bahadur and a group of supporters accompanied him. They traveled for four or five days at a time, without a change of clothes or money in their pockets, touring the distant wards of the village that were higher up the mountain and as far as six hours away from ward four.

When I asked Nar Bahadur and Min Bahadur what they talked about when they campaigned, they insisted that they focused on the party ideology (*siddhānta*). However, other than the conversation between Aama and Bala Ram, I saw and heard little evidence that people perceived the election as a choice between two parties with different sets of ideas. No MNO slogans were listed on the only election poster or painted on houses in the village, and candidates' public statements did not focus on the MNO's ideas.

During local elections, voters paid considerable attention to the particular individuals who were running, rather than to the parties of the candidates. A few days before the election, Padam Bau Gurung, a successful butter trader and MNO supporter, stopped by the *thulo ghar* after the morning meal and reported that he had just come back from campaigning in ward seven with Nar Bahadur and Min Bahadur. There had been only 11 MNO supporters in ward seven, but now there were 43. I asked why all these people had decided to support the MNO. Padam Bau answered that it was because the communist leaders there had stolen money that was supposed to be used for ward projects and people were upset. 'They say that their own party [the Communist Party] is good, but the people are not good. [They say] the MNO's party is not good, but the people [the candidates] in the party are good,' explained Padam Bau. This illustrates what other people in the village also told me: in local elections, it was important to elect good people who would do good work for the village regardless of their party affiliation. People considered whether parties were good or bad, but these were secondary factors in their decisions.

Candidates also campaigned on the assumption that people would vote largely on the basis of their personal ties to the candidates, as I saw in the campaigning style of Sita Aama and Tara Aama, two Gurung women in their fifties who both ran as candidates in ward four. Just before the 1997 local elections, new laws resulted in changes in the composition of the village governments (VDCs). Previously, there had been only one representative to the VDC per ward, whereas under the new laws there would be five ward representatives. There was to be one ward chair and four members, one of whom was to be a woman. Tara Aama, Baje's brother's wife and his wife's sister, was running for the position of ward four chair, which she had held for five years during the Panchayat system. Sita Aama, who had held a position on the Women's Committee during the Panchayat era and ran a popular tea shop in the bazaar, was running for the ward representative seat reserved for women.

Vivacious and outgoing, they were among the few women in the village who were politically active. They were the only women in Maidel who would occasionally walk five hours to Ilam bazaar to attend MNO district committee meetings. They were both grandmothers, with daughters-in-law to do most of the household work, and spent considerable time socializing or participating in various village committees. Both women's husbands were far less active in the social life of the community than they were. Thus, both women had more freedom to participate in politics than most other women in the village.

Sita Aama invited me to come 'visiting around the village to ask for votes' with her and told me that I should arrive at seven o'clock to eat the morning *dāl bhāt* meal with her, as she wanted to get an early start. I arrived at Sita Aama's at shortly after seven as she specified, but no one had started cooking. We finally finished eating around nine, and Sita Aama put on a dressy outfit such as she might wear to visit Ilam bazaar or attend a wedding in the village: a fuzzy cardigan sweater and one of her fancy diaphanous nylon saris, wrapped around her waist, rather than draped over her shoulder as saris are worn in the city. Tara Aama arrived only at ten, also in a nylon sari wrapped around her waist.

Finally we hit the campaign trail, making our first stop at a funeral ceremony. Here, I didn't notice Sita Aama and Tara Aama ask anyone for votes, although people at the funeral discussed the election in a general way. Rather, we sat alongside the other guests in the house and drank the tea and ate the snacks that were offered to us. As we were leaving, Sita Aama pulled a few people aside and, in a hushed voice, reminded them to vote on election day.

Next, we made our way to Phul Maya's house, the first of eight houses that we visited that day where the candidates made clear requests for votes. We found Phul Maya, an elderly woman, sitting by the hearth with her husband, rocking their sleeping grandchild. We sat on low wooden planks (*pida*) by the hearth, and everyone began sharing village news, chatting about things like the Sherpa man who had rented the jeep to bring supplies to build a new house. After Phul Maya served us enamel mugs of sweet smoky milk tea, Sita Aama began talking about the election: 'Well, you both know that we're running for election. We just want to remind you that we're running and to remind you to vote!' she said laughing. 'Of course, of course,' said Phul Maya, also laughing, 'Who else would we vote for but you?' Tara Aama reached into her *paṭukā*, a wide band of cloth wrapped around her waist over her sari, and pulled out a small plastic bag. She removed a crumpled copy of the ballot from the bag and showed the elderly couple their names and election symbols on the grid of candidates' names, positions and election symbols. She explained, 'Okay, when you get to the voting booth, make sure you hold the paper in this direction. Just place your stamp across the bottom row, and you'll vote for the MNO for all positions!' Sita Aama chimed in, warning them that many old people had held their ballot in the wrong direction and thus had accidentally voted only for the chairman. We finished our tea and then headed to the next house.

The conversations at most of the houses we visited were similar. Most of the houses that we visited were clearly already supporters of the party, as they displayed MNO flags. We stopped by a few houses where individuals were rumored to have recently switched their allegiance to the Communist Party. When we stopped by to visit one such family, only an old woman was at home, sitting on the porch of her one-room thatched-roof house and beating some rye off the stalks. Tara Aama greeted the old woman, and squatted on the edge of the porch: 'Grandmother, has anyone else been by to ask you for votes?' The old woman continued her work, and said she wasn't sure. 'Will you vote for us on election day or not?' Again, the old woman gave a non-committal answer. Tara Aama pulled out the ballot again and slowly pointed out their election symbols on the sheet. The old woman squinted and said she was having trouble seeing the pictures. Then Tara Aama quizzed her on how to hold the ballot, as the old woman fingered the crumpled paper for a few moments. We continued on our way without waiting for tea.

I had visited people around the village with Sita Aama on many occasions and these campaign visits were not so different from these other visits. The conversations always began with a lengthy discussion of village happenings, and then eventually the women would briefly, but directly, 'ask for votes' (*vot māgnu*). Tara Aama and Sita Aama had no pamphlets to distribute and offered voters no reasons as to why they should vote for them rather than for other candidates. While the women identified themselves as MNO candidates, they never discussed the MNO's platform with voters, or suggested that electing them would help further the party's goals. Campaigning for these women was primarily about affirming personal connections: they renewed social ties with their villagers, and attempted to instill in their neighbors an obligation to vote for them. They presented themselves as candidates who would be good individuals for the job, and who would remember their neighbors once in office.

There was a huge turnout for the election several days later, with 75 percent of the eligible voters casting ballots. Election results suggested that voters were not merely choosing a random assortment of individuals who seemed best suited for each position. MNO candidates won the chair and vice chair seats, as well as all seats in wards two, four and six. In ward three, the MNO won all but one ward representative chair, won by a Communist Party (UML) candidate. The Communist Party won seats in five wards (wards one, five, seven, eight and nine). This voting pattern suggests that people in Maidel were casting votes along party lines rather than voting for individuals per se. In all but one ward, candidates from a single party won all five seats, indicating that a majority of voters in each ward had aligned themselves with either the MNO or the Communist Party. If voters had been considering each candidate as an individual, then there would have been more wards where candidates from both parties won, like ward three where the Communist Party won one seat and the MNO won four seats.

After the election results were announced, the MNO party committee held a huge victory celebration in the bazaar in ward four: they slaughtered a buffalo and cooked up cauldrons of curry and rice to feed all MNO supporters. Party supporters congratulated victorious candidates with white silk scarves used in Buddhist rituals (*khata*), garlands of flowers and red powder (*abir*). Despite the merry-making, MNO supporters were dismayed that MNO candidates had lost in two wards where they had won in the 1991 elections. Throughout Nepal, in fact, the Communist Party made remarkable gains in these 1997 local elections. Many people attributed the Communist Party's success in the polls to the popularity of its programs during the time they ran the government from 1994 through 1995.

If voters were not merely choosing candidates as individuals, neither were they strictly choosing candidates based on the ideology of the parties they represented. Although voters were voting along party lines, these parties had not asserted a particular set of issues during the campaign. This suggests that voters were actually voting along faction lines, and that party politics after 1990 were an extension of the system of factional politics that was in practice during the Panchayat system.[3]

By factional politics, I refer to political systems in which individuals are bound together in networks of mutual obligation: individuals pledge their political allegiance to faction leaders, who in return assist these individuals in their times of need. Leaders of sub-factions, which were brought under larger factions, were known as 'influential people' (*prabhāvik mānchhe*). Nar Bahadur explained to me that the first step in establishing support for the party in the village was to convince influential people from each ward to join the party: 'If we convince these people, they'll bring the whole ward.' He explained that it was not wealth alone that made a person influential; rather, influential people demonstrated leadership skills in resolving local disputes, and in working on behalf of the ward. Yet they certainly had more economic resources than others, as they were patrons who assisted other people during their times of need. They served as brokers between villagers and people in positions of greater power.

Party activists placed much importance on persuading influential people to join their own party because political party affiliation stemmed at least partly from circles of *āphno mānchhe*, literally, one's 'own people', groups of people who relied on each other for labor exchanges and for mutual assistance. When influential people joined a party, they brought a whole entourage of their *āphno mānchhe* with them. Due to this phenomenon, all political parties in the village were composed of people from across the class spectrum. Many villagers told me that they experienced social pressure to join a party that one's established circle of *āphno mānchhe* joined; people spoke about how they feared being the only one in their '*ṭol*', or hamlet, to belong to a different political party.

In the post-1990 multi-party system, it was difficult to distinguish between parties and factions. Political party affiliation had been mapped onto affiliation to factions that had existed earlier. People in Maidel alluded to a long-standing rivalry between Baje and Moti Lal, another Gurung man who was one of the wealthiest individuals in the village. I was not able to learn much about the particular events that led to or deepened this rivalry. However, Moti Lal had challenged Baje for the position of village chairman in the last election of the Panchayat system, and won, and he was now a staunch Congress Party supporter. When Baje was convinced to run for village chairman as an MNO candidate, people who were loyal to him and his faction were brought into the MNO. For this reason, many Maidel MNO supporters attribute the MNO's success in the local elections to Baje's decision to join it. As one elderly Gurung woman told me, 'we would have voted for him whatever party he was in.'

I was not able to observe MNO campaigns for national elections, but MNO activists insisted that in these, conveying the party's ideology to voters was important for winning votes. Although I began this portion of my fieldwork after the 1994 election, I saw evidence from this campaign, such as election pamphlets, cassette recordings of speeches delivered at mass-meetings and slogans on people's homes that clearly enunciated the MNO's goals and ideology.

MNO ideology and support for the party

In Nar Bahadur's narrative of how the MNO became popular in Maidel, he suggested that the party's ideas play a key role in bringing people into the party. It was on the basis of listening to Kiran Akten's speeches that nearly all of the 50 people who accompanied him to the MNO mass-meeting in Alubari bazaar decided to turn in their old party memberships and become members of the MNO. This narrative suggests that the party's ideas were at the heart of party success in the village, an idea that is central to the way that MNO supporters represented the party. Here, I consider the question of why the MNO's ideology was compelling to people in the village, even if this alone cannot be taken as the sole reason for the party's success.

The Alubari mass-meeting was not the first time that people in the area had heard the MNO's ideas, though Nar Bahadur's narrative may give this impression. Nar Bahadur and many others were already familiar with the basic ideas of the party because they had read Gopal Gurung's book, *Hidden Facts in Nepalese Politics*. Many Maidel villagers recalled that a single tattered copy of the slim, blue paperback book had circulated through Maidel just prior to the end of the Panchayat regime. Individuals such as Jan Bir Gurung, the MNO candidate who was elected as the ward four representative to the Village Development Committee (VDC), spoke passionately about their experiences of reading the book. When visiting Jan Bir, a stern, sinewy farmer in his late thirties, in the dark kitchen of his thatched-roof house, I asked how he first heard about the MNO. He enthusiastically recalled how he encountered *Hidden Facts*:

JB: I heard about the Mongol party about a month and a half before the multi-party system came [February 1990], from the book that Gopal Gurung wrote, *Hidden Facts*.... A friend brought the book back from Naya Bazaar. I had gone out strolling in the village, that's what you do in the village, right? And [when I met my friend] I wondered what book he was reading. When I looked closely I saw that it was *Hidden Facts*. And I had to read it secretly. Then I gave it to someone else, and they passed it to someone else, and from there it reached as far as ward eight! Who knows where that book went, circling around like that. And then the multi-party system came, as well.

Q: There was only one copy in Maidel?

JB: There was only one, at first. It was old from everyone sharing it. When I finished it I gave it to someone else; when they finished it, they gave it to someone else, and so on...

Q: So what did you think of this book?

JB: It was really surprising! Gopal Gurung wrote that Chhetri-Bahuns had kept us *matwālis*[4] down in all these different ways; they oppressed us. [He wrote] about who gets seats at the upper central level, and who has reached there up until now. It's all true too, you see! In Nepal, Marich Man Singh Shrestha was the only Mongol Prime Minister!... And they blamed him for all kinds of things and didn't allow him to stay in power for more than six months. They removed him suddenly, and again there were Chhetri-Bahuns. I felt very satisfied, reading the things that were written about Bahuns in *Hidden Facts*. It was really believable and that book tells about the analysis of true things.

Jan Bir's enthusiasm for Gopal Gurung's description of the inequality between high-caste Hindus and Mongols was further illustrated by an MNO slogan painted in red clay on his front door: 'Let's not become the horses of the 20% Chhetri-Bahuns; Let's work to uplift the 80% Mongols!' (*20% chettri-bāhun ko ghoḍa nabanau. 80% Mongol ko utthan garde jau!*). MNO supporters throughout the village echoed these ideas, describing themselves as exploited (*śoṣit*) and oppressed (*dabāb; thicho-micho*) by high-caste Hindus.

However, in the village of Maidel, relations between resident high-caste Hindus and Mongols did not conform to the MNO's depiction of social relations. Few high-caste Hindus lived within the boundaries of the VDC and they had negligible political power within the village. Class boundaries also did not map onto ethnic boundaries: the high-caste Hindus had no economic power over other villagers and were no wealthier than others overall. Many MNO activists asserted that the MNO was more successful in VDC elections in villages with few high-caste Hindus. They explained that if there were more Bahuns, they would dominate the local political scene and would never allow the MNO to gain power.

How, then, did the MNO's ideas about high-caste Hindus as oppressors make sense to people in a village where local high-caste Hindus are relatively powerless? MNO supporters in Maidel insisted that high-caste Hindu dominance (*bāhunbād*) existed at 'higher levels'. As one Magar MNO activist in Maidel explained, 'Supporting the MNO doesn't mean that we are going to criticize or attack these [local] Chhetris and Brahmans – that's not the situation. Our struggle is another type of struggle, reaching to the highest level. Our struggle is with the higher levels of the state.'

In Maidel, or when they traveled to the district headquarters and Kathmandu, villagers encountered representatives of higher levels of the state who were mostly high-caste Hindus. Most government positions in Maidel were filled with high caste Hindus from two neighboring VDCs. The school headmasters, over half of the schoolteachers, the postman who came three times a week, the health workers from the health post in the next VDC and the VDC secretary (the only salaried, government-appointed position on the VDC) were all Bahuns who commuted to Maidel from neighboring villages. MNO supporters in Maidel consistently noted that the government offices that they visited in Ilam bazaar were 'filled with Bahun-Chhetris'. This situation was not particular to Ilam; as shown in Chapter 2, Bahuns are over-represented in state positions throughout Nepal.

Because 'Mongols' had little contact with the high-caste Hindus who were permanent residents of Maidel, the only high-caste Hindus that they regularly interacted with were representatives of the government. Local people in positions of power were selected by villagers and were all 'Mongols', while outsiders in positions of power were selected by people from higher levels of the state and were '*bāhune-bāhun*' (totally Bahun). This situation contributed to local MNO supporters' conviction that high-caste Hindus dominate Nepal's government. For MNO supporters, one of the main goals of the party was placing Mongols into these government offices.

In explaining why they supported the MNO, many villagers described negative encounters with high-caste Hindu state representatives, focusing on the education system and government offices. Villagers frequently recounted unpleasant experiences when visiting government offices. As Ram Bahadur Gurung, a farmer who lives in a thatched-roof, one-story home that he decorated with MNO slogans during the national election, told me, 'Whenever we go to offices, we see only Aryans. If we need to do some work that would only require 5,000 rupees, they'll make us pay 10,000 to get it done. If I have to pay 20 rupees tax on my land, they'll make us pay 40 rupees. We are oppressed by Chhetri-Bahuns here.' Ram Bahadur could have interpreted this as evidence of the problems of corruption in the government. Instead, he attributed the problems in the government to the dominance of high-caste Hindus in it. While government employees may have demanded bribes from high-caste Hindus as well as from 'Mongols', Ram Bahadur interpreted this as illustrating oppression by high-caste Hindus.

Many villagers talked about experiencing ethnic discrimination in the education system, one of the main sites in which the state sought to remold its heterogeneous population into a unified Nepali nation. People recounted incidents in which high-caste Hindu teachers, who made up the majority of teachers in the state-run schools, discriminated against 'Mongol' students. Tara Gurung, a vivacious 18-year-old who had been attempting to complete high school for the past several years, told me how she had done well all school year in her classes until after she gave a speech at an MNO rally. She failed her exams, and believed that this was because her Bahun teachers were angry with her for giving this speech.

Even older people who had never attended school themselves yet occasionally visited schools, like Man Maya Gurung and her sister Purnima, two unmarried elderly women who had raised one of their nephews, said that they had witnessed discrimination against Mongols there. 'We learned that Chhetri-Bahuns are ahead from looking at nearby examples. Just look at the school,' noted Man Maya. 'The children of Chhetri-Bahuns go ahead, ours fail.' Purnima exclaimed, 'In Alubari school, they even put our Mongol kids in the back of the classroom.... They have to stretch from the back to see the teacher.'

Nar Bahadur told me about a painful incident of discrimination by a high-caste Hindu that happened when he was preparing to take the grueling, comprehensive School Leaving Certificate (SLC) examination that students must take at the end of tenth grade and must pass in order to continue on with their education, and to be eligible for most government jobs. Before they take the SLC, students must pass a qualifying exam that people refer to as the 'sent-up' exams, using an English phrase:

> One very clear thing that happened with Chhetri-Bahuns that really made me angry took place while I was studying, in 2041 [1984]. In 2041, I was at the school in Chiso Pani and I had given the grade 10 sent-up exam. My studying was very good, you see?... I didn't know English that well, and didn't know math that well. But in all other subjects I knew everything completely, from top to bottom.... And the school's headmaster and other masters were good people. All of the masters were Chhetri-Bahuns. After the sent-up exam was finished, those Bahuns told me that I definitely wouldn't fail, that my general knowledge was good and that my studies were also good, they gave me this kind of hope. And after I took the sent-up exam, I also believed it, I had hope that I really would pass, and I was thinking that I really would pass.... Before the results were out, I was already prepared to give the final.... When the results came out, I was short one mark in the subject of history, in one subject.... I did well in all other subjects.... I failed because I needed to get one more mark in history.
>
> And I thought, perhaps the number count [calculation] might not be correct. The headmaster wrote me a letter so that I could go to Ilam ... to have my notebook rechecked. He wrote a letter saying that we would meet at such and such a place in Ilam, and that he himself was surprised, and that he had hoped that I would pass. I went at the time that he called me and the headmaster was in Ilam. I went to the District Education Office to have my exam rechecked. The DEC [District Education Chairman] was a Bahun, I forget his name.... When we went there, he wouldn't recheck it, he wouldn't look at the exam. What he said was to get a bank voucher [money order] for ten rupees, and come back. I didn't have much experience with banks, of course. The headmaster went – he was a Poudel, a Bahun. But even though he was a Bahun, he was very friendly to me.... He brought the voucher for ten rupees from Nepal Bank and the DEC rechecked the exam. When he rechecked it, he said, 'it's right, he needed one more mark in

history.' The headmaster took the DEC to an upstairs room and said, 'Look sir, this younger brother has a lot of general knowledge and his other subjects are also good. It's just that he fell short by one mark in history. One mark is not such a big deal, it's not that important of a subject. Nothing bad will happen if you make this decision and give this younger brother a chance to take the final.' When the headmaster said this to the DEC, the DEC said directly, 'Looking at his face, he's not the type of person who studies.' Saying by looking at his face, he's not the studying type, that's how he made the decision on this subject!

Later, after the multi-party system came, after I saw Gopal Gurung's book, I knew. Eh! So that's what that meant! I realized later that actually, if he had seen a Chhetri-Bahun face he would've given the one mark.... At that time, I didn't understand what he said, I only understood later. I was really angry at that time and said I wouldn't study and I just quit my studies.

While Nar Bahadur framed the story as an example of 'something that happened with Chhetri-Bahuns that made me really angry', his representation of high-caste Hindus was ambiguous. He described 'good' high-caste Hindus, the 'friendly' Bahun headmaster who went out of his way to help him and the Bahun teachers at his school, as well as the one Bahun man, the chair of the District Education Office, who discriminated against him. Having failed the 'sent-up' exam was clearly a humiliating experience for Nar Bahadur. He was angry about failing the exam by such a small margin, and he had expected that the chair of the District Education Office would bend the rules for him, especially as his headmaster was there with him. As Nar Bahadur recalled, it was the DEC's statement about Nar Bahadur's face that suggests that he was discriminating against Nar Bahadur as a Mongol.

Nar Bahadur stated that he did not understand what the DEC meant when he referred to his face, and learned the meaning of his statement only after reading Gopal Gurung's book. The MNO's ideas about racial discrimination offered Nar Bahadur a new lens through which to interpret one of the most disappointing and significant events of his life. Nar Bahadur regretted not continuing with his studies and suggested that he might have tried to take the sent-up exam again the next year if he had understood the meaning of the DEC's comment.

Harka Bahadur Gurung told me about facing discrimination in his attempt to get a teaching job in a local school:

I took the SLC [School Leaving Certificate] exam in 2039 [1982]. When I took it, I didn't pass in two subjects. At that time if you passed the SLC or if you didn't pass two subjects, you could become a temporary teacher. I heard from the school board that there was an opening at the school in ward two here. After I heard that, I went to Ilam to give my application. I went to ... the District Education Office. When I went to that office,... I said, 'I need a job. I hear there is an opening at such and such a place. You should give this job to me. I've taken the SLC exam. I failed this year but I'm going to take the exam again.' The situation is that there's no chance for someone who hasn't taken the SLC. That would be the end. Well, I couldn't go on repeating myself, it was very uncomfortable, this topic.

I had a class friend who was in grade nine; he's the son of an Adhikari Bahun. What he did is that he failed grade nine and went right away to Banaras. He went to Banaras or someone gave him a certificate. I'm not sure what happened.... He went there [to the District Education Office] and the next day he was a teacher in a school here in Maidel. So that's to say, how easy it is [for him]. We passed the test and took the SLC, we didn't get it. He didn't pass grade nine or take the SLC, but brought a certificate, and he became a teacher. And after some time, he was fired, but still he got some economic benefit from that.

Harka Bahadur asserted that there should have been no chance for his Bahun classmate to get this job, as he had not taken the SLC. However, his classmate used his connections with high-caste Hindus to land the very job that he himself had been unable to get. By saying that his classmate went to Banaras, a city in India that is a famous Hindu pilgrimage site, to get a certificate saying he had completed high school, Harka Bahadur implied that it was through his connections with other high-caste Hindus that he was able to secure the certificate. He described how playing by the rules led him nowhere, while a Bahun classmate was able to use connections and bend the rules of the system in his favor.

Not everyone who supported the party could apply its ideas about high-caste Hindu dominance to their own lives in this way, as I saw in my conversation with two elderly Limbu men called Dambar Bau and Buddhi Man. Dambar Bau puffed on a fat hand-rolled cigarette and wore glasses with one of the ear pieces replaced by a string, one lens cracked down the middle, and the other lens held in the frame with a yellow rubber band; his Limbu neighbor Buddhi Man sported a frayed *topi* (cloth cap), and rubber flip-flops so worn they were perfectly molded to his feet. When I asked what they thought about the MNO, Buddhi Man answered in a slow, melodic voice, 'We don't understand that well, eh? When democracy came, everyone joined the Mongol party, so we did too. We will stick with this party as long as it is operating. We 80 percent Mongols are a bit oppressed (*dabāb pareko*), so in order for others to hear our voice (*āwāj*), we joined this party.' 'How are Mongols oppressed?' I inquired. Buddhi Man, again, responded slowly, 'Well ... we haven't read history ... we've heard this idea from leaders and activists.'... Dambar Bau chimed in, boisterous and impatient, 'Eh! What do we know? We are totally mute! (*laṭo*) Blind! (*andha*).' Buddhi Man spoke again in measured tones: 'Even if we don't know much, I feel in my heart that the fact that Nepal is in the hands of the 20 percent Aryans could be true.'

Although these men did not see a connection between their own lives and the ideas of the MNO, they understood the concept of democracy as allowing others to hear their voices.

The way that Harka Bahadur, Nar Bahadur and others view social relations did not spring directly from 'experience'. Rather, the MNO taught individuals how to apply the MNO's ideas about high-caste Hindu dominance to interpret their own life experiences. Nar Bahadur talked explicitly about having been able to understand his encounter with the DEC as an instance of discrimination by high-caste Hindus only after having read Gopal Gurung's book. He and others learned how to think of their life experiences through the lens of MNO ideology. Begona Aretxaga's conceptualization of experience 'as an ongoing construction always placed within the arena of existing discursive fields and social practices' is helpful in understanding these narratives of experience as interpretations (1997: 17). Individuals' experiences are shaped by interpretations that they forge within particular cultural and political contexts.

I do not mean to suggest that high-caste Hindu dominance did not exist without these narratives. Rather, given a different interpretive lens, these people might have seen these experiences as examples of other forms of power at work: for example, they could have interpreted these incidents as examples of class inequality or of the failures of state. People drew upon MNO ideology as an interpretive framework for their narratives of experience, suggesting that the MNO changed how people identified themselves.

Relations between Mongols in Maidel

The MNO asserted that the myriad ethnic groups who made up the Mongol category must unite in order to gain political power and freedom from the oppression of high-caste Hindus. While MNO slogans calling for Mongol unity, 'Let all Mongols be one!' (*sabai Mongol ek hau*), were scrawled on several stalls in the bazaar area of Maidel, few people were attempting to build this unity on a level of everyday interactions in the village. Many people who supported the MNO did not view people from other Mongol ethnic groups as their equals. The MNO attributed this problem to the influence of the Hindu caste system.

In the course of daily life, people interacted most closely with people from their own kin, and thus their own ethnic group. For example, when a group of Gurung women gathered to form *parama* work groups, a cooperative form of labor exchange in which a group takes turns working on the land of each individual in the group, it was most often with kin from neighboring households. Only when a family needed to hire day laborers (*khetālo*) for large tasks such as bringing freshly cut rice stalks from the paddy fields an hour down the hill would they hire Limbus from a poorer hamlet in Maidel.

People from some ethnic groups held negative stereotypes about people from other groups. As I was closest to the Gurung community in Maidel, I often heard how Gurungs talked about other ethnic groups in the village. The day after I had spent a day in ward six interviewing Limbus, who were the majority there, I became sick. When I told Aama I wasn't feeling well, she immediately blamed it on the tea that I drank in the Limbu homes the previous day. 'Those Limbus just drink alcohol all the time and they make terrible tea!' she opined. Later, Tara Maya stopped by to visit Aama, her sister, and when I told her that I'd visited ward six, she looked horrified and exclaimed, 'Alone?! That Limbu village is a strange place.' I asked what she thought was so strange about it. She replied, 'Well, their speech is strange; the tea they serve is strange: they keep pigs and they're dirty.' Her daughter Tara chimed in, smiling: 'But Kiran Akten is probably very clean!' Recalling my friendship with Kiran, these women made an exception to their general stereotype of Limbus.

The influence of a Hindu world-view is evident in the comments that these Gurung women made about Limbus. Alcohol consumption was in fact widespread among all ethnic groups in Maidel except for high-caste Hindus, yet many people associated alcohol consumption, or at least in excess, with low social status. This view recalls the fact that the state categorized most indigenous nationalities groups as alcohol drinkers (*matwāli*) in the 1854 legal code, and used that cultural practice to justify their lower ranking in the social hierarchy. Gurungs generally do not keep pigs and most often do not eat pork, and many Gurungs viewed this as an argument for their ethnic group to have a higher status than ethnic groups who do consume pork. These kinds of prejudices complicated the MNO's plans to form a solid political alliance among all Mongols. The idea of Mongol unity had little meaning in everyday interactions between villagers, and became salient only in opposition to the high-caste Hindus who represented the state.

In the post-1990 political system, political party affiliation became a central part of social identity in the village. Maidel residents were highly aware of who supported which party, and fellow villagers' shifts in party affiliation were a favorite topic of gossip. While some people denied that party affiliation had any meaning in daily life in the village, I saw evidence that it was central to social interactions. Each house was marked with a political party flag, particularly during election times. Furthermore, when people formed work groups to plant rice or hoe potato fields, they often selected people from their own party to join their group. When I strolled with Sita Aama on her daily rounds through the village to visit neighbors for tea, she would comment on the party affiliation of every house we passed, gripping my arm and hissing 'Communist's house!' in my ear when we walked by one of her opponent's homes. She occasionally would call out and chat with these people if they were outside their homes when we walked by, but we never went in for tea at one of these homes. Her closest friends and relatives were all fellow MNO supporters.

While the MNO hoped to unite all Mongols as followers of their party, political party affiliation created rifts within the village. One clear example of a social fracture due to conflicting party affiliation was the ostracism of Talli Bahadur Gurung, a man who lived in the small bazaar, where nearly all of the other residents were MNO supporters. Talli Bahadur had recently left the MNO and joined the Communist Party. When Talli Bahadur's son was married, he invited his neighbors to attend, as was expected in the village. Weddings were the most joyous and well-attended social events in the village, as the hosts invited their entire circle of relations and acquaintances and served them a feast of meat and alcohol. Yet on the day of the wedding, Talli Bahadur's house was forlornly quiet, while his neighbors in the bazaar busily carried on with their daily chores.

When I asked Aama, the grandmother of the house I lived in, why no one was at the wedding, she chortled, 'Who would go to a communist's wedding?' The poor attendance at Talli Bahadur's son's wedding was the topic of many fireside conversations over the next few days; women exclaimed to each other with satisfaction, 'No one went to that wedding!' On other occasions in this village, people from opposing political parties did attend each other's weddings, so it seemed that Talli Bahadur was ostracized because he had previously belonged to the MNO. The message to all MNO supporters was that anyone who left the MNO to join another party would lose the support of their neighbors.

This antipathy between supporters of the Communist Party and the MNO was exacerbated by several incidents of violence between members of these parties in Maidel just after 1990. Communist Party supporters beat and nearly killed an MNO activist, and MNO activists retaliated by setting fire to the house of a low-caste communist supporter. It was these events, rather than the platform of the Communist Party, that many MNO supporters recounted when explaining their dislike of the Communist Party. Violence in Maidel did not have an ethnic character; rather, it took place between party-based communities, and between groups of people that the MNO sought to unite as Mongols.

These political rifts led some people to recall the partyless Panchayat system with nostalgia. Bhauju, Nar Bahadur's wife, reminisced about how peaceful things had been in the village before the multi-party system: 'The Panchayat era was better because there were no conflicts between neighbors and other villagers. Now there are lots of parties and lots of conflicts along with them.' Bhauju and others who fondly recollected the Panchayat era had forgotten that the apparent peace of those days was the result of fear and a lack of political freedom, more than of genuine contentment.

Conclusion

The institution of a democratic political system in 1990 created both possibilities and limitations for rural political actors who sought to create political changes. Contradictions between party ideologies and practices appeared at several different levels. The MNO's ideology of creating ethnic equality through radically transforming the state was at odds with the party's role in maintaining the state's presence in the village. When MNO representatives served on VDCs they did not try to obstruct the operations of the state, despite their party's strong critiques of the state. Like all village government representatives, the MNO representatives were excluded from decision-making processes at the center. Yet this situation was exacerbated for the MNO representatives, as their party was not represented in the higher levels of the government. Nonetheless, these elected officials tried to run the village-level offices much as individuals elected from other parties did, resolving local conflicts and bringing development to the village in the form of health posts, new schools and water taps.

Winning seats on the VDC did little to help the MNO achieve its party's grand plans of creating structural changes in the state, as this would require power at the national level. Yet the MNO presence on the VDC still served a purpose for the party. MNO activists and leaders pointed to the MNO candidates serving on village governments to demonstrate that Mongols were capable leaders and should be widely included in the formal political process and institutions. Furthermore, they argued that winning these seats showed that there was popular support for the MNO's long-term goals and potential for the party's growth.

The more open political culture in the post-1990 multi-party system enabled the MNO to freely circulate a new discourse of ethnic rights. The MNO was able to recruit supporters from a variety of ethnic groups, and to instill in these people the idea that they shared a Mongol identity and together formed a political community. Yet the new democratic ideals of political action as driven by a commitment to ideas existed alongside the persistence of personalized ties as a major factor in determining political affiliations. Thus, in village-level elections in particular, the MNO candidates emphasized their individual qualities and connections to voters and paid little attention to their party's platform of ethnic rights. The party's goal of creating Mongol unity was crosscut by divisions between different Mongol ethnic groups in Maidel and the fact that many people supported other political parties. To overcome these divisions, the MNO attempted to define a unified Mongol identity through cultural productions, as we see in the next chapter.

5 'Our own heartbeats'

The politics of culture in the MNO

On a blustery spring afternoon in a village in central Ilam district, 40 men and women and many schoolchildren sat on a grassy hilltop. To the south, the plains were faintly visible beyond the hills, and on the northern horizon, a tiny piece of the snowcapped Kanchenjunga peeked through the clouds. The crowd intently listened to Kiran Akten sing this song:

> Wake up Mongols, this country is ours,
> The mountains, hills and plains are all ours.
> We shouldn't wander this way and then that way.
> Let's learn to live by our own heart beat.
> Let's live taking care of our own villages and huts.
> Let's recognize our relatives and all live in harmony.

With songs like this, the MNO sought to create a sense of belonging to the Mongol community. Through representations of Mongols in songs, calendars and rituals, the MNO aimed to transform practices of everyday life and reconfigure people's sense of self.

In its cultural representations, the MNO sought to redefine the identity of the Nepali nation. As Kiran Akten explained to me, 'To save Nepal's identity, we like to separate ... our people from Hindu culture (*sanskar*). We would like to identify our people as we were before, just as our ancestors were, living with their own identity.' He described Nepal's current identity as threatened because the markers of national identity are Hindu, and are also used in India. By expunging Hindu culture from their lives, Mongols could remove Hindu domination and gain political power, ruling themselves as their ancestors once had. The assertion of a Mongol identity and of Mongol culture was a political act that lay claim to the political control of Nepal. As the MNO song above indicated, the MNO saw Mongols as the rightful proprietors of the country: 'this country is ours, the mountains, hills and plains are all ours.'

Being Mongol meant adopting Mongol cultural traditions, referred to as 'our own heartbeats' (*ā- āphnai ḍhukḍhukīharu*) in the title of an MNO cassette. Hearts and heartbeats are common metaphors of identity in Nepal. However, defining 'our own heartbeats' was a challenging proposition for the MNO, due to the extreme diversity among the groups of peoples that the MNO aimed to unite as Mongols. This chapter examines the dilemmas that the MNO encountered in trying to represent the identity of Mongols, as well as the oppositional dimensions of the MNO's cultural productions.

Here, I examine three distinct forms through which the MNO sought to substantiate the idea of a Mongol community: an MNO calendar, an MNO leader's celebration of the Tihar holiday and MNO songs.

The calendar and songs as texts and the Tihar celebration as a ritual could be reproduced, enabling the people who engaged with them to have a sense of participating in a shared Mongol community. Calendars and holidays are examples of invented traditions, representations of the past which play an important role in the construction of ethnic and nationalist identities (Hobsbawm and Ranger 1983; Mosse 1975). Instilling in people a new sense of their relationship to the past, invented traditions encourage people to re-imagine their identities.

Debates over culture are often part of political struggles and are an integral part of efforts to redefine the meanings of political systems and to change the distribution of power in society (Alvarez *et al.* 1998: 7). Due to the connection between controlling the meanings of social practices and accruing or maintaining power, cultural revitalization plays a central a role in the indigenous nationalities movement. The MNO and other organizations frequently expressed the urgency of uplifting 'our language, religion and culture' (*hāmro bhāsā, dharma, sanskriti*), which they saw as threatened by the dominant high-caste Hindu culture.[1] This ubiquitous phrase challenged the central tenets of Panchayat era nationalism: the Nepali language, Hinduism and 'the high caste cultural tradition represented by the monarchy' (Des Chene 1996: 124). Activists in the movement also spoke of their right to practice their own culture, highlighting the freedom of cultural expression as a central part of the concept of democracy.

The project of specifying what is meant by 'our language, religion and culture' involves 'cultural objectification' (Handler 1988), the selection, promotion and reification of one of many possible forms of culture to represent the entire culture of a particular group. Cultural objectification in the indigenous nationalities movement was accomplished through such means as the frequent 'cultural programs' *(sanskritik kāryakram)*, in which people performed dances and sang songs while wearing clothing that indexed the identity of the entire group, and articles on language or religion in magazines published by the indigenous nationalities organization (Des Chene 1996).

Cultural objectification was a challenge not just for the MNO, which aimed to unite multiple ethnic groups, but also for the indigenous nationalities organizations. While these organizations aimed to promote a sense of cultural unity within one ethnic group, tremendous cultural heterogeneity exists within all groups. Ethnic groups in Nepal, like those elsewhere, are not culturally and linguistically bounded, stable communities (Guneratne 2002; Holmberg 1989; Levine 1987).

In defining Mongol identity, the MNO aimed to create unity between diverse groups of people, while still affirming their heterogeneity. MNO activists and supporters emphasized that Mongol identity should encompass, but not erase, the identities of the different ethnic groups within the Mongol category. The MNO did not attempt to replace identities such as Rai, Gurung and Limbu; rather, it recontextualized and redefined these identities, by asserting that these ethnic groups all belonged to the Mongol race and that they therefore should form a political community. Thus, the MNO could not represent Mongol identity through selecting a cultural practice that specifically signifies the identity of one Mongol ethnic group, such as Limbu or Gurung.

The MNO encouraged Mongols to reject Hinduism and rely less on the Nepali language. Yet, unlike the indigenous nationalities organizations, the MNO never indicated which specific language, religion and culture Mongols should embrace. Many MNO supporters saw the indigenous nationalities organizations as providing them with their 'own language, religion and culture'. In the 1990s, many MNO supporters participated in the organizations that were active in eastern Nepal, such as the Limbu organization *Kirat Yakthung Chumlung*, and the Rai organization *Kirat Rai Yayokkha*. Some people joined the MNO after getting involved in the indigenous nationalities organizations, while others said their participation in the MNO led them to get involved in these other organizations. These MNO supporters perceived the work and goals of the indigenous nationalities organizations as complementary to the MNO's goals as they raised people's awareness and encouraged them to break away from Hinduism.

The relationship between the MNO and the indigenous nationalities groups became a point of conflict among MNO members towards the end of 1996, when MNO leaders increasingly criticized these organizations. MNO leaders like Kiran Akten, who had earlier participated in these organizations, began to urge other leaders to refrain from taking part in them. MNO leaders worried that these organizations would mislead people into believing that the goal of activism was merely cultural revival, rather than gaining political power. Cultural revival would be ultimately meaningless without the power to institutionalize the use of these languages and cultures at the state level, they argued; 'like growing cash crops without a market to sell them in,' as Kiran Akten explained.

MNO leaders also criticized the indigenous nationalities organizations for promoting the identities of individual ethnic groups rather than the identity of Mongols as a whole. As Nar Bahadur stated, 'We are fighting for the freedom of all Mongols, not just of one group.' Leaders perceived these organizations as threatening to the MNO's political project, and argued that these organizations could fracture the Mongol community, preventing Mongols from acting as a unified political force. The MNO's efforts to define a shared Mongol culture were largely in reaction to the growing popularity of the indigenous nationalities organizations. Two of the MNO cultural productions examined here – the calendar and the Tihar celebration – were direct responses to projects initiated by indigenous nationalities organizations.

The creative force behind many of the MNO's cultural productions was the influential and charismatic leader, Kiran Akten. Because of Kiran's prominence within the MNO, his creations often came to be adopted by the whole party.

Thus, Kiran's songs became well known as people learned them from hearing him sing at mass-meetings, during his visits to their villages or from listening to the cassette he recorded. Kiran wrote poetry and songs, as well as political pamphlets. He is a talented musician who plays the guitar, *bā̃surī* (bamboo flute), *sārangī* (small violin), harmonium, *mādal* (a two-sided, cylindrical drum) and electric keyboard. He has a haunting voice and recorded several folk songs for Radio Nepal in the mid-1980s, a project that won him a degree of local fame as one of the songs was a standard on Radio Nepal's folk tune play list. Although Kiran, his wife and two children subsisted by farming their land in the hot, lush plains of southern Ilam, he gave minimal attention to farming during my visits to his home. While other villagers plodded away at daily chores, Kiran passed days lost in thought as he wrote in his diary, worked out the melody of a song or sat under a tree in the forest and taught himself to play the mandolin, finally squeezing farm work into a few frenzied days. Kiran also traveled frequently, always carrying at least one musical instrument, and spent weeks walking through the hills to attend party events or meet with party supporters in far-flung villages.

Developing the cultural content of Mongol identity was an important project for Kiran. He established several organizations within the MNO in his home village, such as a Mongol youth club and a Mongol National Cultural Society to support these projects. As he stated in one public meeting, 'Actually, cultural programs and music … are more dangerous than an atom bomb.' By using the metaphor of weaponry to talk about music and cultural programs, he highlighted the efficacy of cultural productions in political struggles.

Constructing a Mongol calendar

In most homes and shops in rural Nepal, calendars distributed by the district government or by businesses hang on the walls, alongside posters of Bollywood film stars, scenes of Switzerland and baskets of kittens. In the mid-1990s, calendars distributed by indigenous nationalities organizations were ubiquitous elements of home décor in rural east Nepal. While en route to Maidel from Ilam bazaar, I stopped at a teashop in a tiny bazaar, and saw a calendar from the Tamang Ghedung, one of the indigenous nationalities organizations. When I commented on the calendar to the friendly shopkeeper, he began talking about the impending loss of Tamang language, religion and culture. These calendars proved to be reliable indicators of people who were involved in or at least influenced by the indigenous nationalities movement.

Nearly every indigenous nationalities organization produced a calendar during the 1990s. Calendars as displayable artifacts were important to these organizations because they publicized and promoted the organizations' names and goals, and because of their symbolic force in creating national communities. In Anderson's (1991 [1983]) classic formulation, nations are created through certain modes of representation, such as novels and newspapers, that he calls 'print capitalism'. These forms produce a sense of belonging to the nation because they can be reproduced and widely disseminated, enabling disparate people to simultaneously engage with them and share something with people they will never meet (Anderson 1991 [1983]: 22). Like the forms of print capitalism that Anderson discusses, calendars produce a sense of belonging to the nation. Through calendars, citizens come to imagine themselves as participating in a sequence of events shared by all throughout the nation. The calendar structures what Anderson calls 'homogenous, empty time', the crucial backdrop upon which people can imagine the national community (p. 33). Furthermore, a calendar is a 'spectacular site of collective memory' (Zerubavel 2003: 316), and shapes the ways people imagine the past. While calendars bind a national community to a particular interpretation of the past, they also provide a grid for the future. Calendars thus invoke the nationalist configuration of time, in which the nation is represented as sharing a golden past that will be reinstated in the future when the nationalist movement is successful (Smith 2004: 221–223). By suggesting that each nation or ethnic group has a unique system of structuring time, a particular history and a unique set of cultural practices, calendars create chronological homelands.

As calendars can effectively create communities, political movements often attempt to revise calendars in order to make political statements (Zerubavel 1981: 2003). For example, the Italian Communist Party sought to ritualize history through creating its own calendar with dates emphasizing the party's interpretation of history (Kertzer 1996: 19–20), while the French Republic calendar initially replaced a seven-day week with a ten-day week in an effort to secularize post-revolution France (Zerubavel 1981: 82–95). Similarly, the MNO and indigenous nationalities organization activists expressed their opposition to the Nepali state's definition of Nepal as a Hindu nation by forwarding their own calendars. The official calendar of Nepal, at least since the late eighteenth century, is the 'Hindu' vikram calendar (*vikram sambat*), although the Gregorian calendar has been used concurrently since at least the 1950s. This calendar system dates to the coronation of King Vikramaditya in India (Majupuria 1981: 14). The MNO party manifesto called for abolishing this calendar because it is 'anti-national', as it is a Hindu calendar used by India.[2]

Many ethnic groups in Nepal have their own calendrical systems, which have largely fallen into disuse. By reviving these calendars, the indigenous nationalities organizations contested the dominance of the 'Hindu' *vikram sambat* calendar. These calendars exemplify what Homi Bhabha (1990) calls 'counter-narratives of nationalism', as displaying them was an act of symbolic opposition to the dominant model of the nation, regardless of whether or not people actually gauged their lives by these calendars.

In 1996, several years after the proliferation of indigenous nationalities organization calendars in eastern Nepal, MNO leaders decided that their party should also create a calendar. In place of the calendars representing single ethnic groups, the party sought to create a calendar that would create alliances among all Mongols. At an MNO conference for activists held in his village in May 1996, Kiran gathered input from party activists on the issue of creating an MNO calendar. About 50 people, including Gopal Gurung and myself, attended the conference, which took place in a crumbling government office building, marked with an MNO flag for the day, where we perched on narrow benches in the stifling heat for nearly seven hours. At the beginning of the program, Kiran explained the issue to the activists: 'Yakthung Chumlung, Yayokkha [a Rai organization] and many different organizations have brought out their own calendars. In this way, we should use our own Mongol National Organization calendar. But how would it be appropriate for us to create this calendar? For example, what scripts should we use? How should we arrange the "design"? What should the form, the shape and the structure of the calendar be?' For Kiran, the central question was how to create a calendar that could belong to the entire Mongol population, without prioritizing any one ethnic group.

In their responses, most people offered suggestions on how to represent 'Mongol' languages on the MNO calendar. These suggestions included the usual strategies available for representing a nation or ethnic group, from trying to represent the entire range of diversity within the group, to using a few markers of difference to stand for the whole group. Some people stated that all of the languages spoken by Mongols should be represented, like one elderly man who suggested: 'As many scripts of the indigenous peoples (*mūlbāsī*) of Nepal as there are, all of them should be written on the calendar, just like there are many scripts written on bank notes in India.' Several other activists stated that the language and script on the calendar should be Mongol in origin, yet did not specify which or how many languages should be used. For these individuals, having a 'Mongol' language on the calendar was primarily of symbolic importance.

Others rejected the strategy of using one language to symbolize difference, as it posed a potential threat to Mongol unity. As Kiran's older sister, Sangita, told the crowd:

> We Mongols are multi-ethnic and multi-lingual. If we put words of Mongol origin on the calendar we cannot represent everyone. So words from only one group (*jāti*) may be included. At the same time, many people may criticize us ... for promoting only one group. For example, if the Gurungs' script is used in the calendar, the Rais and Limbus may criticize it, saying it only promotes Gurungs. Similarly if we only put Magars or Tamang [scripts], it may turn out in the same way. Then our people may lose faith in the party. From that perspective, maybe it's better to use the language we are speaking now [Nepali]. To publish this calendar our party must think carefully.

Sangita's suggestion that the calendar use Nepali overlooked the fact that this would reinforce the dominance of this language, and thus undercut the MNO's project of redefining Nepal's national identity as Mongol.

Other speakers considered ways of representing Mongol unity that did not rely on language, for example by depicting the types of oppression that Mongols have faced, by showing how Hinduism has dominated Buddhism. Many speakers cited party identity, represented by pictures of the MNO flag and Gopal Gurung, as the best way to unite Mongols. As one young Limbu activist from Jhapa district stated: 'I am requesting that we Mongols always have to put either the flag or the president because we are multi-ethnic, multi-lingual and multi-cultural.'

The MNO calendar, produced in 1998, reveals that MNO activists resorted to representing Mongols primarily through party identity rather than through cultural symbols. Simply designed, the calendar was printed in red and blue ink on a single sheet of white paper, bound at the top with a strip of metal. On the top were the letters 'MNO', while in the upper right-hand corner sat a picture of Gopal Gurung with the caption 'Founder President' (see Figure 5.1).

The central graphic of the calendar depicted the MNO flag mapped onto the territory of Nepal, symbolizing the MNO's goal of redefining Nepal as a Mongol nation. The upper, blue half of the flag, filling in northern Nepal, contained the white five-pointed star found on the MNO flag and a row of symbols of various religions: a stupa to represent Buddhism; a cross for Christianity; a mosque for Islam; and an oil lamp framed with two vases of flowers, presumably to represent the Limbu and Rai religion, Kirat Dharma (*Satya Hangma*), though it could

Figure 5.1 MNO calendar.

also stand for Hinduism. In the lower, red half of the flag, covering the southern tier of Nepal, was the *khukuri*, a knife with a curved blade, as it appears on the standard MNO flag. Beneath the grid of months and days, the words 'Mongol National Organization Central Committee, Kathmandu' were written in the Devanagari script used for Nepali.

Above this grid was a quote in the Nepali language: 'For followers of all religions to live free from civil war, and for all Nepali communities to live equally, let everyone participate in making Nepal a democratic (*loktantra*) state.' The word *loktantra* is used to refer to democracy rather than the term *prajātantra*, which was commonly used until 2006. The MNO argued that the term *prajātantra* meant literally 'power to the king's subjects (*praja*)', whereas *loktantra* means power to the people (*lok*). To use the term *loktantra*, then, was to call for the end of the monarchy and a truer form of democracy.

While the MNO intended to create an alternative calendar to the state endorsed *vikram sambat* calendar, it retained some elements of the *vikram* calendar, using parts of the Gregorian calendar to mark it as different. The names of the months appeared prominently in English, yet were also written in a smaller font in Nepali. Arabic numerals were large and bold, while the Devanagari numerals were smaller. The names of the days of the week appeared only in English. The sequence of the months approximated the *vikram* calendar, as the calendar year began with the month of that calendar's new year, April. But the calendar began on April 1, rather than April 14, the first day of the *vikram sambat* year. Despite the MNO's opposition to the hegemonic *vikram* calendar, they could not imagine marking time outside of its boundaries.

Kiran explained to me why the Gregorian calendar was preferable to the *vikram* calendar:

> The *vikram* calendar is a foreign calendar. The Newari calendar is from here. We should use that or the Buddhist calendar, this is what we've said. Or there is the calendar that is presently used in the world ... We should use this. Because the world is using it, using this won't have any effect. If we directly use everything that is foreign India's, we'll lose our identity.

Kiran asserted that because the western calendar system is so widely used, it 'won't have any effect' on the national identity of Nepal. He viewed global cultural practices not as forces of homogenization but as empty signs that could be incorporated anywhere. Thus he used the term 'foreign' to refer only to the *vikram* calendar, not to the western calendar. Kiran saw the western calendar as distinguishing Nepal from India, failing to recognize that it is widely used in India.

The MNO calendar used no Mongol languages, instead of selecting a few and risking animosity between Mongols. Rather, it combined English and Nepali, employing the English, Gregorian calendar terms for the names of the months and days of the week. The MNO calendar, like most MNO publications, used Nepali for the most complex linguistic information on the calendar, the phrase under the map of Nepal. Even though they proclaimed that Mongols should look for and use their own languages, the MNO relied on Nepali as a medium of communication. Many Mongols did not speak their 'own languages', and no Tibeto–Burman language could serve as a lingua franca.

The use of English here appears to contradict the party's emphasis on reviving local languages yet was an effort to avoid relying solely on Nepali. MNO activists like Kiran often suggested that it would be better for the national language of Nepal to be English than Nepali, believing that English was a more neutral, less symbolically powerful language within the borders of Nepal. This is the same logic that Kiran used in explaining his preference for the Gregorian over the *vikram* calendar. As Sonntag (2003: 93) notes, this view of English was common among advocates of multilingualism in Nepal.

In the calendar, there were no clear references to the cultural distinctiveness of Mongols. The MNO calendar listed no holidays; this could have provided a sense of a shared Mongol culture, if there were holidays that all Mongol groups celebrated. Kiran attempted to reclaim and celebrate Tihar as a Mongol holiday, as discussed in the next section, but perhaps this reinterpretation of Tihar was not widely enough shared throughout the MNO to include it on the calendar. The calendar did not represent Mongols through opposition to Hindus as it did in the party's main slogan, 'We Mongols are not Hindus'. The epigraph on the calendar suggested that civil war and inequality could occur in Nepal without democracy (*loktantra*), yet did not state the MNO's charges against the post-1990 political system. Only the multiple religious symbols on the calendar suggested that Mongol was more than a political identity, and evoked the MNO's commitment to a secular state. These symbols, however, could represent any followers of these religions, not just Mongols. Ultimately, unlike the indigenous nationalities organizations' calendars, the MNO calendar did not provide people with a sense of Mongol identity beyond the identity of the political party.

A Mongol reinterpretation of Tihar

Public celebrations are a key component in building national identities, as mass participation in rituals binds people together. Hansen argues that such enactments of the national community are key in allowing people to identify with the nation: 'the nation can only proliferate as a mass phenomenon if crystallized around a nondiscursive kernel of social practices, such as rituals and festivals...' (1999: 210). Rituals also create a shared sense of history by creating links with a common past (Hobsbawm and Ranger 1983).

The MNO and other organizations in the indigenous nationalities movement gave new meanings to two holidays that the Nepali state had forwarded as markers of national identity, Dasain and Tihar. Dasain, a ten-day long festival in the fall, is the major national holiday. Tihar follows shortly after Dasain and together these holidays last nearly a month, forming the festival height of the year. They are considered Hindu and national holidays; participating in them enacts a belonging to the Nepali nation. The MNO and the indigenous nationalities organizations called for boycotting the Dasain holiday, as I discuss in

Chapter 6. However, many activists in the indigenous nationalities movement embraced Tihar as a holiday that originally belonged to them but was appropriated by Hindus.

Kiran Akten, his brother Khadga and their extended family members were the main architects of the celebration of Tihar as a Mongol holiday that I observed. This celebration was in part a reaction to efforts by an indigenous nationalities organization, *Kirat Yakthung Chumlung*, to celebrate Tihar as a holiday that belongs to Limbus. Kiran and his family attempted to orchestrate a celebration of Tihar that would provide a unifying cultural identity for Mongols. It was one of the few efforts to create and perform a specifically Mongol culture, and reveals some of the central dilemmas in defining Mongol identity. This recoding of Tihar ultimately celebrated the political identity of the MNO more than it created a concrete cultural identity for Mongols.

Before describing this reinterpretation of Tihar as a Mongol festival, I describe the standard celebration of the holiday. Of course, Tihar is not celebrated in exactly the same way everywhere, and changes over time. I present Tihar as I witnessed it in Kathmandu in the 1990s.[3]

Through performing various rituals during the five-day Tihar festival, people seek to ward off Yama, the god of death (Majupuria 1981: 108–115). On each of the first four days of Tihar, people make offerings to a different animal. On the first day, people perform *kāg pujā*, making offerings to crows (*kāg*), who are considered to be Yama's messengers. On the second day, *kukur puja*, people make offerings to dogs, the guardians of the gates to the kingdom of death. Though they are generally scorned and often kicked, on this day dogs receive flower garlands, *tikā* on their foreheads and leaf plates heaped with cooked rice. On the third day, people worship the cow and Laxmi, the goddess of wealth. During the day, people offer cows flower garlands and food, while at night people set out small oil lamps and tiny candles along the paths and in windows to welcome Laxmi into their homes to secure prosperity in the coming year. In the evening, groups of young girls play *bhailo*, roaming from house to house, singing and collecting money.

On the fourth day of Tihar, *goru puja*, people make offerings to bulls (*goru*). At night, people light oil lamps and candles again, and groups of people play *deusī*. They go from house to house singing a call–response song in which the leader improvises verses from a set of standard lines and the group responds with the chorus '*deusī re*'. In the song, the group pleads for donations of money, food, and alcohol from each household. If the group feels that the initial offering it receives is too paltry, they continue singing and demand more. One year I played *deusī* with a group of Gurungs in Kathmandu who sang all night at their relatives' houses and collected cases of beer, dozens of fried rice flour doughnuts (*sel roṭī*) and thousands of rupees. While the group considered using the money to improve the school in their ancestral village, they ultimately decided, as many *deusī* groups do, to spend the money on a community picnic.

The fifth day of Tihar is *bhai ṭikā*, when sisters worship their brothers and pray for their long lives. This ritual commemorates the story of a girl who prayed to the god of death and convinced him not to take her brother's life. Sisters, or women adopted as sisters for the ritual, offer garlands and trays of food, especially *sel roṭī*, to their brothers. They also give their brothers a multi-color *ṭikā* of red, green, blue and yellow dots in a vertical line on their foreheads. In exchange, brothers offer their sisters gifts or money. Groups continue to play *deusī* throughout the day and night.

Kiran and his family altered their celebration of Tihar so that it was marked as a Mongol rather than a Hindu holiday. 'You must come to celebrate Tihar with us, Susan *bahini*. This is very important for your research, and it will be fun too,' Kiran informed me when I spoke to him from a public telephone in Ilam bazaar, shortly before the holiday. My arrival was delayed for several days by a transportation strike in the dusty bazaar town of Birtamod, in the southern plains region, from where I usually took a rickety bus through the sweltering plains and lush jungles of the inner Tarai to reach Kiran's village. I passed the time in Birtamod in a bookstall that specialized in indigenous nationalities publications, chatting with the owner and the members of the indigenous nationalities organizations who often gathered there. Activists in the Limbu social organization *Kirat Yakthung Chumlung*, middle-aged men who were teachers, accountants and retired soldiers, told me about their organization's plans for Tihar. They were printing pamphlets so that people could sing *deusī* in the Limbu language, in the 'traditional' Limbu way, using the Limbu terms *laringke* and *namlingke* instead of the typical Nepali refrain *deusī re*. The Limbu language song printed in the pamphlet told the story of how Bali Hang, a Limbu king, outwitted the god of death. The activists hoped that they and other people would raise money for their organization during the Tihar festival.

When I arrived in Sukrabare several days before the Tihar festival, I told Kiran, who is Limbu, about the *Kirat Yakthung Chumlung*'s plans. He had heard about this, but was visibly displeased with my interest in the Limbu organization's program and dismissed my queries about it. 'Actually, this is not really relevant for you, sister,' he instructed me curtly.

Kirat Yakthung Chumlung identified Tihar with Limbus alone. However, Kiran sought to recode Tihar as a Mongol holiday by narrating a history of the festival that rooted it in a shared Mongol past. Kiran explained that he had heard the story he told me from his father. The source of the story is the Mundhum, a Limbu religious text, according to the Limbu historian Iman Singh Chemjong, who offers a translation of the story in his widely read book, *History and Culture of the Kirat People* (Chemjong 1967: 77–81). Activists in other indigenous nationalities organizations told similar versions of this history, and Gopal Gurung also included an abbreviated version of the story in *Hidden Facts in Nepali Politics* (Gurung 1994: 67).

Kiran told the history of Tihar to me and a small group of MNO activists one late afternoon during the beginning of Tihar, as the stifling heat of the day began to subside. Folk narratives like these change with every retelling, depending on who is telling them, the context in which they are told, and on the composition of the audience of listeners (Narayan 1989). It was important for Kiran to identify this as a story about Mongols because of the audience who was listening to the story on that occasion, a group of MNO activists and me. While Kiran's version of the Tihar story retained the same basic framework and sequence of events of the tale translated by Chemjong (1967), and included in the *Kirat Yakthung Chumlung*'s pamphlet, he presented it as Mongol rather than Limbu history.

In his lengthy recounting of this tale, Kiran emphasized that Tihar celebrates an historical occasion when a community of Mongols came together to save their Mongol king, Bali Hang, from the god of death, Jemaraja. The narrative was set in a golden past during which Mongols ruled Nepal and were not divided. Kiran portrayed the government during this era of Mongol rule as benevolent even though it was a monarchy, an implicit critique of the Hindu monarchy. In the narrative, the god of death threatened to take the king away when night fell. In response, the people kept the arrival of darkness at bay by lighting lamps, thus changing night into day and thwarting the god of death. Kiran noted that, 'the world looked completely different' because of their efforts. This transformation of night to day symbolizes the social transformation that the MNO aims to create. By showing how a unified community could achieve the near impossible and ward off the god of death, the story demonstrated the power of Mongol unity, and offered a model for contemporary Mongols to follow in attempting to restore Mongols' political power.

Kiran's narrative of Tihar informed the way that he and his family celebrated Tihar that year. Kiran's story explained three of the rituals that are usually performed at Tihar: lighting lamps, caroling and *bhai ṭikā*, the climactic event of the festival when sisters worship their brothers. The worship of the crow, dog, cow, bull and Laxmi were excised from his narrative of Tihar. The celebration of Tihar in Sukrabare that year followed the ritual map presented in Kiran's narrative, as Kiran and his family lit lamps, caroled and performed the bhai tika ceremony but refrained from celebrating crow, dog and Laxmi *pujā*.

By selecting certain elements as representative of the authentic history of Tihar, while eschewing other rituals as inauthentic Hindu practices that had been mixed in with the true Tihar, Kiran and his family redefined this event as a Mongol holiday. Kiran argued that the crow, dog, cow, bull and Laxmi *pujās* were inauthentic features of the festival that Hindus had added to Tihar to mark it as a Hindu festival. Kiran explained:

> this giving the dog a garland, and the cow a garland, and giving the crow food, they made this up. This is the Mongols' culture, their true original culture but the Hindus said we must take that. They have tried to appropriate (*hastachep*) it, saying, 'this is ours'. Because in Nepal alone, we are 80 percent Mongols. They can't get rid of the 'culture' of the 80 percent. So what they did is that they mixed a little bit of their culture with it. In the political area, they are in the high level of power, right? So they mixed it in this way. So they started to claim it was their culture. Slowly, in this way, they appropriated this.

Kiran's discussion of cultural appropriation emphasizes the close links between controlling political power and controlling meaning. Redefining Tihar was clearly marked as a political project.

Kiran and his family took pains to mark their celebration of Tihar as different from the dominant celebration by altering even some minor details. On the second day of Tihar, Kiran's family began decorating the courtyard between his house and his mother's house. Khadga and Antari, one of his sisters, pasted rectangular strips of brightly-colored tissue paper on strings and suspended the long lines of flags between the two houses. Kiran and Khadga told me that in previous years they had cut the strips of tissue paper in triangles, rather than in rectangles. High-caste Hindus cut their tissue paper decorations in triangles, they insisted. 'In order to not copy the Chhetri Bahuns, we've introduced this new style of cutting the paper!' Kiran explained. Khadga announced that these rectangles were the 'Mongol style'. Khadga did not offer any explanation of the symbolic link between Mongols and rectangles, or between triangles and high-caste Hindus. Rather, rectangles became the 'Mongol style' solely because they were not triangles, and thus represented a break with previous Tihar celebrations.

I wondered whether anyone would notice their slightly different decorations. Yet the next day, a neighbor remarked, '*Abei*! Why did you cut them like that? So plain!' Khadga launched into his explanation about how these were the 'Mongol style' of streamers. Such seemingly unimportant differences became significant as they alerted people to the different meanings of this celebration, and gave Kiran and his family a reason to tell other villagers about their celebration of Tihar as a Mongol holiday.

Another difference in their celebration of Tihar was that it included a non-Hindu religious ceremony. That year, Kiran organized a ceremony for the Limbu mystic Falgunanda's birthday, which fortuitously fell on the day of Laxmi puja.[4] Falgunanda (1885–1948) founded the Satya Hangma religion. In its early formation, this revitalization movement promised that Limbus could regain their former land and power in eastern Nepal if they reformed their religious practices, by renouncing animal sacrifices and alcohol, and speaking only Limbu (Caplan 1970; Jones and Jones 1976: 45–46).[5] Satya Hangma lost popularity after Falgunanda's death, yet resurfaced towards the end of the Panchayat era, when Guru Atmananda, a descendant of Falgunanda, began to preach and predict future events. By the mid-1990s, many Rais and Limbus throughout Ilam, including many MNO supporters, had joined Satya Hangma. I accompanied Kiran and other MNO activists to a festival at a Satya Hangma temple complex in southern Ilam where thousands of people gathered to celebrate Guru Atmananda's birthday, and to hear the Guru tell of his visions for the future.

Most Satya Hangma followers were Rais and Limbus, but the Satya Hangma leaders I spoke with envisioned the religion as one that could appeal to all of the indigenous nationalities, and interpreted 'Kirat' to mean not just Rais and Limbus, as most people used the term, but to include all indigenous nationalities. Satya Hangma had close ties to the indigenous nationalities movement, and was promoted by the organization *Kirat Dharma Tatha Sahitya Utthan Sangh* (the

Organization for the Upliftment of Kirat Religion and Literature), founded in 1979. It contributed to the revival of the Limbu language as all of the religious texts are written in the Sirijanga Limbu script. Satya Hangma leaders argued that this language was actually the original language of all Kirati people, who include not just Rais and Limbus but all Mongol peoples. When people became Satya Hangma priests, they learned to read and write in Sirijanga. By joining Satya Hangma, Rais and Limbus marked a shift in their identity and embraced the indigenous nationalities movement's concern with saving their 'own language, religion and culture'. Despite its growth in popularity, Satya Hangma's status as the 'real' religion of the Rais and Limbus was contested, as many Rais and Limbus argued that it was not the religion of their ancestors.

On the morning of Falgunanda's birthday, Kiran and his brother constructed a bamboo altar at the side of the courtyard to display a framed picture of Falgunanda. They attached a loudspeaker and microphone to a car battery, and arranged mats on the ground for a seating area. Kiran invited about 50 people, including his relatives and some Rai, Gurung, Magar and Newar neighbors, to arrive at noon for the *pujā*, and he instructed everyone to fast that morning so they would be in a state of purity for the ceremony. While waiting in the scorching sun for the service to begin, a boom box blared the cassette of MNO songs that Kiran had recorded.

At about two o'clock, Kiran picked up the microphone and introduced the ceremony as an event that had meaning both for the MNO and from a religious perspective. Kiran talked about the life of Falgunanda, describing some of the miracles he had performed. While Kiran presented Falgunanda as a Limbu, he stressed the relevance of his teachings for all Mongols. Mongols have 'bad habits' of drinking alcohol, and sacrificing animals when they make offerings to the gods, but Falgunanda said we must not drink alcohol and that we should only make offerings of flowers and fruits to the gods, Kiran told the crowd. After this speech, everyone in the audience went up to the altar and offered flowers, fruits and sweets to Falgunanda, following Kiran's lead. Then, Kiran played the mandolin, accompanied by his cousin Maita on the drum, and sang a devotional song he had written, 'Hey Mahaguru Falgunanda'. At the end of the ceremony, the *prasad*, the fruits and sweets offered to the altar were redistributed to the audience.

Although this ceremony replicated many of the central features of Hindu worship, such as fasting, making offerings and receiving *prasād*, Kiran and other followers of Satya Hangma saw this as a non-Hindu religion, chiefly because the central religious authorities, Falgunanda and Atmananda, were Limbu rather than Bahun. By celebrating Falgunanda's birthday on the day of Laxmi puja, Kiran and his family drew attention to their opposition to Hinduism. Holding this substitute celebration was Kiran's attempt to replace the focus on securing wealth in Laxmi *pujā* with Satya Hangma's message of moral, social and political reform.

Another way in which Kiran's family marked Tihar as Mongol was by lighting lamps only on the fourth evening of Tihar, rather than for Laxmi *pujā* on the third day. The day after the Falgunanda ceremony, Kiran's wife, who I call

Bhauju, was crouched over sweeping the floor. Suddenly she straightened up and exclaimed, '*Lo*! We were supposed to light the oil lamps last night!' Kiran also became concerned and got up to check the calendar. After a few minutes, he spoke confidently, 'No, we did the right thing. It was Falgunanda's birthday and we have no business celebrating Laxmi *puja*. We're supposed to light the lamps tonight!' Whether or not this absence was intentional, Kiran explained it as part of a defiant boycott of Laxmi *puja*.

On the night of the fourth day of Tihar, Kiran and his brothers constructed a bamboo railing around the perimeter of their shared courtyard. Antari and Kanchi, the youngest sisters of the family, placed small clay oil lamps on the railing, and as soon as it grew dark we lit the lamps. Khadga, who had just returned from working in Malaysia, arranged newly purchased plastic chairs and tables in the courtyard and invited Kiran, Bhauju and I to join him for bottles of beer and fried meat, luxury items in the village. Later that night, a group of about 20 teenage men and women, and a handful of men in their early thirties gathered at Kiran's house and began practicing to play *deusi*. Kiran and his cousin Maita played MNO songs on guitars and mandolins, while a young Magar man played the drum. Later in the evening, Kiran and some of the older men set out to sing MNO songs at each house.

The *bhai ṭikā* ceremony the following morning, wherein I became a fictive sister in Kiran's family, was similar to other ceremonies I have participated in elsewhere in Nepal. I fasted and bathed along with the sisters in the morning, then lit incense and offered gifts, food and *ṭikā* to each brother and his wife. After eating, we took turns dancing to MNO songs and folk songs that Kiran and his cousins played, as well as Nepali film songs played on the portable stereo.

Later in the day, I joined a *deusī* group of young people that Kiran and his cousin Maita led towards the dusty bazaar, where they began dancing and singing under the intense mid-day sun. Pairs of men and women took turns dancing in front of each MNO supporter's house in the bazaar, singing strident songs calling for a Mongol revolution, somber verses mourning the lost lives of Gorkha soldiers, and jubilant tunes celebrating the party flag and leader. A crowd gathered around the performers, while Bahun and Chettri shopowners watched quietly, their arms folded. After the group performed three or four songs, people in the targeted house offered the group money, uncooked rice and *sel roṭī*. When night fell we took a short break for the evening meal, then the group reconvened and performed throughout the night, returning home only the next morning.

I had imagined that an MNO version of *deusi* would either use the basic *deusī* song but substitute verses about Mongols for the more common verses, or would use the Limbu terms *laringke* and *namlingke* in place of the usual refrain, *deusī re*. Instead, Kiran, Khadga and a group of boys sang new and old MNO party songs, many of which Kiran had composed. Because people usually sang these songs at MNO gatherings, singing them during Tihar explicitly marked this part of the festival as a party event. The celebration was further linked to the party because the MNO youth club planned to use the donations they collected to support the first MNO conference, slated to be held later that year.

In his narrative of Tihar, Kiran described how people had sung the Limbu words *laringke* and *namlingke*, yet he did not incorporate this in the Tihar songs in Sukrabare. Kiran wanted Tihar to become a holiday that united Mongols, and if he had insisted upon having people sing these Limbu terms, it would have been marked as a specifically Limbu festival. As was the case in the MNO calendar, Mongol identity was closely linked to identity of the party through the performance of MNO songs in the Mongol Tihar. Tihar was also an occasion for retelling and commemorating an historical narrative of a time when Mongols were rulers and worked together to achieve great things.

MNO songs

Kiran performed MNO songs in a wide variety of venues: after district-level meetings, while giving speeches at mass-meetings, at his home when relatives and neighbors stopped by to visit, and during festivals like Tihar. Songs were important tools for political mobilization for him. As Kiran told me:

> I see the role of songs and music in politics in this way: music is the heart of politics, the backbone of politics. People will not gather just to hear someone giving a speech, but if you have good music, they will come to listen to it. When they come to listen to the music, you can sing a little bit, and at the same time you can express your political ideology. And then you sing again. When you do this, you make a big impact on people. The other thing is that the political power depends upon the youth of a country, on the younger generations. Youthful people have a romantic outlook; they like to make jokes. At this age, they like songs, music and dancing, so if you sing songs and perform dances, young people will gather.

As Kiran noted, he could draw people to listen to the MNO's message through songs more easily than through speeches.

Strong, historical connections between music and politics exist in Nepal. Throughout the Panchayat era, in particular, students learned songs that celebrated the Nepali nation as part of the standard school curriculum. In its use of songs to mobilize people for oppositional political action, the MNO followed in the footsteps of the Communist Party of Nepal, which had strong support in eastern Nepal through its underground organization during the Panchayat era. The Communist Party launched a cultural organization, the *Jana Sanskriti Manch*, in which people traveled and performed political songs (Stirr 2009). Leftist musicians, most notably Shambu Rai, created a corpus of 'progressive songs' (*pragatisil git*) to voice opposition to the Panchayat government (Grandin 1996). Like these other forms of political music, MNO songs conveyed ideology and provided an entertaining means of mobilizing party support.

Mongols and masculinity in MNO songs

Masculinity is the central theme in the construction of Mongol identity in MNO songs. Ethnic and nationalist movements often employ gender as a way of representing the identity of a community because gender suggest ways in which individuals can enact and embody the nation (Mosse 1985; Parker *et al.* 1992; Yuval-Davis and Anthias 1989).

These MNO songs defined Mongols as masculine warriors through the prominent use of two symbols: the Gorkha soldier and the *khukuri*, a knife with a long, curved blade. Images of Gorkha soldiers in the army and the plight of the mercenary soldier who must fight battles in foreign countries were central in MNO songs and poems. The appeal of the image of the soldier for the MNO derived from the fact that many men involved in the MNO served in the British or Indian armies, or had family members who did. This image also recalls the British colonial construction of the many ethnic groups as martial races to justify their recruitment into the British army, as described in Chapter 2.

The song titled 'Carrying cold rifles in their hands' (*Hāt mā chiso rifle bokera*) exemplifies the way the MNO uses the figure of the soldier to evoke the sorrows of Mongols. This song was sung to a rather mournful tune, and accompanied by a *mādal*, the cylindrical Nepali drum that is ubiquitous in folk music, played at a slower pace than most other MNO songs. When I first heard this song outside Kiran's home one moonlit night, adolescent girls and boys danced in the courtyard and sang in unison:

CHORUS: Carrying cold rifles in their hands,
        Mongols go to other lands;
VERSE 1: Forgetting their sons, daughters and families,
        Memories spill in the form of tears.
        Mongols go to others' borders,
        Carrying *khukuris* and rifles to eliminate the enemies.
        Making their lives targets for bullets,
        Sons and daughters cry hearing the news.
(CHORUS)
VERSE 2: Becoming a slave for a few days in that country,
        they give up their lives for another's cause.
        Mongols go but their thirst for this country grows.
        With a bullet in the chest, their lives go.
(CHORUS)

In this song, the word 'Mongol' refers exclusively to men, particularly those who join foreign armies. The song mourns not only the lost lives of the many soldiers who have died in battle, and the hardship of war, as evoked in the image of the 'cold rifles', but also the fact that these Mongols were fighting in 'other lands' and 'gave up their lives for another's cause'. The song laments that this practice has resulted in a loss for Nepal, in that Mongols were not fighting for or in Nepal. However, the song suggests that this situation will soon end as 'their thirst for this country grows'.

Unstated but implied in this song is the idea that Mongols should deploy violence for the sake of their own cause rather than in another country. Songs such as 'Time will never forget' (*Yugle kahile bhuldaina*) elaborate this theme, suggesting that Mongols should emulate these soldiers, but they should now fight for the benefit of Mongols:

CHORUS: Time will never forget,
            We should never forget.
            We must dig out the true history
            Of the rocks and soil here.
            Time will never forget.
VERSE 1: Mongol brothers made the world recognize
            That Nepalis are brave,
            Showing the world that they take bullets
            In the target of their chest.
(CHORUS)
VERSE 2: If we have to sacrifice our blood to the soil,
            Let us sacrifice it to the soil here.
            If we have to sacrifice our blood to the rocks,
            Let us sacrifice it to the rocks here.
(CHORUS)

This song implores listeners to remember the 'true history' of Mongols, which includes the former golden age when Mongols ruled Nepal, and the centuries of oppression by high-caste Hindus. In the second verse, Mongol brothers are hailed as soldiers who have earned Nepal international fame. The song asks Mongols to follow the model of bravery demonstrated by these soldiers, but to fight in Nepal, rather than in other countries. Mongols should be willing to sacrifice themselves for their own cause, which is tied to the cause of the Nepali nation. The possibility of using violence to achieve the MNO's goals was validated by the representation of Mongols as soldiers.

The Mongol youth club that Kiran founded performed this song at an MNO conference in Sukrabare. A young man sang and played the guitar, accompanied by two teenage women who sang in the high-pitched voices favored in much South Asian music. Two men carried MNO flags while another two held *khukuris*. Combining dance and skit, they marched in place, moving the flags in a series of formations and carving the air deliberately with *khukuris*. In this performance, these young men enacted the ideal of Mongols as masculine soldiers, fighting for their own political cause.

This song also invoked the bravery (*bīr*) of Mongols, another key symbol of Mongols as warriors. Bravery also held an important place in state-sponsored nationalist constructions (Onta 1996b). Yet bravery is more closely associated with 'Mongol' ethnic groups than with other groups in Nepal. The names 'Bir' and 'Bahadur', which both mean 'brave', are a frequent component of men's names, such as Jit Bahadur or Kul Bir, in 'Mongol' communities in Nepal. Few Brahmans give their sons these names.

Another ubiquitous symbol for the MNO is the *khukuri*, represented on the MNO flag as well as in songs. This curved, wooden-handled knife is used almost exclusively by men. Most village men in the hills of east Nepal carry *khukuri* encased in leather sheaths, tucking them into a length of material wrapped around the waist or on a strap slung across the shoulder. The *khukuri* is used to cut branches or meat, to whittle pieces of bamboo or for self-defense. The *khukuri* evokes rural society, since few employees in government offices or people in the cities carry them, and represents bravery, martiality and the threat of physical violence.

The MNO's manifesto described the meaning of the *khukuri* emblazoned on the lower half of the flag: 'The *khukuri* is the Gorkha or Mongol's symbol of bravery. Even in the world wars, in the midst of all modern technological weapons, the *mūlbāsī* Mongols of Nepal carried this very old weapon and fought, advanced and were victorious' (Gurung n.d.). The *khukuri* is a symbol of the past and MNO songs often referred to it as 'our ancestors' weapon' (*purkāko hatiyār*). The *khukuri* connected Mongols to their ancestors, who once ruled Nepal, giving them the force to regain power.

Amidst these songs celebrating masculine warriors, women were featured only rarely. During Tihar in Sukrabare, I heard one MNO song that featured women:

CHORUS: Hey Mongol brothers, please listen
          To the women's lament.
          Hey Mongol brothers, please listen
          To the women's lament.
VERSE 1: Our lives are finished,
          but tyranny isn't finished.
          Others' women crossed hills,
          Your women stayed behind.
          Others' women live smiling,
          Your women live crying.
(CHORUS)
VERSE 2: Come my Mongol brother,
          we'll give you help.
          Rather than living quietly in tyranny,
          it is better that we shed our blood.
(CHORUS)

The song uses the sorrow of women to motivate Mongol brothers to fight for the Mongol cause. The position of women symbolizes the oppression of Mongols as a whole: Mongol women have 'stayed behind' while other women have 'crossed hills'. Evoking the status of an entire community by referring to the status of that community's women has been a common way of representing women. British colonizers in India, for example, cited the low status of women in India to justify their colonial presence (Mani 1989). Women are expected to re-energize Mongol masculinity, rather than take action to end their own sorrow. Representations of Mongols as masculine warriors thus positioned women as peripheral actors in the political struggle. The centrality of masculinity as a mode of representing Mongols reflected the male dominance within the party. Most of the people who constructed and disseminated MNO ideology were men. Although many women supported the party, their ideas rarely entered into the public discourse of the MNO.

All of these songs linked masculinity to violence and encouraged Mongols to shed blood for the MNO's cause. While the MNO has not taken up arms, these representations may make MNO activists more likely to participate in violence, as I discuss further in the Conclusion.

The 'Our Own Heartbeats' cassette

Notes slowly swell from a synthesizer, accompanied by sound effects that mimic wind blowing through a forest, a babbling stream and chirping birds. Over the music, Prakash speaks in a breathy voice: 'Aha! How beautiful this place is! How nice this is. Nowhere is there any chaos, nor is there any fighting. How peaceful this place is. And ... and along with the sweet tune of the waterfall that flows from the lap of the beautiful Himalayas, playing as it falls, many colored birds and other wildlife are also enjoying speaking their own languages, aren't they Kiran brother?' Kiran responds in a hushed, serious tone, 'Yes, Prakash brother, these birds and other animals are speaking their own languages and dancing, and even so, it's so peaceful, they are so contented.'

This melodramatic dialogue begins the cassette of Mongol songs titled *Our Own Heartbeats* (*ā-āphno ḍhukḍhukiharu*). Kiran Akten and Prakash were recording this cassette at a studio in Kathmandu when I first met them in 1993. Kiran wrote and sang the songs, in addition to playing most of the musical instruments, while Prakash, a teacher from a relatively wealthy family, produced the project. They made hundreds of copies of the cassette and sold it for 55 rupees. Over the next few years, the cassette became well known among MNO activists and supporters. I heard this cassette played over scratchy speakers at many MNO meetings, saw drunk old men dance to it at the weddings of MNO supporters, and listened to it on a day-long hike to a party event in a distant part of Ilam district, when an activist played it from a portable tape deck.

The dialogue at the beginning of the cassette refers to the MNO's vision of the Nepali nation. In the short dialogue, Kiran and Prakash described numerous living creatures 'speaking their own languages' and peacefully inhabiting the forest. They emphasized that multiple species and languages co-exist peacefully, challenging the Panchayat state's proposition that encouraging multiple languages and cultures would create conflicts in the nation. Harmonious diversity is depicted as part of the natural landscape of Nepal.

This cassette celebrates the linguistic diversity existing in Nepal, presenting songs in five languages. Five songs were in Limbu, three were in Rai, one each was in Magar and Tamang and two songs were in the Nepali language. The Nepali language was referred to as 'Khas', a way of disassociating this language with the identity of the Nepali nation, and emphasizing that it originally belonged to the Khas people.

The inclusion of songs in multiple languages on the cassette could have been intended as a way for the MNO to communicate its message to multiple ethnic groups. However, there are many different Rai languages, and there are at least two mutually unintelligible dialects of Tamang languages. Not all people who identify with one of the five ethnic groups represented on the cassette could speak or understand 'their own language'; for example, Nepali was the first and only language of Magars in Maidel.

However, the multiple languages served to represent the cultural plurality of Mongols. Even without understanding the words of the lyrics in the different languages, listeners could understand these songs as expressing ideas of ethnic difference and diversity. The musical qualities of the songs also indexed the ethnicities of the groups they represented. A Rai language song on the cassette followed a popular style of song, called *chandi nach*, that most listeners would readily equate with Rai-ness (Stirr 2009).

Of the 12 songs on the cassette, only the two songs in Nepali became popular. People sang them, usually without the cassette, while working in their fields and homes. While Kiran wrote many songs in the Limbu language, he usually sang songs in Nepali at MNO gatherings. While the MNO suggested that Nepal should be like a jungle filled with many varieties of birds and animals each making their own sounds, it was not effective for the MNO to use these various languages to communicate its messages to the diverse population it sought to mobilize.

Conclusion

The calendar, reinterpretation of Tihar and songs served multiple purposes for the MNO. Through these cultural productions, the MNO challenged the dominant discourse about the Nepali nation, and argued that the national identity should embrace pluralism and reflect the identities of Mongols. They gave people a sense of how Mongol identity could be put into practice in life, and revealed to people the political dimensions of everyday culture, such as holidays and calendars. Indigenous nationalities organizations instigated a wider range of cultural changes than the MNO did, by offering lessons in the Limbu language or promoting a standard traditional Gurung outfit, for example. However, the MNO gave these cultural changes a direct and different political meaning. For the MNO, the point of transforming culture was not to preserve the culture and identity of one ethnic group but rather to change people's identities so they would become politically engaged, and seek power for Mongols as a whole.

While the MNO attempted to substantiate a unified cultural identity for Mongols that would encompass the diversity of Mongol ethnic groups, this project often proved to be challenging. Cultural unity was difficult to represent without drawing on the particular cultural forms of one ethnic group and thus excluding others. Thus, Mongol identity was represented as an embodied racial or gendered identity, as it was in the songs; as rooted in a shared history, as it was in the Tihar narrative; or, more often, as a political identity, inseparable from the identity of the MNO, as it was in the MNO songs sung at Tihar and in the MNO calendar.

People in the MNO developed many ways of marking themselves as Mongols by expressing their connection with the party. People in Maidel and other villages made and wore MNO clothing, including scarves, hats, badges, woven bags, and even neckties, inscribed with the letters MNO or the party flag and colors. The MNO created a party salute, '*Jaya* Mongol!' accompanied by a fist raised in the air with the thumb up, to represent the unity of Mongols. In the late 1990s, MNO leaders created identity cards for party members so that people would know who was a 'real' Mongol, Kiran explained. While these practices allowed people to express a political identity, they did not answer the question of what it meant for Mongols to have their own culture.

6 Becoming not-Hindu
Religious and political transformations

On my first visit to Maidel, my companion Vivek Rai, an MNO activist from a neighboring village, led me to a *chautārā* (a stone bench resting place) at the edge of the Gurung settlement. While I surveyed the colorful wooden homes scattered across the hillside, Vivek drew my attention to an inconspicuous thatch-roofed structure of weathered white-washed mud walls next to the *chautārā*. He exclaimed, 'This is the *gumbā* that the Gurungs built during the Panchayat time. The police came and locked it up. They wouldn't let the Gurungs practice their own religion!'

This was the first of many times that I heard about this *gumbā*, a Buddhist temple or monastery (see Figure 6.1), that the Gurungs had built, and about local state authorities' opposition to the Gurung practice of Buddhism. Gurungs in Maidel became Buddhists during the end of the Panchayat era, after having followed Hinduism for generations. Religious identity in Nepal is intrinsically political because the state has defined Nepal as a Hindu nation. Thus, the Gurung's religious transformation became loaded with oppositional meanings, especially after conflicts emerged between the community and local authorities.

The Gurung adoption of Buddhism in the late 1980s was symbolically connected to the emergence of democracy in the minds of many villagers. Given the strong Hindu identity of the Panchayat state, people linked the rejection of that Hindu identity to opposition to the Panchayat system; in turn, they interpreted the adoption of Buddhism as a veiled effort to create a more democratic polity. Religious freedom was associated with democracy, and people saw the possibility of following their 'own religion' (*aphno dharma*) as an indicator of political freedom in the post-1990 multi-party era.

This chapter recounts the history of how Gurungs began practicing Buddhism, and how local state authorities reacted to the Gurungs becoming not-Hindu. Gurungs interpreted their practice of Buddhism as a way of identifying themselves both as more authentic Gurungs, and also as not Hindus. I avoid using the term and concept of 'conversion' to describe and understand the Gurung shift from Hinduism to Buddhism, as it obscures the local meanings of this change in religious identification. Gurungs framed it as a return to their ancestral religion and a rejection of Hinduism, rather than as the adoption of a new religion. It was through the category 'not-Hindu' that many Gurungs forged

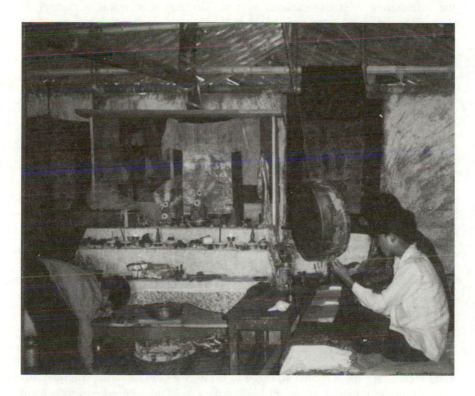

Figure 6.1 The Gurung gumbā in Maidel.

connections between the religious shift to Buddhism and the political mobiliza-tion of the MNO in Maidel. The MNO defines Mongols as 'not-Hindu', as illus-trated in an MNO slogan, chanted before MNO gatherings and inscribed on many party signboards: 'We Mongols are not Hindu' (*Hāmi Mongol Hindu Hoinan*). The meaning of being not-Hindu became contested in the Gurung com-munity when the MNO called for Gurungs and other Mongols to 'boycott' (*bahiskār*) the national Hindu holiday.

The history of the Gurung shift to Buddhism and the *gumbā* controversy

Gurungs in Maidel embraced Buddhism a few years prior to the end of the Pan-chayat era. In Maidel and the surrounding area, the Gurung movement to the Nyingmapa sect of Tibetan Buddhism began in 1987, when His Holiness Rinpoche Karma Wanchuk Gurung, a reincarnated lama, came from Darjeeling to teach Gurungs in east Nepal about Buddhism. Gurungs in the area had first made contact with this Rinpoche through a Gurung organization in western Nepal eight years earlier. In 1979, the year of relative political freedom before the referendum on the Panchayat system, Gurungs in Butwal, a district in western Nepal, sent a letter to Gurungs in Ilam inviting them to an event held by the Gurung Buddhism Assistance Committee (*Gurung Bouddha Dharma Sewa Samiti*). Man Gurung, the postman in a nearby village, saw the card and began corresponding with Gurungs from this organization. Gurungs from west Nepal sent him books on the Gurung language and culture, and put him in contact with the Rinpoche.

On his first visit to Maidel in 1987, the Rinpoche, as villagers referred to him, stayed at the home of Moti Lal, a prominent Gurung man, and performed ceremonies there and at other homes in the village. The Rinpoche returned to Maidel several times over the next four years, and his visits inspired a group of Gurung men to form an organization called the Organization for the Promotion of Buddhism (*Bouddha Dharma Prachar Samiti*).[1] About 30 men from Maidel and two neighboring villages were involved in the organization. The most active members were four men from Maidel, who ranked among the village elites. Moti Lal Gurung, the wealthiest individual in the village by many villagers' estimates, had been an elected representative from his ward to the village-level government, and at that time was the *Pradan Panch*, or head of the village administration. Khom Bahadur Gurung had been a ward member for 14 years, and supported the Congress Party during and after the Panchayat era. The other two men, Bhim Bahadur and Dilip, were involved in the underground Communist Party in the Panchayat years.[2]

Later in that same year, with the assistance of the Rinpoche, these four men and others in the organization arranged to bring two Gurung lamas from the primarily Gurung Ramghat Monastery in Pokhara to Maidel in order to train local young boys to become lamas. After the lamas from Pokhara were living in Maidel and had begun teaching pupils, the Organization for the Promotion of Buddhism decided to found a small '*gumbā*'. Although the term '*gumbā*' is often translated as monastery, the Gurung community did not build a structure to house a monastic community. The Maidel Gurungs followed the Nyingmapa sect of Tibetan Buddhism, which does not require lamas to be celibate and the Gurung boys who have been trained as lamas serve as ritual specialists for the community while living and marrying within the community (Ortner 1978: 30). The local community referred to the building as both a *gumbā* and a school. Like most 'monasteries', it served as a site for conducting rituals, and teaching young lamas.

Soon after the *gumbā* was founded, the police began to monitor the activities of the organization. Moti Lal recalled, 'During the Panchayat time, police used to come and sit at our *gumbā* meetings and take notes on whatever we said.... We had to submit copies of reports to the police. We had a committee to look after the *gumbā* and used to raise money to pay the guru a fee of 500 rupees a month for teaching. But the police told us that we could not collect money and give it to a guru.'

After a year, the *gumbā* was closed on orders from the Chief District Officer (CDO) of Ilam district. During the Panchayat era, CDOs occupied the most powerful position in the district, with authority over all government offices there. Following orders from the Bahun CDO, a Tamang policeman put a padlock on the door and informed the Gurungs that they needed to register their *gumbā* before it could be opened. Then the CDO sent arrest warrants to the four men from Maidel who were leaders in establishing the *gumbā*, and they were brought to his office in Ilam's district center. Although they feared they would be put in jail, the CDO merely interrogated them and ordered them to register the *gumbā*.

Local state authorities also tried to remove the *gumbā*. The District Superintendent of Police (DSP) came to Maidel and told the local people that they needed to place a police post on the prominent hilltop occupied by the *gumbā*. As the DSP works under the CDO, and regularly receives orders from him, it is highly likely that this action was also ordered by this CDO. Surprisingly, the local community successfully resisted the DSP's demands, and provided land at the foot of a hill for the police post.

In order to get registration for the *gumbā* at the Home Ministry as the CDO had ordered, Moti Lal traveled to Kathmandu. Moti Lal recalled that the civil servants there were uncooperative and told him he needed a recommendation from the CDO in order to get the registration. Attempting to fulfill these typical bureaucratic demands, Moti Lal made the long trip between Kathmandu and Ilam several times.

Despite their efforts, the Gurungs never found out whether or not they received their registration and the *gumbā* was never unlocked. As Khom Bahadur explained,

> We spent money to go to Kathmandu many times in order to get the registration, but it wasn't possible to get it, because the Panchayat system was difficult. They didn't give it and there were just a lot of expenses. And it went along in this way and in the year 2048 (v.s.) [1990], the multi-party system also came. From then on it was peaceful. Happily, no one looked for the registration or anything else.

While the *gumbā* was no longer controversial once the multi-party democracy was established, the locked building had fallen into disrepair. It was demolished and a new thatch-roofed *gumbā* was built in its place. Memories of the opposition to the *gumbā*, though, were not replaced so easily.

Interpreting the *gumbā* controversy

The central question that arises from the story of the *gumbā* controversy is why the local authorities reacted to the *gumbā* as they did. As I could not obtain documents on this issue written by the local state authorities, my knowledge of the authorities' actions and words is limited to what I learned from Gurung villagers and the documents they wrote.[3] Villagers offered three explanations of why the *gumbā* was closed. First, the *gumbā* founders accepted the local authorities' explanation that the Gurungs were required to register the monastery. However, there was never a law that required monasteries to register with the government. There was a voluntary system of registering monasteries through a government committee called the Monastery Management and Development Committee (*Gumbā Byabastha Tatha Bikas Samiti*), formerly run under the Home Ministry and later under the Local Development Ministry. This committee was formed to keep track of the number of monasteries within Nepal, and to distribute funds to restore monasteries in disrepair. Files of correspondence that Khom Bahadur kept indicate that Gurungs had tried to register their *gumbā* through this committee, via the Home Ministry. Whether or not the CDO at the time knew that the registration was optional remains unclear, but the leaders of the organization and many other Gurungs believed that registration was mandatory.

Second, villagers suggested that closing the monastery was part of the Panchayat state's policy to suppress all public organizing. The CDO objected to the *gumbā* founding because it appeared to him to be an organized effort at politics, and thus outside of the boundaries of permissible activities. Khom Bahadur suggested that the *gumbā* was closed because officials interpreted it as political party activity:

> It was the Panchayat system at that time. In the Panchayat system, no one was allowed to talk with many people at once. For example, at that time, crowds of people weren't allowed to walk in a line, or talk or they'd be called a political party. After the *gumbā* was opened, they accused us of starting a political party.

The meetings that Gurungs held could have come under suspicion merely because they entailed a group of people meeting and talking together. This incident also occurred at the end of the Panchayat era, when the regime steadily grew more unpopular, and the political climate increasingly tense. Furthermore, the involvement of a prominent communist activist, Bhim Bahadur, may also have raised their suspicion that this was a form of political activity.

Many villagers who were not among the four who were brought in to the district office, reported that the CDO had said 'it is a *bahudal* (multi-party) *gumbā*, not a *Bouddha* (Buddhist) *gumbā*' when he closed it. This play on words implies that the CDO perceived the *gumbā* as established for political rather than religious purposes, and as posing opposition to the non-party (*nirdal*) Panchayat system. While the CDO may not have said this, the circulation of this idea demonstrates that villagers linked the idea of religious freedom to the idea of multi-party democracy.

Third, Gurungs suggested that the local authorities did not want the Gurungs to become not Hindu. Moti Lal recounted that the CDO was critical of the Gurung shift to Buddhism because it represented a shift away from Hinduism:

> the CDO office gave orders to close the school, because they wanted us to follow Hinduism. The CDO said we have to follow Hinduism. He told us if we wanted to practice Buddhism, we could do it in our own homes, individ-

ually, but not as a society in one place, not at a public *gumbā*. The CDO office called us there and told us that there was a limit to how we could practice Buddhism, and that it should be less than Hinduism. He also told us that we needed to have the *gumbā* registered at the Home Ministry. He also said that in the name of religion, there shouldn't be any political activities.

Here Moti Lal's assertion that the CDO objected to the practice of Buddhism 'as a society in one place', 'at a public *gumbā*' and as a guise for political activities supports the idea that the CDO's opposition to the *gumbā* was part of the Panchayat state's efforts to suppress all forms of popular organizing. Moti Lal also explained that the CDO told them to keep following Hinduism, and to make the practice of Buddhism a secondary activity.

Moti Lal asserted that the CDO's orders to lock up the *gumbā* stemmed from the CDO's views of Buddhism as a threat to Bahuns as Hindu priests: 'I think the CDO gave us this order because most of the people working in the offices are Bahun-Chhetris ... the Gurungs would stop using Bahuns, and as a result, their income would decrease. So Buddhism was like a disease for them.' Although Moti Lal was not an MNO supporter, his interpretation of the CDO's opposition to the *gumbā* as an effort to maintain high-caste Hindu dominance echoed the MNO's ideas.

Most Buddhist institutions in operation in Nepal in the Panchayat era operated without controversy, further supporting the idea that local authorities closed this *gumbā* because they objected to Gurungs becoming 'not Hindus'. The Sherpa community built a new *gumbā* a few years before the Gurungs built their *gumbā*, just an hour up the hill from the Gurung *gumbā* in Maidel, yet they were not hassled by local authorities. The central difference between these two *gumbā* foundings, as one elderly Sherpa man told me, is that the Gurungs were previously Hindus, whereas the Sherpas were not.

The high-caste Hindu rulers have long thought of Gurungs as allies, as they served in the army that helped Prithvi Narayan Shah conquer Nepal. Sherpas, however, have been portrayed as more distant from the state. Thus, the Gurungs' shift to Buddhism may have signaled to local authorities that Gurungs were abandoning their position of being allies of the state.[4]

The Panchayat state had a negative view of religious change. Although there were no laws against leaving the Hindu religion, or changing one's own religion, an injunction against proselytizing was introduced in Nepal's third constitution, promulgated in 1958 (2015 v.s.), and it remained in the constitution of 1990: 'Every person shall have the freedom to profess and practice his own religion as handed down to him from ancient times having due regard to traditional practices: Provided that no person shall be entitled to cause another person to change from one religion to another' (HMG 1990: Article 19 (1)). The law also does not expressly protect the rights of individuals to change their own religion. Burghart (1996a) perceives this discomfort with religious 'conversion' or change as stemming from the Hindu view of society as 'an auspicious ritual unit' and argues that in Nepal, 'religious conversions are not a private matter; rather they disturb society as a whole' (p. 297). Local authorities may have perceived the Gurung move to Buddhism as likely to 'disturb society as a whole' because it implied a rejection of belonging to the Hindu-defined Nepali nation.

By closing the *gumbā*, the local state authorities ironically fortified the political dimensions of the Gurung shift to Buddhism. Villagers took this act to clearly illustrate the Hindu bias of the state. The leaders of the Organization for the Promotion of Buddhism who were instrumental in bringing Buddhism to Maidel said that they did not intend the religious movement and establishment of the *gumbā* to create the political meanings that it generated. As Bhim Bahadur, stated, 'When we started this, we were thinking of *dharma ko utthan* (raising up religion) not *jatiya utthan* (raising up our ethnic group).'[5] None of the founders ever supported the MNO and it seems that they did not intend to create support for ethnic-based politics. However, the narrative of this shift to Buddhism became intertwined with the narrative of MNO mobilization in Maidel. By the 1990s, people's discussions of the move to Buddhism and the *gumbā* incident were infused with MNO discourse.

MNO narratives of the Gurung shift to Buddhism

When telling this story, MNO supporters connected the *gumbā* incident and shift to Buddhism with the political ideas forwarded by the MNO about Hinduism in two main ways. First, they represented the local authorities' actions and statements as an illustration of religious oppression and Hindu domination. Second, villagers described the shift to Buddhism as a rejection of Hinduism, and asserted that this opposition to Hinduism was simultaneously an acceptance of a Mongol identity.

The MNO supporters represented this event as a clear, local illustration of the Hindu bias of the state and of the lack of religious freedom in Nepal for Gurungs and other Mongol ethnic groups. The MNO asserted that high-caste Hindus dominated the state. Many MNO supporters regarded the *gumbā* closing as not just the act of a few state officials, but attributed it to all high-caste Hindus, 'Aryans'. As Ganesh Gurung, an elderly MNO supporter, explained: 'The Aryans also didn't let us follow Buddhism. Before the multi-party system came, we were oppressed by their religion ... they didn't let us build and use the *gumbā*. Actually, they didn't let us follow our religion openly.' MNO supporters refer to the local authorities' reaction to the *gumbā* as the 'banning' of the *gumbā*. An elderly Gurung man stated, as many others did, that: 'They didn't let us practice Buddhism. They "banned" our *gumbā*!' The use of the English word 'banned' expresses the idea that the local state authorities did not merely close and lock the building: they officially forbade the practice of Buddhism.

MNO supporters linked the MNO's success in the area to these events. People told me about the 'banning' of the *gumbā* when recounting why they joined the MNO. When I asked Nar Bahadur why so many people in Maidel had joined the MNO, he said this incident showed people that 'the Gurungs' religion was oppressed'. MNO supporters from other ethnic groups, including Limbus, Rais and Magars, also described the *gumbā* controversy as creating support for the MNO. As Mavi Resami, a lanky Magar man in his early twenties who is a village-level MNO activist, told me:

> Even before democracy came, there were people in Maidel who criticized Bahuns. The Gurungs and Magars used to use Bahuns, but later stopped.... They were 'fed up' with Bahuns. The Gurungs opened a small 'school' to teach children how to become lamas. But it was closed from above, and they arrested some people. The multi-party system came soon after that, and the MNO came along with its ideas about ethnic upliftment and religion, and people here said, 'Aha! This is what's happened to us! We haven't been able to practice our own religion!' So everyone immediately liked the MNO.

The MNO asserted that the rejection of Hinduism is necessary to escape oppression from Bahuns. MNO supporters saw the adoption of Buddhism as a move away from using Bahuns as priests and a rejection of Bahun domination. As one Gurung MNO supporter stated, 'We understood that we had been forced to follow the Aryan's religion. So, now we follow Buddhism.' He characterized Hinduism as an outsider's religion, imposed on their community; by contrast they chose to follow Buddhism.

Many MNO supporters perceived the shift to Buddhism to be closely connected to the MNO's political movement. When I asked people why they joined the MNO, they frequently told me about the Gurung move to Buddhism. MNO supporters suggested that, by beginning to practice Buddhism, the Gurungs had already accepted the idea of Mongol identity before the party was established in Maidel. As the MNO leader Nar Bahadur explained, 'The Gurungs had accepted that "we're not Hindus, we're Buddhists" in the Panchayat era, before the "party" came. In relation to that, we had already changed our religion, brought lamas and quit Hinduism, and built a *gumbā* in the Panchayat era.' Nar Bahadur's phrase 'we're not Hindus, we're Buddhists' echoes a popular MNO slogan.

In the story of the Gurungs' shift to Buddhism, the category 'not-Hindu' contains multiple meanings. First, becoming not-Hindu, to the *gumbā* founders and other Gurungs in Maidel, meant asserting a more authentic, Gurung identity. The shift away from Hinduism was represented as a return to Buddhism, the religion of their ancestors and Gurungs in western Nepal. Second, to the local officials, becoming not Hindu implied political defiance and a rejection of the Hindu national identity. Finally, for MNO supporters, becoming 'not-Hindu' meant embracing a political identity that incorporated a wide spectrum of ethnic groups, and critiques the dominance of high-caste Hindus.

Gurung practices of Buddhism in Maidel

One morning, I accompanied Aama to the monthly *pujā* that the Gurung community held at the *gumbā* on Dasami, the tenth day of the lunar fortnight. A crowd of about 30 elderly men and women prepared and drank tea outside the building, while their young grandchildren played. Inside, three young Gurung lamas chanted as they read from Tibetan texts. Aama moved towards the back of the *gumbā*, where two large *thangka* paintings of the Buddha hung above the altar, and added offerings to the heap of fruit, fried rice flour doughnuts (*sel roti*), packages of hard candy, puffed rice, and arrowroot and glucose biscuits. She lit a package of incense, waved it in wide circles three times, and stuck it in a dish of uncooked rice. She performed a series of three prostrations in front of the altar, bowed to each of the books at the long, low table where the lamas read, and then admonished me, 'Why didn't you bow? Go ahead!' I awkwardly copied Aama's movements, and found a place among the people sitting on the floor. The lamas continued to chant for an hour or so, occasionally playing a large drum that hung from the ceiling, cymbals and brass bells, while the crowd of elderly women gossiped, drank tiny steel glasses of salty, milky tea, and appeased their grandchildren with candy.

The high point of the ritual came when it was time to light the 108 butter lamps. Suddenly the size of the crowd doubled, as younger people, who were more burdened with household work than the older folks, arrived to make offerings and light butter lamps. The people outside rushed in, pressing forward to light a lamp and bow at the altar. One of the younger lamas brought the offerings outside, where several people divided the food into equal shares, and distributed it to everyone in attendance. The lamas soon completed the chanting, and people drifted homewards.

I attended many similar Buddhist *pujās* while living in the village of Maidel. While such rituals were by then a regularized part of village life, these Gurungs had been following Buddhism for less than ten years. This Dasami *pujā* was one of the few regular Buddhist rituals performed in the village, aside from marriages and funerals. Most Gurungs in the village only performed rituals at community events like this *pujā*. Only a few Gurung households had permanent altars or *pujā* rooms in their houses, where the oldest person in the house made offerings on a daily and individual basis. The entire community came together twice a year for Buddhist rituals: on Buddha Jayanthi, in May, to celebrate the Buddha's birthday; and in February, to celebrate Lhochhar, the Gurung new year. When rituals were not taking place, prayer flags (*lungtā*), long narrow strips of white cloth with wood block printed prayers that flutter on tall bamboo poles outside every Gurung house, served as a reminder that this community now followed Buddhism. The performance of Buddhist ritual in Maidel, then, is largely a way in which people enacted their belonging to the Gurung community in the village.

The Gurung lamas at the Dasami *pujā* defined Buddhist practice and identity for this community. People often asserted 'now we use lamas for rituals' when describing their shift to Buddhism. In 1997, in Maidel and the two neighboring villages, there were 11 young Gurung men who had undertaken years of learning and initiation rituals at large monasteries in Kathmandu and Pokhara, and were eligible to lead rituals. These young men in their late teens and early twenties were responsible for conducting all of the Buddhist rituals for Gurungs who lived in this area. Though young, and not from families of economic or political stature, they were highly respected.

Gurungs emphasized practices, rather than beliefs, when describing the shift from Hinduism to Buddhism. For Gurung lay people, being Buddhist means using lamas for rituals, performing new rituals and celebrating new holidays, such as Dasami, Buddha Jayanthi and Lhochhar, the Gurung new year. Although Lamas instructed people to perform rituals and occasionally explained the meanings of these rituals, most lay people had only an elementary knowledge of Buddhist philosophy. Lay people, unlike the lamas, underwent no initiation rites to become Buddhist, nor did they receive any formal instruction about Buddhist philosophy. As Bhim, one of the Gurung lamas told me, 'When people in the village join Buddhism, all they have to do is start using lamas.' When I asked lay people about why they held rituals for Dasami every month, they replied, 'it is part of Buddhism' or 'we wouldn't know that, you should ask the lamas'.[6]

None of the Gurung lay people saw their shift to Buddhism as the adoption of a new set of religious beliefs. People seemed confused by my questions about how their beliefs had changed since they became Buddhist. Rekha, a young daughter in law, answered me impatiently: 'Whichever religion you're in, you believe in that religion. When we followed Hinduism, we believed in that. Now we follow Buddhism, and we believe in this.' She suggested that the Gurungs' change in religious beliefs followed their change in religious affiliation.

My search for evidence of changing religious beliefs reflects mistaken assumptions that lurk in the concept of conversion, as social scientists use it. As Comaroff and Comaroff caution, the concept of conversion relies on the Protestant ideals of 'spiritual individualism' that emphasize an individual's rational choice between religions, represented as mutually exclusive systems of belief (pp. 249–251). The concept of conversion thus should not be used to interpret all forms of religious change. Gurungs did not view their religious shift as resulting from a choice between two systems of belief.

The adoption of Buddhism did engender a shift in subjectivity for these Gurungs, even if it was not inspired by Nyingmapa Buddhist doctrine. By becoming Buddhists, these Gurungs enacted a new form of Gurung identity that was inspired by the transnational Gurung movement to uplift Gurung culture. From the mid-1950s onwards, Gurungs in Nepal and Darjeeling, as well as those working abroad with the British army, began organizing to preserve Gurung religion, language and culture. The promotion of Buddhism as Gurung's real religion was one goal of this movement (Gurung 2039 v.s.).

Gurungs in Maidel discussed the shift to Buddhism as a shift to a more authentic Gurung culture. Rekha explained the shift to Buddhism as many Maidel villagers did: 'We found out that Hinduism wasn't really our religion. Our religion is actually Buddhism.' Gurungs located this more ancestral, authentic Gurung culture in western Nepal, the Gurung heartland from which they migrated. As Moti Lal explained:

> We Gurungs are Buddhists. Gurungs in the west are all Buddhists. We are
> trying to maintain our old identity.... At first, a long time ago, our ancestors
> followed Buddha dharma in west Nepal. Later on, many years ago our
> ancestors came from the west to the east. At that time, because there were
> no lamas, we followed the Hindu religion and used Bahuns. For 100 to 150
> years we followed the Hindu religion.

Here, he depicted the Gurung move to Buddhism as an act of preservation,
insisting that it continued old traditions. By becoming Buddhists, Gurungs were
maintaining their 'old identity' rather than trying out a new religion, he suggested, overlooking the fact that Gurungs in eastern Nepal had followed Hinduism for generations.

By shifting to Buddhism, Gurungs in Ilam asserted their belonging in a wider
Gurung community. Links between Gurungs across the country and between
Nepal, Darjeeling and Sikkim were intensified. Gurungs in Maidel assert that
practicing Buddhism created unity among Gurungs within the village as well as
across the country. As Moti Lal explained:

> we have connections up to the national level but before we never met people
> from other areas. Gurungs from different areas in Ilam wouldn't meet that
> often before Buddha dharma. We never used to have meetings regarding our
> own identity.

Gurungs were interested in Buddhism primarily as a new way of expressing their
identity as Gurungs. Following Buddhism did not bring the Gurungs into closer
relations with other Buddhist ethnic groups in the village, such as the Sherpas. This
Sherpa community of about 13 households, which neighbored the main Gurung
settlement in Maidel, had always practiced Buddhism, and thus had extensive religious resources that the Gurungs might have shared. The Sherpas had constructed a
large, elaborate *gumbā* about an hour's walk uphill from the main Gurung settlement. Yet Gurungs never used the Sherpa *gumbā*. There were several experienced
Sherpa lamas who also followed the Nyimgmapa school of Buddhism. Even though
the Gurung community was suffering from a shortage of Gurung lamas, Gurungs
rarely employed Sherpa lamas in their rituals. Of the 11 young Gurung men who
had become lamas in Maidel and the surrounding area, only three were in the villages, while the others pursued additional training in monasteries in Kathmandu,
Pokhara, Darjeeling and Sikkim. One young lama was run ragged trying to meet
the numerous requests for him to perform rituals. Gurungs and Sherpas also never
combined celebrations of major holidays of the Buddhist calendar.

Gurungs acknowledged that their religion was the same as the Sherpas' religion, yet they insisted that the practice of Gurung Buddhism should be a distinct
enterprise. Phul Maya, an unmarried, elderly woman who lived with her sister,
explained that while Gurungs and Sherpas have the same books and the same
religion, they each needed their own *gumbā* and their own lamas because 'we
are separate societies'.

Implied but not stated here is the fact that many Gurungs viewed themselves as superior to Sherpas. Several Gurungs told me that, initially, many Gurungs had not liked the idea of following Buddhism because of its association with culturally Tibetan ethnic groups, who are disparaged by those culturally dominant groups in Nepal. As Yem Lal explained, 'When we changed to bringing lamas, people didn't understand. People hadn't thought that this is our religion.... People said, *Hat!* This is the Bhote lama's religion!' While the term 'Bhote' literally means people from Tibet, or Bhot, as it is called in Nepali, it has negative connotations of dirtiness and otherness. As culturally Tibetan peoples, Sherpas can also fall within the category 'Bhote'. Gurungs had internalized the nationalist idea of Hinduism as the standard and respectable religion to follow. In order for Gurungs in Maidel to be convinced to practice Buddhism, it had to be distanced from association with 'Bhotes' and framed as a distinctively Gurung practice.

In describing the shift to Buddhism, Gurungs emphasized that they were no longer following Hinduism. When people talked about what it had meant for them to be Hindu, they emphasized practices rather than beliefs, describing the types of rituals that they had performed as Hindus, under the direction of Brahman priests, rather than a set of Hindu ideas. When following Hinduism, Gurungs in Maidel had employed Brahman, or 'Bahun', priests from a neighboring village, as there were no priests among the few households of Bahuns in Maidel. As followers of Hinduism, Gurungs could never perform their own religious rituals. As Man Gurung explained, 'We had Bahuns do rituals for 100 years, and not one Gurung ever became a priest. Even if we studied for 20 years, we could never become a priest. But now our Gurungs study to be lamas for two or three years and are lamas.' The switch from Bahun priests to Gurung lamas defined Buddhism for most Gurungs.

Many Gurungs said that they preferred Buddhism because it eliminated the high costs involved in practicing Hinduism and because they were not financially supporting Bahuns. Maya, a middle-aged woman, told me, 'We were oppressed by Chhetris and Bahuns because Hindu dharma was using a lot of money. For our own dharma we don't need money to worship.' Buddhist rituals did involve some expenses, but lamas and villagers stressed that people could give whatever amount they liked to lamas, and that lamas could not request or insist on a particular fee. Furthermore, the lamas always made a point of returning a small amount of what people had offered them. Buddhism enabled the Gurungs to keep resources within their own community. People also mentioned that practicing Hinduism required them to behave in a subservient manner to Bahuns, as they had to bow to them. The shift to Buddhism undermined one source of local Bahuns' power.

The Gurung practice of Buddhism had contradictory meanings within the community in Ilam. Gurungs who supported the MNO sought to link the meaning of 'not-Hindu' primarily to the category 'Mongol', and to support for the MNO, and only secondarily to 'Gurung'. However, while all Gurungs in Maidel practiced Buddhism, not all of them supported the MNO. Gurungs in the Congress or Communist Parties did not accept the idea that being 'not-Hindu' was equivalent to being 'Mongol' and supporting the MNO. Instead, for them, being 'not-Hindu' only meant revitalizing their Gurung identity. These conflicting meanings were highlighted in the boycott of Dasain in Maidel.

The Dasain boycott

The boycott of Dasain has been one of the most widely embraced cultural practices put forth by the post-1990 ethnic political movement, particularly in eastern Nepal. While MNO activists credit their president Gopal Gurung with first calling for Mongols to boycott Dasain, and attribute the widespread non-celebration of Dasain to the efforts of the MNO, people involved in different parts of the indigenous nationalities movement have also called for and practiced the Dasain boycott.[7]

The Dasain boycott must be explained in the context of the dominant meanings and celebration of the holiday. The Dasain holiday lasts for about two weeks during the Nepali month of *Asoj* (September–October), when the monsoons have ended, deep blue skies frame the mountains, fields of marigolds are in bloom and the rice is harvested. Employees often receive an extra month's salary to help meet the many expenses that come with the holiday, and ten to 15 days of vacation, as offices are closed for the full length of the festival. In anticipation of the festival, people repair and paint their houses. Butchers arrange for the delivery of herds of goats, as people consume large amounts of meat on a daily basis during Dasain, while during the rest of the year middle-income families may have meat about once a month (Bennett 1983: 136–141). Families from communities that have no restrictions against alcohol brew large quantities of *raksī* to serve during the holiday. Since everyone in the family receives one new outfit, clothing shops and tailors have some of their busiest days. It is the most important holiday of the year for many people and, until recently, the majority of people in Nepal celebrated this holiday.

Two hegemonic myths are tied to the Dasain holiday, both of which assert that the holiday celebrates an occasion on which a god or goddess vanquished a demon after ten days of battle. In one account, people cite the source of the Dasain story as the Ramayana, a Sanskrit epic. In this interpretation, the ten main days of Dasain commemorate a ten-day battle between the king-god Ram and the demon Ravana, and celebrate Ram's killing of Ravana on the tenth day. The second mythical account of the Dasain celebration refers to a battle between the goddess Durga and a buffalo demon called Mahisasur, which ends with Durga vanquishing Mahisasur and his army (Bennett 1983: 264–265; Parish 1994). The major rituals of the Dasain holiday are supposedly linked to these myths. On the eighth day of Dasain the demon was slain, and people re-enact its slaying through performing a sacrifice on this day in the festival; the tenth day of Dasain celebrates the victory of the god or goddess over the demon, enacted in the joyous exchange of *ṭikā*.

In practice, Dasain is more about reaffirming connections with kin than about commemorating the victory of deities over demons. Most importantly, it is a time when people gather with their families. The entire transportation system is flooded during this mass pilgrimage homewards, as people travel to their parents' homes from wherever they are in Nepal, and women travel to their natal homes for part of the festival to receive *ṭikā* from their own parents. Dasain is not merely about gathering with family members. Rather, as Bennett describes it, 'Dasai [*sic*] is above all, a celebration – an enactment – of the complex status relationships that bind kinsmen together' (p. 137). As people receive *ṭikā*, blessings and food from relatives who are their superiors, an individual's place within the hierarchy of the family is acknowledged and affirmed during Dasain.

There are also political dimensions of the holiday. Political hierarchies are reaffirmed and acknowledged during Dasain, drawing on the idiom of hierarchy in the family that is affirmed through the ritual of *ṭikā*. Just as individuals receive *ṭikā* and blessings from their higher-ranking kin, so individuals receive *ṭikā* from their political superiors. Dasain played a 'legitimating role' in the political realm of Nepal, as Tamang headmen, for example, would receive *ṭikā* from princely overlords in the early state (Holmberg 1989: 226). Every year at Dasain, district-level government employees were reviewed and either reappointed or terminated (Caplan 1975: 34). Throughout the Panchayat era, villagers brought gifts to and received blessings and *ṭikā* from village headmen during Dasain (Holmberg 1989: 46; Sagant 1996: 156). This offering of gifts, such as meat, fruit, liquor, farm implements or pheasants, and taking *ṭikā* was a way through which 'all dependents renewed their allegiance to the *subbā* [Limbu headman]' (Sagant 1996: 156). The Dasain holiday was also closely associated with Nepal's royal family. On the tenth day, the king and queen personally gave *ṭikā* to ministers and central government officers, as well as to anyone who waited in the long line outside the palace.

Dasain also has political meanings as a national holiday. The state supports the celebration of the holiday by closing all government offices for about 15 days, thus halting all government business, including the postal service, during the festival. More importantly, Dasain has become a centerpiece of the Hindu identity of the Nepali nation. Those who did not celebrate Dasain were perceived to be 'outsiders to greater Nepalese society' (Holmberg 1989: 226). If this mere non-participation in Dasain casts people as marginal to the nation, the boycott of the festival clearly challenged the very definition of the nation.

In the 1990s, indigenous nationalities groups throughout Nepal were fiercely debating whether or not they should boycott Dasain. People in the village of Maidel stopped celebrating Dasain, not after the Gurung shift to Buddhism, but after the arrival of the MNO. As Buddhiman told me, 'After we joined the MNO, we stopped taking *ṭikā* on Dasain.' During the first couple of years of the multi-party system, from about 1991–1993, MNO activists took the lead in organizing Dasain boycott activities. They published and distributed pamphlets to fellow villagers, explaining why they should not celebrate Dasain, and delivered speeches over car battery-operated loudspeakers on the main day when people receive *ṭikā*. During these years, the MNO led an oppositional and highly politicized boycott of Dasain.

MNO activists proposed that, since Mongols are not Hindus, they should not celebrate Hindu holidays, including the prominent Dasain festival. This was indeed the most frequently-voiced explanation of the Dasain boycott among MNO supporters in the villages. When people talked about being Mongol and about supporting the MNO, they always referred to the fact that they had stopped celebrating Dasain.

Through the Dasain boycott, Mongols performed 'a not Hindu' identity. MNO activists opposed the status of Dasain as a national holiday. Kiran Akten pointed to the ways in which Dasain symbolizes the Hindu identity of the Nepali nation:

> Other evidence that this Dasain is not our festival is that every year, Radio Nepal says that Bijaya Dasami [a more formal name for Dasain] is the great festival of the Hindus only. If Radio Nepal said that Bijaya Dasami is the great festival of Nepalis, then we would all celebrate it. We would have had to celebrate it, but they say that it is only the Hindus' festival, not the Nepalis'. When they say it is the Hindus' festival, that is directly saying that it is not for the Buddhists, Muslims, Christians, Sikhs, Jains and other non-Hindus. There is no reason for non-Hindus to celebrate a Hindu festival!

Kiran rejected the state-sponsored radio's equation of Hindu with the Nepali nation, pointing to how the assumption that Hindu equals nation excludes many Nepalis from identifying with the nation.

MNO activists never referred to the political dimensions that the Dasain holiday acquired in the administration of the Nepali state. Yet, the holiday's history as an occasion when the hierarchical relationships between representatives of the state and local peoples were affirmed may inform the MNO's opposition to Dasain. Through the Dasain boycotts, MNO activists refused to legitimize the power of the state.

In explaining why Mongols should boycott Dasain, MNO leaders analyzed the mythical history of the holiday. They asserted that Dasain celebrates the Hindu conquering of Mongols in both mythical and more recent historical times. In these narratives, the Dasain festival became a symbol of the entire history of high-caste Hindu domination of Mongols. Kiran Akten recounted, over the course of several hours, a history of Mongols that spanned from mythical time to several hundred years ago.

First, Kiran asserted that the dominant myths of Dasain, which tell of the victory of a goddess over a demon, actually refer to battles between Mongols and Aryans. His narrative suggested that the MNO's struggle against high-caste Hindus began in ancient times. The portrayal of Rawana and Mahisasur as demons in these myths reflects Hindu discrimination against Mongols, as these so-called demons were actually Mongols. Thus, MNO activists, recast Mahisasur as the 'ancestral father' of all Mongols. Gopal Gurung also described Rawana as a non-Aryan, and thus as the real hero of the Ramayana, in *Hidden Facts in Nepali Politics,* where he writes, 'Ironically, we celebrate the Dasai [*sic*] festival to commemorate the death of a non-Aryan king Rawan by a Hindu Aryan king Ram where as it should be the reverse, a time of mourning. It is shameful that we are helping their cause' (Gurung 1994: 63). The MNO's version of this myth may draw from other anti-high-caste Hindu political movements in South Asia, which have also interpreted Rawana as a symbol of subaltern communities (Richman 1991).

Second, Kiran described Dasain as marking the day when Mongols began to lose the rule of their land to the high-caste Hindus. In recounting this history, he began 800 years ago, with the tale of how Hindus fleeing Muslim invaders in India came to Nepal as refugees. A kind and generous Magar king, Khadka Magar, allowed the Hindu refugees to stay in his country. Trouble began when the Hindus began to spread their religion and the idea of the caste system. Through the influence of the caste system, the Magar community was divided into elite and lower groups, who began to fight each other. While the Magars were fighting, the Hindus forged a plan to conquer the weakened Magar kingdom. They started digging a secret path to the Magar king's palace and, on the seventh day of digging, they reached the palace. The next day, the eighth day, one of the Hindus, Drabya Shah, killed King Khadka Magar. On the following day, the ninth day, Drabya Shah called a meeting of the Hindus to decide what to do with Khadka Magar's corpse and blood. And on the tenth day, Drabya Shah announced that they would mix the Magar king's blood with uncooked rice and would wear it as *ṭikā* to celebrate their victory. Drabya Shah was crowned king on that day, and he proclaimed, as Kiran tells it, 'From this year onwards, on the day on which we won this war, everyone will wear *ṭikā*, red *ṭikā*.' Thus both Dasain and the reign of the Shah monarchy were established.

In this narrative, Dasain memorializes the Hindu vanquishing of Mongols. This history counters the dominant nationalist narrative of how Nepal was unified under the leadership of the royal family's ancestors by describing this as a process through which the original Mongol rulers lost power. For the Mongols, the eighth day of the Dasain festival, when the goddess Durga slayed the demon Mahisasur in the dominant myth, is a tragic day on which a great Mongol king was murdered.

Thus, the *ṭikā* symbolizes the Hindus' victory over Mongols. Some MNO activists particularly scorned the use of red powder in *ṭikā*, as symbolic of their ancestors' blood, but argued that if they took white *ṭikā*, uncooked rice and yogurt without the vermilion powder, that the meaning of the *ṭikā* was changed. Other activists felt that taking any form of *ṭikā* during Dasain was unacceptable. Kiran argued that Mongols should not only refrain from taking *ṭikā* themselves; rather, they should also insist that high-caste Hindus not wear Dasain *ṭikā*. As Kiran told me:

> we say that we should not just boycott [Dasain] *ṭikā*, but if Chhetri-Bahuns walk around in front of us wearing *ṭikā*, we are getting ready to fight with them. Because, who wouldn't get angry, seeing them walking arrogantly in

front of us, wearing the blood of our ancestor, who they killed? The time is coming when we will 'challenge' them, when during Dasain, we will say: Don't wear *ṭikā* in front of us! Stay inside and wear *ṭikā*, but if you come out on the street in front of us, you will be hit with rocks and things, you'll be struck with *khukuris* and batons.

Kiran demanded that high-caste Hindus recognize the Mongol interpretation of Dasain, and threatened violence as a way of imposing this meaning on the festival.

The MNO connected the holiday to an ancient history of antagonism between Mongols and Aryans that has continued through to the present day. This interpretation emphasized the mythical and historical political dimensions of the holiday, obscuring some of the holiday's meanings in practice. The Dasain boycott attempted to rearrange how people associated the festival with the past. MNO activists asked people to replace their lived memories of Dasain, as a grand celebration of kinship ties and an enjoyable time of plenty, with a singular, collective history of domination.

By 1994, when I began my research in Maidel, MNO activists had convinced virtually the entire population of 'Mongols' in the village to stop celebrating Dasain, regardless of whether or not they supported the MNO. Most MNO supporters understood the Dasain boycott as a way of marking their identity as 'not-Hindus'. Some MNO supporters also spoke of Dasain as memorializing the Hindu vanquishing of Mongols. As Saila, a Limbu teenager told me, it was wrong to take *ṭikā* and celebrate Dasain because 'Our ancestors were killed then. We should actually be sad on that day, the tenth day of Dasain.'

However, the earlier defiant protests of Dasain had faded into a mere non-celebration of Dasain. When I asked Nar Bahadur about the Dasain boycott, he said that no one celebrated Dasain anymore, but that there were no plans for anti-Dasain activities this year. 'We haven't had time,' he said. Activists probably felt that since people had stopped celebrating Dasain, it was no longer necessary to explain to them why they shouldn't celebrate it. When I asked Buddhiman if the MNO held programs to protest Dasain, he responded, 'That doesn't happen, it's just that we don't take *ṭikā*. It's just like an ordinary day, just like always.'

Though there were no protests against Dasain, people perceived themselves as diligently observing Dasain boycotts by abstaining from taking *ṭikā*. Yet contrary to Buddhiman's statement, the days of the Dasain boycott were not just ordinary days, and were filled with many of the activities that people remembered in association with Dasain.

During the days of Dasain that I spent in the village in October 1995, people participated in many activities associated with the holiday. Prior to the Dasain period, families white-washed their houses and repainted the colorful strips of red mud along the bottom of the houses. Several buffaloes and goats were slaughtered in the village, and we ate heaped plates of meat with tender rice from the new harvest at every meal throughout this time. Children twirled through the village in the new clothing their parents bought for them. Relatives visiting from Kathmandu and Kalimpong packed the house where I lived. On the eleventh day, Bhauju and her children donned new clothing, and visited her natal home on a neighboring mountain ridge, just as she had in the years before the Dasain boycott. However, once these activities were unmoored from the occasion of Dasain, they lost their significance. Aama and other older people in the village in particular expressed a sense of loss, as they sighed and commented to me and to each other during conversations, 'Well, this is how it is, now that we quit celebrating Dasain.' 'Ah, well, that's how it is, what can you do about it?'

That year, however, Gurungs in Maidel began holding weddings during Dasain for the first time, instead of during November and December (*Mangsir*) as they did in the past. Four weddings were held in the Gurung community during Dasain that year. I was invited to attend the two weddings that were held on the tenth day of Dasain. At each of these Buddhist weddings, teenage Gurung lamas performed the rituals in front of an altar constructed in the courtyard of the house, chanting from sacred texts in Tibetan script, playing instruments, and occasionally pausing to instruct the guests, bride and groom about their next steps in the ceremony.

Although the wedding was labeled Buddhist, as Gurung lamas were officiating the ceremony, all of the key symbols of a Hindu marriage were used in it. Both brides wore red and gold silk saris, and each groom placed red vermilion powder on his bride's forehead and a *tilhari*, a carved gold ornament on strings of glass beads, around her neck. Towards the end of the ceremony, guests and relatives placed *khata*, white silk scarves given to demonstrate respect in Buddhist ceremonies, around the necks of the newlyweds. Most significantly, the closest relatives of the bride and groom placed a red *tikā*, a mixture of vermilion powder, rice and yogurt, on their own foreheads, then gave the newlyweds *tikā* and blessings.

When I asked Nar Bahadur why people had begun holding weddings during Dasain, he suggested that it was a way for people to covertly continue to celebrate Dasain: 'People feel like something is missing when they don't celebrate Dasain. During Dasain people exchange *tikā* and during weddings people give *tikā*. This is the first year there have been weddings on Dasain. You can't really tell who's wearing a *tikā* for Dasain and who's wearing a *tikā* for the weddings.' He then said that a few Gurungs who claimed to be Buddhist still occasionally secretly called Bahuns for rituals. His interpretation of these weddings is supported by the timing of the weddings, all of which were held on days when people could receive Dasain *tikā* from relatives.

Nar Bahadur saw these weddings as potentially threatening to the meanings that he and other MNO activists gave to the boycott. Yet, the weddings did not necessarily contradict these meanings. These weddings were a way for people to replace their lived memories of Dasain with another set of lived memories. The exchange of *tikā* was revived but it was no longer a Hindu practice in the context of Buddhist weddings. The resuscitation of *tikā* in this new guise illustrates the power of enactment as a way of remembering (Connerton 1989). The weddings turned the boycott of Dasain and the history of Mongols that it stands for into something that people could enact. It connected the boycott with a lived memory as well as with a reified, collective memory.

The weddings were also a way for Gurungs who did not support the MNO to disassociate the non-celebration of Dasain with support for the MNO. Several of the families who held these weddings supported parties other than the MNO. One wedding involved Moti Lal, a staunch Congress Party supporter, whose niece was married. When the MNO emerged in the village, the party asserted that boycotting Dasain was a way of affirming their political beliefs and agenda. For those Gurungs who did not support the MNO, this presented an awkward, somewhat contradictory situation. As Gurungs who practiced Buddhism, they were not supposed to celebrate Dasain. Yet by not celebrating Dasain they affirmed the MNO's interpretation of the holiday and political agenda. By holding weddings on Dasain, these Gurungs could assert an alternative religious identity without aligning themselves with a Mongol 'not Hindu' identity.

Conclusion

Throughout the narratives about the Gurung shift to Buddhism, people connected the idea of democracy with the idea of religious freedom and choice. In describing Hinduism as a religion that was not really theirs and that they had been forced to follow, they linked it with the authoritarian dimensions of the Panchayat state. According to villagers, the CDO shut down the *gumbā* because, he interpreted it as a form of political activity that expressed opposition to the Panchayat system: he thought they were starting a political party and said it was a *bahudal* (multi-party) instead of a *Bouddha* (Buddhist) *gumbā*. People viewed the CDO's closing of the *gumbā* as evidence of the lack of freedom in the Panchayat era.

Gurungs initially interpreted their adoption of Buddhism as a rejection of Hinduism, and a return to their ancestral religion. Although the MNO did not instigate this move away from Hinduism, the party capitalized on it and heightened the political meanings of these events. For the MNO, this religious movement was an example of how all Mongols should reject Hinduism and oppose the high-caste Hindu dominance of the state. The party saw these cultural transformations as a necessary step in the process of gaining political power for Mongols. People suggested, in fact, that the success of the MNO in mobilizing support in this area of Ilam was related to the religious movement and the controversy surrounding it, preceding the MNO's arrival. Villages in Ilam with the strongest support for the MNO also had the highest population of Gurungs in the district, and this may have been one of the factors that drew Gurungs to the party.

Even if religious change was a powerful force in motivating people to join the MNO, religion played a contradictory role in the party. People interpreted the MNO as 'our own religion's party', in the words of one Gurung woman. However, the MNO could not promote any one religion; it could only insist that

Mongols were not Hindus. While the MNO attempted to link the rejection of Hinduism to support for its party's goals, the Dasain boycotts was one of the only ways that the MNO could substantiate this shared not-Hindu identity. However, Gurungs who supported other parties were able to reinterpret their non-celebration of Dasain as an affirmation of their identity as Gurungs, rather than as supporters of the MNO's politics. Furthermore, different ethnic groups practiced many different non-Hindu religions. Some Limbus and Rais followed Satya Hangma, Gurungs could practice Buddhism, while Sherpas followed a similar but separate Buddhism. These ethnic groups could privilege their affiliation with these religions over belonging to a more inclusive Mongol not-Hindu identity. Religion could unify the disparate Mongol peoples as 'not-Hindus', while also fracturing them into followers of their own religions.

Conclusion

Ethnic parties in a new Nepal – the Constituent Assembly elections and the future of the MNO

Nepal's indigenous nationalities movement has made considerable progress since 1990, when marginalized ethnic groups began demanding greater representation in the state and an end to high-caste Hindu dominance. Dominant groups considered demands for ethnic equality to threaten the state during the Panchayat years, and paid little attention to these demands during the early years of the post-1990 multi-party democracy. With the rise of the Maoists after 1996 and the second people's movement in 2006, ethnic equality became part of the dominant political discourse. Between 2006 and 2008, some of the movement's major demands were adopted by the state: Constituent Assembly (CA) elections were held, and the work of drafting a new constitution commenced, Nepal was declared a federal democratic republic, and many symbols of Nepal as a Hindu nation were removed: the monarchy is gone, the state is now secular and a new national anthem, penned by a member of an indigenous nationalities group, was adopted.

Ethnic political demands shifted substantially in the period between 1990 and 2008. In the 1990s, movements by indigenous nationalities, Dalits, and Madhesis sought to extend rights that were supposedly guaranteed by the new democratic state to these marginalized populations. By the early 2000s, they demanded a complete restructuring of the state. Since the formation of the constituent assembly in 2008, such movements have aimed to ensure that these identities provide the framework for the structures and policies of the state, through a federal system, proportional representation and reservations.

Ethnic movements became increasingly politicized in response to the rise of the Maoist movement and its adoption of ethnic demands. The Maoists addressed issues of ethnic inequality more directly than any other large political party, and targeted and gained the support of many people in indigenous nationalities communities (Lecomte-Tilouine 2004; Shneiderman and Turin 2004). Building on the growing expression of ethnic grievances through the indigenous nationalities movement, the Maoists voiced their support for ethnic issues just before launching the People's War in 1996. Later, the Maoists announced a plan to establish nine autonomous ethnically-based regions. In 2004, they declared eight such regions in their areas of control, beginning with the Magarat Autonomous Region in an area of 20,000 square kilometers in western Nepal (Ogura 2008:

198–207). The party also established or incorporated about 20 ethnic liberation fronts to advance ethnic issues, establish ethnic autonomous states and to play a role in running these states, according to the Maoist central committee member Gopal Kiraty, who spoke with me in August 2008. This chapter examines how the MNO has fared in this changing context, and then concludes with some thoughts about the MNO's experience of democracy during the 1990s.

The MNO and other ethnic parties in the Constituent Assembly elections

One indicator of the heightened politicization of ethnic movements is that ethnic political parties played an expanded role in the April 2008 Constituent Assembly elections. The increased mobilization of these movements led to an increase in the number of ethnic parties. In the 1990s only three ethnic parties ran in elections whereas 11 ethnic parties participated in the 2008 elections. These included three new parties representing indigenous nationalities in addition to the MNO; four Madhesi parties; one party that defends the interests of people of hill origins in the Tarai; and two parties representing a coalition of marginalized groups. Many ethnic parties were formed in response to the structure of the CA, which did not allow for representation of civil society organizations. Ethnic activists feared that without a political party to represent their issues in the CA, they would not be able to gain support to secure ethnic federalism and the right to self-determination for indigenous nationalities in the new constitution. Overall, ethnic parties performed better in these elections than they had in the 1990s. However, the MNO failed to win any seats.

Two factors in addition to the increased politicization of ethnic movements can explain the increased formation and success of ethnic parties in the 2008 elections. First, ethnic parties could more easily get on the ballot than in the elections in the 1990s. Ethnic parties were allowed to register with the Election Commission. The interim constitution of 2006 maintained the same restrictions against ethnic parties that existed in the 1990 Constitution, but apparently they were no longer enforced. Thus, after 18 years of effort, the MNO successfully registered its party with the Election Commission, along with several other ethnic parties. In her study of ethnic parties in Latin America, Van Cott similarly found that 'improved access to the ballot for aspiring parties' is a necessary, but not sufficient, condition for the formation and success of ethnic parties in a political system (2005: 8).

Second, Nepal's adoption of a new 'mixed' electoral system increased the likelihood of small parties, like ethnic parties, gaining representation on the CA. In this system, 240 seats were elected by the first-past-the-post system (FPTP), while 335 seats were elected by proportional representation (PR). In the PR system, the entire country was a single electoral constituency and parties received seats based on the proportion of total votes that they received. Prior to the elections, parties submitted lists of potential candidates who could be appointed to fill any seats the party won via the PR elections. Parties were required to fulfill quotas in the composition of these lists to increase the representation of women, Dalits, indigenous nationalities, Madhesis and other marginalized groups. Nine ethnic parties received seats via the PR elections.

The MNO expanded its activities by the 2008 elections, as it put forth candidates in more districts than it had in the past. In the 1990s, the MNO had no more than six candidates in three districts and was mainly confined to Ilam and Jhapa. In the 2008 FPTP elections, 17 MNO candidates ran for election in 12 districts: Panchthar, Ilam, Jhapa, Sankhuwasabha, Morang, Solukhumbhu, Ramechhap, Sindhuli, Rasuwa, Dhading, Makwanpur and Kathmandu. Gopal Gurung ran from Ilam, just as he had in the past. The other candidates in Ilam and Jhapa had been involved in the party since the 1990s. In the other districts many candidates were members of a new sister organization to the MNO that began operating in 2006, as I discuss below, and they ran for election from their home districts.

While the structural changes to the electoral system benefited other ethnic parties, the MNO won no seats in the CA elections, either from the FPTP or the PR elections. In the FPTP elections in Ilam, the number of votes for MNO candidates increased slightly by comparison with 1999, although its portion of total votes cast declined slightly (see Table 2.1, Chapter 2). Gopal Gurung won more votes than any other MNO candidate, just as he had in the past national elections. This suggests that the MNO continues to be centered on Gopal Gurung's charismatic leadership. None of the other candidates in any other districts won a significant number of votes.

The MNO's loss of vote share in the Ilam elections between 1999 and 2008 is related to the participation of new powerful parties, including the Maoists. The Maoists won no seats in Ilam even though they won 120 out of 240 seats in the FPTP elections, more than any other party. However, they created new competition for the MNO and this was probably one of the main reasons why the party could not increase its vote share in Ilam. The victorious candidates in Ilam were from the Nepal Communist Party (UML) in constituencies one and two, and from the Nepali Congress Party in the other constituency. While analysts deemed the election to be free and fair at the time, Lawoti (in press) suggests that the Maoists used threats to influence the election outcomes, due to the large percentage of votes that Maoists were able to capture in some areas. Yet the Maoists came late to Ilam and, according to Gopal Gurung, they were not able to maintain total control of the district for more than about two years. This was a major factor in the Maoists' third-place position in the Ilam elections, behind UML and the Congress Party (see Table C.1). The arrival of a new ethnic party in Ilam, the *Sanghiya Loktantrik Rastriya Manch* (Federal Republic National Front, or FRNF) created further competition for the MNO.

The FRNF is a front for four autonomous political organizations – the Federal Limbuwan State Council, Tamangsaling Autonomous State Council, Tharuhat Autonomous State Council and Khambuwan Autonomous State Council – which aim to establish autonomous regions for particular ethnic groups. The FRNF gained strong support in Ilam as it includes the Federal Limbuwan Autonomous

Table C.1 Constituent Assembly election results for the top six parties in Ilam district

Ilam 1		Ilam 2		Ilam 3	
UML*	17,655	UML*	17,748	Congress*	16,286
Nepal Congress	13,774	Nepali Congress	14,044	UML	14,695
NCP Maoist	10,917	NCP Maoist	8,916	NCP Maoist	8,474
RaPraPa	2,167	FRNF	1,678	MNO	2,377
MNO	916	MNO	779	RaPraPa	516
FRNF	624	RaPraPa	330	NCP (United Marxist)	250

Source: Election Commission (2008), at: www.election.gov.np/reports/CAResults/reportBody.php.

State Council, which has played a leading role in the movement for Limbu territorial autonomy since 2006. Ilam falls within the territory that would be Limbuwan. In Ilam constituency one, this party came in sixth position, just behind the MNO, while in constituency two, it came in fifth position, just ahead of the MNO. The FRNF did not place a candidate in constituency three, where the MNO ran its strongest candidate, Gopal Gurung (see Table C.1). This data suggests that these parties were in direct competition with each other. In the 1990s in Ilam, the MNO had many Limbu supporters who may have later joined the Limbuwan movement, and switched their allegiance to the FRNF. However, the number of voters for the MNO did not drop between 1999 and 2008 and without further research it is not possible to determine whether former MNO supporters voted for the FRNF.

In the PR portion of the elections, where the MNO might have had a better chance of gaining a seat, it won no seats, with only 11,578 votes. As Table C.2 illustrates, nine ethnic parties won enough votes to gain seats. Parties representing Madhesis did very well, both in the FPTP and PR elections. One party representing Madhesis – the *Nepal Sadbhavana Party* – ran in elections in the 1990s. The rise of the Madhesi movement after 2006 is the clearest explanation of their electoral success (Lawoti 2008 [2065 v.s.]).

Ethnic parties that were more successful than the MNO in the CA elections exhibit two characteristics that distinguish them from the MNO. First, some of these parties expanded their targeted constituency to include other marginalized groups besides the indigenous nationalities. The *Rastriya Janamukti Party* (RJP) and the *Dalit Janajāti party* fall into this category. Second, other parties made ethnic territorial autonomy their central demand, such as the FRNF, *Tamsaling Nepal Rastriya Dal* and *Nepa: Rastriya Party*.

The *Rastriya Janamukti Party* is the only one of these parties besides the MNO that participated in the elections in the 1990s. It won no seats via the FPTP elections but won two in the PR elections. This party is much larger than the MNO, and put 84 candidates up for election. While the RJP earlier represented only indigenous nationalities, it expanded its party platform to represent all marginalized groups, including Madheshi and Dalits, and religious minorities like

Table C.2 2008 Constituent Assembly election results for ethnic parties in proportional representation elections

Party name	Total votes	Number of seats in CA
Madhesi Jan Adhikar Forum	678,327	22
Tarai Madhesi Loktantrik Party	338,930	11
Sadbhavana Party	167,517	5
Sanghiya Loktantrik Rastriya Manch	71,958	2
Nepal Sadbhavana Party (Anandidevi)	55,671	2
Rastriya Janmukti Party	53,910	2
Dalit Janajati Party	40,348	1
Nepa: Rastriya Party	37,757	1
Churebhawar Rastriya Ekta Party Nepal	28,575	1
Tamsaling Nepal Rastriya Dal	20,657	0
Mongol National Organization	11,578	0

Source: Election Commission, at: www.election.gov.np/reports/CAResults/reportBody.php.

Muslims, in addition to indigenous nationalities. The RJP's wider target constituency is reflected in the diverse list of 100 candidates from many different marginalized groups that the party submitted to the Election Commission for the PR election. The *Dalit Janajāti Party* similarly aimed to mobilize a broader group, including both Dalits and indigenous nationalities. It won 40,348 votes and thus one seat in the PR elections. The MNO cannot easily adopt this strategy as long as it constructs the identity of the people it represents along racial lines, excluding Dalits and other marginalized groups. A more inclusive stance could help the party win more votes.

The issue of ethnic territorial autonomy galvanized considerable support for ethnic parties that represent indigenous nationalities. Ethnic-based federalism and rights of ethnic groups to self-determination have become central demands for most of the organizations in the indigenous nationalities movement. The movement promotes ethnic territories as a way to achieve the decentralization of the state and ensure that marginalized groups gain access to political power.

Many of the new ethnic parties demand particular ethnic territories. The FRNF won 71,958 votes and two seats under PR allocation. The *Nepa: Rastriya Party*, which seeks an autonomous region for Newars, won 37,757 votes and thus earned one seat on the CA through the PR system. Another ethnic party called the *Tamsaling Rastriya Dal* (TRD), established by a former general secretary of NEFIN, Parsuram Tamang, was not able to win any seats in the CA but won 20,657 votes in the PR elections, far more than the MNO's 11,578. While the TRD's election manifesto claims that the party represents all indigenous nationalities groups, it is centrally concerned with Tamangs, as the party's name refers to Tamasaling, the ancestral homeland of Tamangs that many propose should become an ethnic autonomous region. Even the RJP and *Dalit Janajāti Party* support ethnic federalism; they propose to combine it with other measures like reservations to ensure that Dalits who lack a territorial basis would not be excluded from the polity.

In emphasizing territory, the claims of these parties are comparable to those of the Madhesi parties, which represent a Tarai-based regional identity and seek to establish a single Madhesi state in the new federal system. The Madhesi parties did extremely well in the 2008 CA elections, winning 42 seats in FPTP elections and 40 seats in PR elections. The largest Madhesi parties – the *Madhesei Jan Adhikar Forum* and the *Tarai Madhesi Loktantrik Party* – gained support by spearheading the Madhesi movement in the winter of 2008, before the CA elections. Another Tarai-based political party, the *Chure Bhawar Rastriya Ekata Party Nepal*, formed in opposition to these Madhesi parties to support the interests of people of hill origins in the Tarai region, and won one seat through the PR elections. In the 1990s, the Madhesi movement received little popular attention, but it was more politically focused and electorally successful than the indigenous nationalities movement. The *Nepal Sadbhavana Party* was the only ethnic party to win representation at the national level in the 1990s. The greater electoral success of Madhesi parties can be attributed at least partly to their focus on the issue of territory.

The MNO's lack of support for ethnic federalism may be a key factor in its weaker election performance than other ethnic parties. The MNO has long advocated a federal structure in Nepal yet, unlike all of the ethnic parties discussed above, it does not advocate dividing or naming territories on the basis of ethnicity. Ethnic federalism could undermine the MNO's efforts to create unity among Mongols, Gopal Gurung explained. While many other parties and policy makers have drawn up maps and plans of how they would divide and name the states in a federal structure, the MNO never did this, leaving its concept of federalism less clearly defined than that of other parties.

The social composition of MNO supporters may be one reason why the party has not supported ethnic federalism. Many MNO supporters in Ilam and Jhapa, as well as Gopal Gurung, were in fact living outside their ancestral ethnic homelands. These Gurungs, Magars, Tamangs and other ethnic groups had ancestors who migrated to Ilam in the wake of state unification in the eighteenth or nineteenth centuries. The MNO's formulation of identity along racial rather than cultural lines may have been particularly appealing to these groups, who were removed from their ancestral cultures and lands. Gurungs and these other ethnic groups might oppose ethnic-based federalism on the grounds that they would be cultural minorities in the Limbuwan state that Ilam would join under this model.

Although it has operated much longer than most other ethnic parties, the MNO had less success at the polls. The MNO's plans for establishing a federal republic, a secular state and a constituent assembly were achieved without the MNO coming to power. The MNO was not able to articulate a new solution to the enduring issue of ethnic inequality that was as compelling to voters as that of ethnic federalism and ethnic territorial autonomy.

However, the party did expand its operations and did not lose votes in its earlier base areas of Ilam and Jhapa. This is remarkable given the political upheavals that have taken place since 1999, the last time elections were held. The MNO's performance in the 2008 elections, and its future as a political party, must be understood in the context of the changes that it has gone through since the rise of the People's War, launched by the Communist Party of Nepal (Maoist) in 1996.

The changing shape of the MNO

Like other political parties in rural Nepal, the MNO was challenged by the Maoist party, which eventually gained control of most of the countryside and dramatically changed the course of rural politics. The Maoists built up their base of support by working at the village level. In their stronghold areas, they established district- and village-level people's governments (*jana sarkār*), where they transformed the political, economic and social dimensions of village life, setting up their own elections, legal system, taxation system and holidays, for example (Khanal 2007; Ogura 2008; Sharma 2004: 45–47; Shneiderman and Turin 2004).

The Maoists gained political control of the villages by creating a power vacuum, and then asserting their own authority (Sharma 2004). Maoists attacked police posts, forcing the ill-prepared police to leave the villages, and threatened village government leaders from other parties with abduction, harm or death unless they joined their party. Many village-level leaders and activists fled villages for the city, and probably formed a sizeable portion of the 150,000 to 250,000 internally displaced people.[1] In most villages that were under Maoist control, no other political parties were allowed to operate openly.

Among the reasons for the rise of the Maoists, analyzed extensively elsewhere (Khanal 2007; Ramirez 2004; Thapa 2004), the rural context of the People's War is significant when comparing the Maoists and the MNO. Both the MNO and Maoists worked at the village level to mobilize people around political ideologies that advocated a complete change in the structure of the state. This form of political mobilization was possible due to the state's weak presence at the village level into the 1990s. Both the state and the mainstream political parties remained highly centralized during this time. Village governments had little authority and control over resources and major political parties and the state paid relatively little attention to villages (Khanal 2007: 88–89; Lawoti 2007b: 35–38). This created an opportunity for radical political parties to mobilize support in rural areas.

Through the early to late 1990s, the MNO was rooted in the villages of Ilam and Jhapa districts in eastern Nepal; it had a minimal presence in urban centers in these districts or in Kathmandu. When the Maoist People's War took hold in eastern Nepal in the early 2000s, much later than it did in the rest of the country, the MNO's base areas were disrupted. These events had a severe impact on the MNO as the party had no substantial presence and infrastructure beyond these rural areas.

In Maidel and elsewhere in Ilam, Maoists threatened to kill MNO activists who refused to join their movement, leading many MNO activists to flee the villages. Most of the MNO activists in Maidel left the village after the Maoists arrived in 2002, as Nar Bahadur Gurung told me when I met him in Kathmandu in 2003. He recalled that the Maoists gave him the ultimatum of joining their party, paying them a large sum of money or facing the consequences. Fearing for his life, he hid in the jungle for several weeks, finally escaping in a burlap bag in the back of a truck. He spent the next two years hiding in relatives' homes in Kathmandu and Kalimpong, India. In 2005, he was able to return to Maidel, according to Gopal Gurung. For reasons that are unclear, the Maoists were no longer threatening the MNO by January 2005. At that time, Gopal Gurung toured throughout Ilam and held MNO mass-meetings in Ilam bazaar and in several places in Jhapa district, in an effort to rebuild support for the MNO. Thus the Maoists were ultimately not successful in uprooting the MNO from Ilam.

Despite the conflicts that took place between the MNO and the Maoists at the village level, the MNO has maintained an ambivalent view of the Maoists. The MNO dismissed the Maoists' support for ethnic inequality as disingenuous. In his book *Mongolism-Bahunism-Maoism in Nepalese Politics* (*Nepālī Rājnitīmā Mongolbād- Bāhunbād- Māobād*), Gopal Gurung (2006) argued that the palace launched the Maoist movement to destroy the MNO, advancing a version of the ubiquitous conspiracy theories concerning the royal family in Nepali political discourse. In a conversation with me in 2005, he described the Maoists as yet another example of a political party led by high-caste Hindus that was using Mongols for their own benefit. He told me of a case in Jhapa where Mongols in the Maoists' army met with him and wanted to join the MNO, because they realized that there was *bāhunbād* (Bahun dominance) in that party. He believed that others would have the same realization and eventually come to the MNO.

Aside from these criticisms, the MNO interpreted the Maoists' rise to power as a positive development. The MNO praised the Maoists for their support of establishing a secular state and a federal republic. An MNO poster issued in late 2006, when the Maoists and other major parties were negotiating the interim constitution, proclaimed in bold letters, 'The Maoists' insistence on *loktantra* meaning a republic, secularism and a federal state is at the right time and the right place. This has the full support of the MNO' ('*Maobādiko loktantra arthāt ganatantra, dharma nirpeksha ra prāntiya sarkārko aḍān ṭhik samaya mā ra ṭhik ṭhaŭ mā chha. Esmā MNOko pūrna samarthan chha*'). In 2008, Gopal Gurung said that the MNO was grateful to the Maoists because they had removed the king and the old constitution.

The MNO in Kathmandu after 2006

After the second people's revolution of 2006 restored democracy and led to the end of the People's War, the MNO re-emerged in Kathmandu in a new form. A 'sister organization' of the MNO, the Mulbasi Mongol National Youth Assembly, or MMYA (*Mūlbāsi Mongol Rāstriya Yūwā Sabhā*) was founded by a group of three middle-aged men from three different ethnic groups who had recently come to Kathmandu from villages in eastern Nepal. These three men, Umesh Gurung, Deepak Magar and Resham Bahadur Tamang, met with Gopal Gurung and told him about their plans to establish the organization, but it remained distinct from the MNO.

While it may appear incongruous for middle-aged men to refer to the organization as a youth assembly, the term 'youth' represents the unrealized political aspirations of people rather than their biological age in Nepali political discourse, as Snellinger (forthcoming) argues. Before turning to the MNO, these men had been active in major political parties but none had become leaders. Umesh Gurung had been active in the Congress Party at the district level for decades, and Deepak Magar was involved in the student wing of the mainstream Communist Party (UML). Resham Bahadur Tamang had been a soldier in the Maoist's People's Liberation Army, leaving after peace was declared. They all told me that they had become frustrated with the high-caste Hindu leaders in these organizations, who would not allow them to rise up in the party structure, and with the lack of sincere attention to ethnic inequality within these parties.

The dramatic political changes of 2006 inspired a tremendous sense of political possibility in many people. Many of the goals that the MNO had long demanded became realities, such as the establishment of a secular state, a federal republic and plans for a new constitution. For these three men who founded the MMYA, these changes validated the MNO's ideology and made the party appear viable once again. The success of the Maoists also gave them a sense that a small party could create major changes. In the heady months after the 2006 movement, these men launched a campaign to publicize the MNO, its goals, and its early articulation of the ideas that were now forming the blueprint for a new Nepal. They published thousands of pamphlets and copies of Gopal Gurung's writings, creating a fifth edition of *Hidden Facts in Nepali Politics*, and spent long days distributing these materials on buses and street corners in Kathmandu.

Within several months, they had found a new collection of supporters: college students who had arrived from small towns and villages in eastern Nepal to study at Tribhuvan University or at smaller campuses in Kathmandu. None of these students who form the new cadre of MNO supporters belong to the middle-class in Kathmandu, as Liechty (2003) describes it; they do not come from families who own property in the city or hold professional jobs. Like the three leaders of the MMYA, many of these students were previously involved in other political parties, including the Maoists, and left these parties because they perceived ethnic discrimination to continue within them.

It is difficult to determine the number of people who belong to the MMYA. In the summer of 2006, Deepak Magar estimated that about 19 students are core activists and many more supporters are involved. In 2008, I observed crowds of 50 to 100 people at talk programs sponsored by the MMYA. A handful of young women who were graduate students were active in the MMYA, and attended and gave speeches at these events. One Tamang woman from Jhapa had family members who were long-time MNO supporters; another woman was completing her Master's degree in literature, and analyzing Gopal Gurung's writings in her thesis.

In the 1990s, MNO supporters in rural Ilam and Jhapa were mostly farmers and former soldiers, few of whom had graduated from high school or attended college. The MMYA in 2008 thus attracted a much different type of supporter to its ranks. These individuals and the new urban context made the MMYA's operating style much different from that of the MNO in the 1990s. Every member I met had a mobile phone and an email address, erasing the challenges of communication that the earlier activists in Ilam and Jhapa faced. Drawing on their education, the MMYA members increasingly used the internet to promote the party, posting speeches on a Nepali video website, and maintaining a blog. In August 2008, activists in this organization began publishing a weekly newspaper, the Mongol Vision National Weekly, and established a website to accompany it. MMYA programs took place in campus meeting rooms and bakery cafes, as well as in some large monasteries in Kathmandu, rather than in schoolyards or fields as they had in the 1990s. Unlike the MNO in the 1990s, the MMYA engaged in urban techniques of protest such as demonstrations, taking advantage of its presence in the city.

Many of these students who were studying at Tribhuvan University proposed to establish an MNO student organization on that campus, akin to the organizations that most major political parties have there. Gopal Gurung refused to allow this, however, saying that such a student organization could create splits in the party. He preferred the MMYA as it could include workers and others who were not students, thus enhancing party unity. The student activists tried to publicize the activities of the MMYA on campus to compete with the other political student organizations there.

The MMYA did not confine its activities to Kathmandu, but reached back to the village homes of its members. It held mass-meetings and rallies in Jiri and other towns in eastern Nepal. Several of the founding members of the MMYA were MNO candidates in the Constituent Assembly elections, and ran for positions from the home districts. They campaigned vigorously (see Figure C.1), and expanded people's awareness of the MNO and its message, but neither they nor any other MNO candidates won seats in these elections. This outcome did not dampen the efforts of the MMYA. They predicted that the Maoists would slowly lose their appeal and people would come to the MNO in time for the next elections, or the next revolution.

The MNO and MMYA are not just concerned with their performance in elections. As in the 1990s, the MNO has continued to contest the dominant terms of the indigenous nationalities movement, attacking both NEFIN as an organization and the very term 'indigenous nationalities'. The MNO's continued efforts to critically respond to NEFIN are intriguing because NEFIN and its member organizations are not political parties that are competing for votes with the MNO. These activities demonstrate that the MNO, with its sister organization the MMYA, acts as a social movement, concerned with shaping discourse and creating social change, as much as it does as a party. This dimension of the party and its relationship with NEFIN was evident in the celebrations of the International Indigenous Peoples' Day (*Viswa Ādivāsī Divas*) in August 2008.

In that year, NEFIN sponsored a massive celebration of this occasion in Kathmandu, established as a holiday by the UN in 1993 to promote its commitment

Figure C.1 MNO activists campaigning before Constituent Assembly elections.

to indigenous peoples. On August 8 and 9, thousands of people gathered in the national stadium in Kathmandu to watch different groups of indigenous nationalities perform songs and dances, and hear leaders of the indigenous nationalities movement, government dignitaries and Constituent Assembly members deliver speeches supporting ethnic federalism and the right to self-determination for indigenous nationalities. A joyous and colorful rally of hundreds of people kicked off the second day: many wore traditional dress, danced and played instruments, and carried signs demanding ethnic autonomy and the right to self-determination for their group. Groups sang songs proclaiming, 'We are indigenous nationalities (*ādivāsī janajāti*)'.

At the zenith of NEFIN's celebration, the MNO held a program on the opposite side of town to celebrate the same occasion, which it renamed *Mūlbāsi Diwas* instead of *Viswa Ādivāsī Diwas*. About 50 people gathered in a small conference room at Pashupati campus and listened to a dozen speeches by Gopal Gurung and other activists from the MNO and MMYA. The activists and audience were mainly young men who were college students in Kathmandu. In their speeches, they talked about the continuation of ethnic inequality despite the positive changes after 2006, and vowed to fight for the liberation of future generations. Many of the speeches also criticized the widespread use of the term *ādivāsī janajāti*, continuing the MNO's longstanding argument on this point; as one young Rai man said, 'the word *janajāti* makes us like those who have no home – nomads and gypsies; it is the opposite of indigenous. Indigenous means those who were originally in this country, from the beginning.' This was the first year that the MNO held such a program on International Indigenous Peoples' Day, and the main point seemed to be to respond to and critique the dominance of NEFIN.

Since 2006, the MNO has increased its opposition towards NEFIN and its member organizations. Gopal Gurung began to require all MNO activists to quit their membership in organizations like *Kirat Yakthung Chumlung*, and has thrown some MNO activists out of the party for their involvement in them. The MNO wrote letters to the international development organizations that have funded NEFIN and some of its member organizations, stating that their funding is going to 'nomads who have been swindling in the name of indigenous (*Mūlbāsi*) people'. The MNO warned them to cease their support of the indigenous nationalities or else the 'Mongol Liberation Army will not hesitate to take a strong step against nomad (*janajāti*) people.' Slogans on walls near Tribhuvan University declared in capital letters in English, 'DFID stop aid to Janjati [sic] (Gypsy People)' and 'Janjati [sic] are not indigenous, they are cheaters (MNO).'[2] These activities demonstrate that the MNO is attempting to draw greater public attention to its rejection of this term.

As part of its increased criticism of NEFIN, the MNO has heightened its attacks on the term *ādivāsī janajāti*, asserting that the term means 'nomad gypsies' instead of indigenous peoples, a definition that they claim is supported by the dictionary. A cartoon picture illustrates this new vehemence. It depicts a high-caste Hindu man, grotesque with bulging eyes and a long nose; his caste status is marked by his sacred thread and long strand of hair (*tuppi*) on his shaven head. His head is labeled Bahun, the arms labeled Chhetri, the stomach as Vaishya, the legs as Shudra and the feet as Janajāti. The cartoon thus depicts *janajātis* as the lowest part of the Hindu caste system, a position none of the indigenous nationalities would accept. The main caption reads, 'Those who call themselves the non-Hindu *Mūlbāsi* (indigenous) Mongols have the origins (*utpatti*) of this country, so who are those who are called *ādivāsī janajāti*?' The racialized portrait attempts to incite hatred of high-caste Hindus and to discredit the term *janajāti*. It is disseminated through pamphlets and reproduced in every edition of the *Mongol Vision* newspaper.

Beyond this attack on NEFIN and the *ādivāsī janajāti* label, the MNO does not make the substantive demands for change that it once did. This is because many of its earlier demands have been incorporated into the state, though not through the efforts of the MNO. The MNO continues to try to make these types of arguments but the issues are more minor now: they seek to root out those remaining symbols of Hinduism in the state, call to create a new national flag (claiming that the current design symbolizes the dominance of Hinduism over Buddhism), and establish a new national animal, the musk deer, rather than the cow. Given the post-2006 state's willingness to change the symbols of the nation, as illustrated by the new national anthem that makes no references to the king, it would not be surprising if these changes are also adopted.

Given the success of NEFIN in defining the dominant terms of the movement, and the MNO's repeated electoral defeat at the national level during 18 years of elections, one might expect the MNO to have disbanded by now. Yet, the MNO continues to pursue its elusive goal of gaining political power, and, as of 2009, the party is attracting new supporters through the MMYA. Like millenarian movements that persist long after the predictions of their leaders fail to come true (Dein 1997), the inability of the MNO to win elections has not led to the dissolution of the party. For some members, the MNO's failure to win elections provides evidence of the continuation of high-caste Hindu dominance of the political system; only parties that have Bahuns and Chhetris at the helm can win, they say. The state's eventual adoption of many of the demands that the MNO first articulated in 1990 has led others to view Gopal Gurung as a prophet of sorts; as one man told me, 'The things that he says really come true.' These people say that if Gopal Gurung could foresee the abolition of the monarchy, his conviction that the MNO will come into power one day might also be accurate. This turn of events thus reinforced their support for the party.

The discourses and practice of democracy in the margins

To conclude, I return to the MNO in the 1990s, the main focus of the previous chapters. Here, I consider what the exploration of the MNO in this book reveals about how people in the margins perceived, experienced and participated in the process of democratization in Nepal in the 1990s.

When people demand democracy, their ultimate goal is not the establishment of democratic political institutions. Rather, people hope that the adoption of those political institutions will transform society and achieve justice, freedom, equality and economic progress. When speaking of democracy, people in Nepal, and elsewhere in the world, imagine this form of governance to be a magic bullet that will transform society into a utopia.

Discourses of democracy have varied during different political contexts and when expressed by different political actors in Nepal. In the people's movement in 1990, democracy meant *prajātantra*, primarily an end to the Panchayat system and the establishment of a multi-party system (*bahudal*) in which people could voice their political opinions, form organizations and influence state policies and practices. Democracy was envisioned as a state of freedom, in which people could choose leaders based on political ideas. In the space created by that new multi-party system in the 1990s, the social movements of marginalized peoples insisted that democracy should also entail ethnic equality and an end to the high-caste Hindu dominance of the state. The Maoists launched the People's war to establish a 'new democracy' that would end class inequality, feudalism, and the monarchy. In the second people's movement of 2006, the call was for a new form of democracy called *loktantra* or *ganatantra*, the end of the monarchy. By 2008, the indigenous nationalities movement's ideas of democracy were centered on the right to self-determination and ethnic territorial autonomy. As these examples illustrate, when each change in the state failed to transform society, people called for new versions of democracy. The idea has persisted that, if only power could truly be transferred to the people or, more specifically to the right people – be they the poor, the ethnic minorities or the low castes – a utopian society would finally emerge.

Political actors and theorists tend to view democratization as taking place in a series of stages, and represent the failure of democracy to meet the ideals of the concept as part of the transition process (Carothers 2002). Yet gaps between the ideals and practices of democracy exist everywhere. The democratization of the formal political system is often partial, and does not mean that democratization of society will follow suit. Democracy everywhere is disjunctive and has never existed in its ideal form, as Caldeira and Holston (1999) argue. What is important in studying democratization, then, is not determining how close or far a political system is from a set of ideals, but examining the specific disjunctures in that political system, how people perceive them, and their effects on political action.

While there are many disjunctive features of democracy in Nepal, I focus here on how MNO supporters experienced and perceived disjunctures between the discourse and practice of democracy in the 1990s. For supporters of the MNO, the new democratic system offered practical and discursive possibilities but also presented practical limitations for creating political change in rural Nepal. Foremost amongst these possibilities was that the MNO could operate openly as a political party. MNO activists could hold public gatherings, give radical speeches in public and publish their ideas without being jailed. Political party affiliation was driven, at least partially, by people's understanding of parties as representing sets of ideas and it became a meaningful form of identity.

People viewed democracy as giving them the freedom to assert cultural differences, for example by following a religion other than Hinduism. Democracy provided the space in which the MNO could question hegemonic cultural practices that were emblematic of the nation and part of people's everyday realities, such as the *vikram sambat* calendar, Nepali language, and Hindu religion and holidays. The MNO argued that to continue these practices was tantamount to upholding the Hindu dominance of the state. While other ethnic organizations were equally as involved as the MNO in bringing about these cultural changes, the MNO emphasized political interpretations of culture, enunciating the connection between asserting cultural difference from the dominant group and gaining political power.

Democracy enabled the MNO to encourage people to adopt a new Mongol identity. As many people recalled, they would not have been allowed to call themselves Mongol during the Panchayat era. The MNO defined Mongols as a race, drawing on a social science framework, and as a community with a shared history of conquest and oppression by high-caste Hindus, narrated in their reinterpretations of Tihar and Dasain myths. The assertion of a Mongol identity was a political act that represented the emergence of a new political subjectivity. Mongols were political actors committed to achieving ethnic equality for Mongols by gaining political power.

While the discourses of democracy inspired the MNO to demand changes, and greater political freedom allowed the party to operate and encourage people to make cultural changes, the party's ability to gain power and affect policies was limited by the structures of the political system. From the MNO's perspective, the ideal of democracy as offering total political freedom was not upheld because of the restrictions on ethnic political parties in the 1990 constitution. This prevented the MNO from gaining registration from the Election Commission; thus MNO candidates had to run in elections as independent candidates, resorting to the Panchayat era strategy used by candidates who secretly represented political parties then. Although the MNO could operate openly, many activists feared negative repercussions from the state, and thus concealed information such as central committee membership and district-level meeting times.

The first-past-the-post electoral system also worked to the disadvantage of small parties like the MNO, especially in national elections. It was difficult for upstart parties to gain representation at the national level and even when they did gain seats in parliament, the role of minor parties in the opposition was negligible. The MNO could only gain representation at the village level.

In village-level elections, MNO candidates campaigned primarily as individuals rather than as representatives of a party that offered a particular critical view of the state and society. People would only vote for candidates they knew and trusted, regardless of their party affiliation. This personalized dimension of politics worked in the MNO's favor at village level, as people voted for the influential individuals who joined the MNO, enabling the party to gain seats. While people believed and understood that party ideology should play a role in elections, politics remained highly personalized.

Due to the centralized structure of the state, there was little autonomy for village governments to collect resources, or initiate or implement plans. Thus the MNO could do little to further its goals through running the village government. Ironically, MNO representatives on village governments became caretakers of a state that they sharply denounced. As members of a radical ethnic party, MNO representatives were hampered in their ability to secure resources for the village from the district-level government, whose representatives were all from major political parties. Personal and party ties were central in forging connections between levels of the government.

The disjunctive element of democracy that MNO supporters focused on the most was the gap between the discursive emphasis on the equality of all citizens in democracy versus the continuation of ethnic inequality in the new political system. Despite the redefinition of Nepal as a multicultural nation in the 1990 constitution, the state remained dominated by high-caste Hindus. This fact led MNO supporters to argue that democracy had not really arrived and that democracy would require state institutions to become more equitable, accessible to all citizens and more representative of the diverse population. People identified the problems with the workings of the state – such as corruption, inefficiency, centralization and lack of justice – as problems of ethnic inequality. People assumed if high-caste Hindu state representatives were replaced with Mongols that the state would become more democratic in its operations.

Despite these disjunctive elements of democracy, MNO supporters continued to espouse democracy as an ideal. In addition, the MNO has continued to participate in elections and play the rules of the democratic game. Although the

MNO threatened to stage a revolution if it did not gain control of the government through elections, it has not engaged in any political violence or relied on coercive means of protest. This may not hold true in the future.

The MNO and the possibility of violence

Compared with the Maoist party, the MNO's adherence to peaceful methods of political mobilization is striking. The MNO was also far less successful in mobilizing support and gaining power than the Maoists. Unfortunately, it is likely that the MNO would have gained more power and votes if it had adopted violent tactics.

Violence has played a central role in major political transformations in Nepal and there have been many small-scale incidents of political violence in the country's history (Lawoti 2007a). However, violence became a more widespread feature of political culture and discourse during the era of democracy, especially during and after the People's War. The success of the Maoist insurgency in curtailing the operations of the state throughout rural Nepal and thus gaining political power heightened the appeal of violent political tactics for many political actors. The number of armed or semi-armed groups escalated dramatically after 2006, from about 12 in 2006 to about 69 in 2009, according to one report (Pathak and Uprety 2009). All of these armed groups represent different identity groups and advance claims to territory; most are related to the Madhesi movement, while others represent various indigenous nationalities groups, including the Limbu and Tharu groups that have received some media attention.

Disjunctive features of democracy have exacerbated violence in Nepal. Given the continuation of the centralized structure of the Nepali state after 1990, it was extremely difficult for small parties to gain power through democratic practices and to influence the government. In 1991, several small Maoist parties that eventually became the CPN–Maoist formed the United People's Front Nepal (UPFN) to run in the elections. Although the UPFN gained nine seats in the parliament, making them the third-largest party, they were excluded from the government and had little opportunity to influence the decision-making process, due to the majoritarian political structures in place (Lawoti 2005: 46–54). The party also won many seats at the village level, but was unable to create changes through local bodies, due to the lack of autonomy of these village governments (p. 53). Lawoti argues that the exclusion of the UPFN from the process of governance acted as a catalyst for the Maoists to launch the People's War (p. 56). When the formal political system appears to be an ineffective means of gaining power, political groups will continue to employ violence.

In this context, it is possible that the MNO could adopt violent tactics in the near future. First, even though the MNO was finally registered in 2008, the party has yet to gain electoral success in national elections. This could lead the MNO to abandon the formal political system, as it has long threatened to do. Second, the rhetoric of violence in the MNO speeches and materials has become increasingly prominent. Sometime in the early 2000s, the MNO established a Mongol

Liberation Army (*Mongol Muktī Senā*), which publishes and signs communiqués along with the MMYA, but has not yet taken any violent action. The party has long legitimized the use of violence for political ends in its speeches and cultural representations, such as the songs described in Chapter 5, and it continues to do so. New party slogans such as 'Born as a Mongol, survive as a Mongol, die as a Mongol' exhort party workers to be willing to die for the MNO. These representations may encourage some members of the MNO to engage in violence. Furthermore, ethnic conflicts that are framed as racial conflicts may be more likely to become violent than those that are not based on race, as one analysis of the 1994 genocide in Rwanda suggests (Mamdani 2001).

I am reluctant to end this book by pondering the possibility that the MNO will engage in violence because of the existing assumption that ethnic politics are incompatible with democracy and cause violence. Yet democracy itself is a far more complex, multi-faceted political project than we often assume. Democracy is disjunctive and can take a variety of unexpected and unintended forms, which can include the presence of violence.

Notes

Introduction: democracy and ethnic politics

1 These restrictions are stated in articles 112(3) and 113(3) in Nepal's 1990 constitution.
2 Other districts where the MNO had district committees in the 1990s were: Panchthar, just north of Ilam district; Morang, just to the west of Jhapa and Ilam; Dolakha and Sindhuli, east of Kathmandu; Nuwakot, north of Kathmandu; and Rupandehi, in the Tarai, west of Kathmandu.
3 Van Cott also notes that ethnic parties in Latin America expanded political discourse, 'offering a critique of the state and regime that otherwise might not be represented in ethnic politics' (2005: 229). However, she does not analyze how ethnic parties communicate their messages and how they spur public debate on these issues.
4 Before 2008, only the *Nepal Sadbhavana Party*, which represents Madhesis, an ethnic category based on a Tarai regional identity, won seats in Parliament.

1 Democratization, ethnic diversity and inequality in Nepal

1 According to the official story of this event, Dipendra was outraged with his family for refusing to allow him to marry the girl he loved. Many people in Nepal dispute this, and believe that the murder was orchestrated by Gyandendra, who sought the throne for himself (Riaz and Basu 2007: 60–62).
2 The practices of census takers also changed after 1990. Before that time, census takers were instructed to assign all individuals from many caste and ethnic groups to the Hindu category. This had the effect of increasing the percentage of Hindus in the census (Gurung 1998: 94).
3 One theory holds that the Shahs' ancestors fled to Nepal in the twelfth century to escape Mughal invasions. However, some sources assert that it is more likely that the Shahs were part of the Khas people, who were living in western Nepal as early as the second millennium BC (Bista 1967). Even though the Shahs had held the throne since the second half of the eighteenth century, the king's power was severely curtailed during the Rana rule. The monarchy was abolished in 2008.
4 Mahendra Lawoti (personal communication) explains that there are several meanings of the term Khas. Whelpton (2005) defines Khas as equivalent to Chhetri, while Neupane (2000) uses the term to refer to all high-caste Hindus. Dor Bahadur Bista (1996) used Khas to refer more specifically to an ethnic group Karnali district. Some students at Tribhhuvan University in Kathmandu set up an organization to assert their identity as Khas and to claim that Khas should belong to the indigenous nationalities category.
5 However, the relationship between Newars and the state was largely ambivalent, since Newar kingdoms were also conquered by the Shahs. Furthermore, although many Newars have been part of the ruling elite, others have not. Newars are included within the category of indigenous nationalities.

6 Wealthy Brahmans from newly-annexed territories thus received land grants in exchange for giving loans to the Gorkha government, as well as for acting as envoys for the Gorkhas by negotiating with political elites of newly-conquered territories (Pradhan 1991: 103). Recipients of these *birta* land grants were exempt from paying regular taxes to the state and had the right to rent out their land and tax those who cultivated it (Regmi 1971: 43).

7 Through the world wars, people from these ethnic communities were occasionally forced to join foreign armies (Des Chene 1993: 71).

2 The indigenous nationalities movement in post-1990 Nepal

1 Some of the organizations formed include: *Tamang Bhasa Sanskriti Bikas Samiti, Tamu Dhi Pariwar* (a Gurung organization), *Langhali Pariwar Sangh* (a Magar organization), *Tharu Kalyan Samaj* and *Rai Limbu Samaj Sudhar* (Tamang 1987).

2 National Indigenous Women Federation-Nepal:, www.niwf.org.np/index.html.

3 These organizations have become more political. A federation of indigenous women's organizations, the *Adivāsi Janajāti Mahila Loktantrik Manch* (Indigenous Nationalities Women Democratic Forum), was established in July 2006 with the express purpose of ensuring that indigenous women were represented in the process of drafting a new constitution (Tamang 2006 [2063 v.s.]).

4 Khopangi's loss of legitimacy was sealed when he took Dasain *tika* (a mark on the forehead made of a rice, yogurt and red powder mixture, given along with blessings by high-status people to those of a lower status) from the king along with all of the other ministers, after he had urged indigenous nationalities to boycott the holiday (Khapangi 2060 v.s.; Magar 2060 v.s.; Thapa 2059 v.s.).

5 Since MNO candidates are listed as independent in the official election data, election results for MNO candidates were ascertained by combining information about candidates' names from MNO leaders with official data from the Election Commission. The number of seats on each VDC was 11 in 1992, increasing to 47 in 1997.

6 The *Janajāti Mahasangh* published Nepali translations of the Charter of the Indigenous-Tribal Peoples of the Tropical Forests. *Nepal Tamang Ghedung*, a Tamang organization belonging to the *Janajāti Mahasangh*, published Nepali and Tamang translations of the Universal Declaration of the Rights of Indigenous Peoples.

7 A worksheet used at Budhanilkantha school in the Kathmandu Valley in the 1990s and an English-language textbook (Timothy and Uprety 1995) show that the concept of race is taught in Nepal.

8 The MNO was not the first political organization to employ the term Mongol. During the 1979–1980 referendum on whether or not to retain the Panchayat system, posters appeared in Kathmandu calling for '...the people of "Mongol *jāti*" to shake off the domination of the "Hindus"' (Sharma 1986).

3 Between political party and social movement

1 Gurung recounted that he was interested in writing from a young age. As a schoolboy, he wrote poems which were published in newspapers in India that were associated with organizations that his father took part in, such as the All-India Gorkha League's *Gorkha* paper and the Communist Party-affiliated *Agradut*.

2 In summarizing the book here, I cite the fourth edition, the English translation, which I have carefully compared with the Nepali-language editions.

3 The State Offense Act was first promulgated in the 1880s during the Rana era and defined crimes against the state as crimes against the king, any members of the royal family or the family of the Rana rulers, any attempt to overthrow the Rana government or any acts of treason (Vaidya 1985: 195–207).

4 After Gopal Gurung was released from jail, he re-opened the *New Light* newspaper in 1991 for a short time, but closed it when he decided to devote more time to politics.

5 Gopal Gurung argued that Article 113(2) in the 1990 constitution, which forbids the Election Commission to register ethnic-based political parties, should not apply to his party because, in fact, the entire constitution did not apply to Mongols. The constitution stated that Nepal is a Hindu state, and since Mongols are not Hindus they should not be governed by it, he argued.

6 The composition of the MNO village committees thus directly followed the format of political representation in the village-level government, the Village Development Corporation, as it was at that time.

7 Gopal Gurung had initially envisioned that there would be formal wings (*morcha*) of the party representing different interest groups: students, youths, women and ex-servicemen.

8 For example, Sita Ram Tamang lists the women's independence or matriarchy as one of the defining features of *janajāti* groups (1987: 5). Gellner (1991) looks at this discourse with regard to Newars.

9 Even where telephone service existed, it did not always ensure an easy means of communication. To contact Kiran via the one public telephone in Sukrabare, I had to request the people working at the telephone office to send a messenger to tell Kiran to come to the phone, and then call back 15 minutes or so later, in hopes of getting to speak with him. If the people working at the phone office were so inclined, they told one of the many children who often hung around the office to walk out to Kiran's house or fields and deliver the message. Kiran had to pay the child a few rupees for the service. Kiran said that he rarely received phone calls from MNO activists because the phone office workers, who supported other parties, knew the callers were political activists and refused to send Kiran the messages.

4 Democratization and local politics: an MNO village government

1 Perhaps because of the highly political nature of my topic, I had limited options for living arrangements in the village. Baje's family was one of the few who offered me a place to live when I first arrived. It turned out to be an excellent, if hardly neutral, location from which to view local political operations. The word *thulo* in Nepali carries both the meanings 'big' and 'important'.

2 The game played on a carom board is similar to billiards. Using their fingers, people flick plastic disks across the smooth surface of the board, in hopes of landing them into one of the pockets at the four corners of the board.

3 See Borgstrom (1980) for an extensive discussion of factional politics in a village in the Kathmandu Valley during the Panchayat era.

4 *Matwāli* is an older term that refers to the groups of peoples who the MNO calls Mongols, as discussed in Chapter 2.

5 'Our own heartbeats': the politics of culture in the MNO

1 People also often included script (*lipi*) right after language (*bhasa*) in this litany, pointing to the importance of promoting indigenous nationalities' languages as written languages that could be used as a medium of education or to run the affairs of a state.

2 The *vikram sambat* calendar is not used throughout India. It is used mainly in North India, except for in Bengal, and in Gujarat.

3 A similar festival, Deepawali or Diwali, is celebrated in India at the same time of year but there are many differences between the two festivals. In India, the festival is linked to the Ramayana epic, and commemorates Ram's return to his kingdom after being in exile. It is in the worship of the goddess of wealth Laxmi that Tihar shares the most with Deepawali.

4 Falgunanda's birthday is on the twenty-fifth day of the Nepali month of Kartik, whereas the dates of Tihar are determined according to the phases of the moon; thus, while the festival falls in Kartik, the precise dates change every year.
5 While Satya Hangma framed this change in religious practice as representing a return to old Limbu ways, the call to abstain from meat and alcohol was clearly influenced by Hindu religious practice (Jones and Jones 1976: 45).

6 Becoming not-Hindu: religious and political transformations

1 At that time, this organization was not affiliated with any of the national-level Gurung organizations. After 1990, the founders of the *gumbā* attempted to formally associate this organization with the Nepal-wide organization, *Tamu Chomj Dhim*. However, Gurungs in the MNO contested this affiliation.
2 Bhim Bahadur Gurung was heavily involved in Communist Party activities throughout the Panchayat era and was arrested and tortured after his participation in the violent Farmer's Movement, which took place in Ilam in 1979 (2036 v.s.).
3 At the CDO's office in Ilam, I requested that he let me read any correspondence between people in Maidel and this office for the years during this event. While he agreed, office workers there could not locate any documents. The village and district police were also unable to locate any records. The Gurung men had handed their letters over to a district-level representative but they were never returned.
4 A Panchayat era Nepali school textbook drawing represents different ethnic groups' varying proximity to the central national identity: Gurungs are portrayed as closer to the high-caste Hindu national norm than Sherpas (Pigg 1992).
5 These village elites may have intended to enhance their own power, though, as Sherpa elites saw building Buddhist monasteries as a way to boost their power and prestige (Ortner 1989).
6 After one Dasami *pujā*, Jiban explained to me and the rest of the crowd that the celebration of Dasami commemorates the tenth day after the Buddha's birth, when his *karma* (fruits acquired from deeds in his past life) was finished. It was a particularly effective time to conduct a *pujā*, Jiban explained, because, 'if we light only one lamp on Dasami, it is equal to lighting lamps for 108 days, or if we burn one stick of incense, it is equal to 108 sticks of incense.'
7 For a further discussion of the Dasain boycott, see Hangen (2005).

Conclusion: ethnic parties in a new Nepal: the constituent assembly elections and the future of the MNO

1 The estimate of internally displaced people is based on 'The Internally Displaced Persons: Current Status', available at www.un.org.np/reports/OCHA/2006/IDP-thematic-report/2006–9-7-OCHA-Nepal-Thematic-Report-IDPs.pdf.
2 I thank David Gellner for forwarding photographs of these slogans to me.

References

Adams, Vincanne (1998) *Doctors for Democracy: Health Professionals in the Nepal Revolution*. New York: Cambridge University Press.

Alvarez, Sonia, Evelina Dagnino and Arturo Escobar (1998) Introduction: The cultural and the political in Latin American social movements, in *Cultures of Politics/Politics of Cultures*, S. Alvarez, E. Dagnino and A. Escobar (eds) Boulder, CO: Westview Press.

Anderson, Benedict (1991 [1983]) *Imagined Communities*. New York: Verso.

Appadurai, Arjun (2002) Deep democracy: urban governmentality and the horizon of politics. *Public Culture* 14(1): 21–47.

Aretxaga, Begona (1997) *Shattering Silence*. Princeton, NJ: Princeton University Press.

Baral, Lok Raj (2005) Democracy and elections: trajectories of political development, in *Election and Governance in Nepal*, L. R. Baral (ed.). New Delhi: Manohar, pp. 25–74.

Bennett, Lynn (1983) *Dangerous Wives and Sacred Sisters: Social and Symbolic Roles*. New York: Columbia University Press.

Bhabha, Homi (1990) DissemiNation: time, narrative, and the margins of the modern nation, in *Nation and Narration*, H. Bhabha (ed.). New York: Routledge, pp. 291–322.

Bhattachan, Krishna (1995) Ethnopolitics and ethnodevelopment: an emerging paradigm in Nepal, in *State, Leadership and Politics in Nepal*, D. Kumar (ed.). Kathmandu: Center for Nepal and Asian Studies, Tribhuvan University, pp. 124–147.

Bista, Dor Bahadur (1967) *Peoples of Nepal*. Kathmandu: Ministry of Information and Broadcasting, HMG.

Blaikie, Piers, John Cameron and David Seddon (1980) *Nepal in Crisis: Growth and Stagnation at the Periphery*. New York: Oxford University Press.

Boas, Franz (1938) Race, in *General Anthropology*, F. Boas (ed.). New York: D.C. Heath and Company, pp. 95–123.

Borgstrom, Bengt-Erik (1980) *The Patron and the Panca: Village Values and Pancayat Democracy in Nepal*. New Delhi: Vikas Publishing House.

Burghart, Richard (1996a) Cultural collusion in ethnography: the religious tolerance of Hindus, in *The Conditions of Listening: Essays on Religion, History and Politics in South Asia*. C. J. Fuller and J. Spencer (eds). Delhi: Oxford University Press, pp. 278–299.

Burghart, Richard (1996b) The category 'Hindu' in the political discourse of Nepal, in *The Conditions of Listening: Essays on Religion, History and Politics in South Asia*, C. J. Fuller and J. Spencer (eds). Delhi: Oxford University Press, pp. 261–277.

Burghart, Richard (1996c) The conditions of listening: the everyday experience of politics in Nepal, in *The Conditions of Listening: Essays on Religion, History and Politics in South Asia*, C. J. Fuller and J. Spencer (eds). Delhi: Oxford University Press, pp. 300–318.

Caldeira, Teresa and James Holston (1999) Democracy and violence in Brazil. *Comparative Studies in Society and History* 41(4): 691–729.

Campbell, Benjamin (1997) Heavy loads of Tamang Identity, in *Nationalism and Ethnicity in a Hindu Kingdom: The Politics of Culture in Contemporary Nepal*, D. Gellner, J. Pfaff-Czarnecka and J. Whelpton (eds). Amsterdam: Harwood Academic Publishers, pp. 205–235.

Caplan, Lionel (1970) *Land and Social Change in East Nepal*. London: Routledge and Kegan Paul.

Caplan, Lionel (1975) *Administration and Politics in a Nepalese Town*. London: Oxford University Press.

Caplan, Lionel (1995) *Warrior Gentlemen: 'Gurkhas' in the Western Imagination*. Providence: Berghahn Books.

Carothers, Thomas (2002) The End of the Transition Paradigm. *Journal of Democracy* 13(1): 5–21.

Chandra, Kanchan (2004) *Why Ethnic Parties Succeed: Patronage and Head Counts in India*. New York: Cambridge University Press.

Chatterji, Suniti Kumar (1974 [1951]) *Kirata-Jana-Kriti*. Calcutta: The Asiatic Society.

Chemjong, Iman Sing (1967) *History and Culture of the Kirat People*. Kathmandu: Pushpa Ratna Sagar.

Cole, Sonia (1965) *Races of Man*. London: British Museum of Natural History.

Coles, Kimberley (2004) election day: the construction of democracy through technique. *Cultural Anthropology* 19(4): 551–580.

Comaroff, Jean and John Comaroff (1991) *Of Revelation and Revolution: Christianity, Colonialism, and Consciousness in South Africa*. Chicago, IL: University of Chicago Press.

Connerton, Paul (1989) *How Societies Remember*. New York: Cambridge University Press.

Dahl, Robert (1971) *Polyarchy: Participation and Opposition*. New Haven: Yale University Press.

Das, Veena and Deborah Poole (2004) The state and its margins, in *Anthropology in the Margins of the State*, V. Das and D. Poole (eds). Sante Fe: School of American Research, pp. 2–32.

De Sales, Anne (2002) The Kham Magar country: between ethnic claims and Maoism, in *Resistance and the State: Nepalese Experiences*, D. Gellner (ed.). New Delhi: Social Science Press, pp. 326–357.

Dein, Simon (1997) Lubavitch: a contemporary messianic movement. *Journal of Contemporary Religion* 12(2): 191–204.

Des Chene, Mary (1993) Soldiers, sovereignty and silences: Gorkhas as diplomatic currency. *South Asia Bulletin* 8(1/2): 67–80.

Des Chene, Mary (1996) Ethnography in the *Janajāti-yug*: lessons from reading *Rodhi* and other Tamu writings. *Studies in Nepali History and Society* 1(1): 97–162.

Devkota, Grishmabahadur (2036 v.s.) *Nepalko Rajnitik Darpan* [*Nepal's Political Image*]. Kathmandu: Arjan Bahadur Devkota.

Diamond, Larry (1996) Toward democratic consolidation, in *The Global Resurgence of Democracy*, L. Diamond and M. F. Plattner (eds). Baltimore, MD: The Johns Hopkins University Press, pp. 227–240

Dirks, Nicholas (2001) *Castes of Mind*. Princeton, NJ: Princeton University Press.

English, Richard (1985) Himalayan state formation and the impact of British rule in the nineteenth century. *Mountain Research and Development* 5(1): 61–78.

Eriksen, Thomas (1993) *Ethnicity and Nationalism: Anthropological Perspectives*. London: Pluto Press.

Fisher, William (1993) Nationalism and the Janajāti. *Himal* 6(2): 11–14.

Fisher, William (2001) *Fluid Boundaries: Forming and Transforming Identity in Nepal*. New York: Columbia University Press.

Frechette, Ann (2007) Democracy and democratization among Tibetans in exile. *Journal of Asian Studies* 66(1): 97–127.

Gaenszle, Martin (1997) Changing concepts of ethnic identity among the Mehwang Rai, in *Nationalism and Ethnicity in a Hindu Kingdom: The Politics of Culture in Contemporary Nepal*, D. Gellner, J. Pfaff-Czarnecka and J. Whelpton (eds). Amsterdam: Harwood Academic Publishers, pp. 351–373.

Gaige, Frederick (1975) *Regionalism and National Unity in Nepal*. Berkeley: University of California Press.

Ganguly, Sumit and Brian Shoup (2005) Nepal: between dictatorship and anarchy. *Journal of Democracy* 16(4): 129–143.

Gellner, David (1986) Language, caste, religion and territory: Newar identity ancient and modern. *European Journal of Sociology* 27: 102–148.

Gellner, David (1991) Hinduism, tribalism and the position of women: the problem of Newar identity. *Man*, New Series 26: 105–125.

Gellner, David (1997) Caste communalism and communism: Newars and the Nepalese state, in *Nationalism and Ethnicity in a Hindu Kingdom*, D. Gellner, J. Pfaff-Czarnecka and J. Whelpton (eds). Amsterdam: Harwood Academic Publishers, pp. 151–184.

Gellner, David (2002) Introduction: Transformations of the Nepalese state, in *Resistance and the State: Nepalese Experiences*, D. Gellner (ed.). New Delhi: Social Science Press, pp. 1–30.

Gellner, David and Krishna Hachhethu (2008) *Local Democracy in South Asia: Microprocesses of Democratization in Nepal and its Neighbours*. New Delhi: Sage.

Gellner, David and Mrigendra Bahadur Karki (2008) Democracy and ethnic organizations in Nepal, in *Local Democracy in South Asia: The Micropolitics of Democratization in Nepal and its Neighbours*, D. Gellner and K. Hachhethu (eds). New Delhi: Sage, pp. 105–127.

Gellner, David and Sara LeVine (2005) *Rebuilding Buddhism: The Theravada Movement in Twentieth-century Nepal*. Cambridge, MA: Harvard University Press.

Goldman, Marcio (2001) An ethnographic theory of democracy: politics from the viewpoint of Ilheus's black movement (Bahia, Brazil). *Ethnos* 66(2): 157–180.

Grandin, Ingemar (1996) 'To Change the Face of this Country': Nepalese progressive songs under Pancayat democracy. *Journal of South Asian Literature* 29(1): 175–189.

Greenhouse, Carol J. and Davydd J. Greenwood (1998) Introduction: The ethnography of democracy and difference, in *Democracy and Ethnography: Constructing Identities in Multicultural Liberal States*, C. J. Greenhouse (ed.). Albany: SUNY Press, pp. 1–24.

Guneratne, Arjun (2002) *Many Tongues, One People: The Making of Tharu Identity in Nepal*. Ithaca, NY: Cornell University Press.

Gurung, Amar Bahadur (2039 v.s.) Samsamayik Samajma Gurung Kalyan Sanghko Bhumika [The role of the Gurung Kalyan organization in contemporary society]. *Tamu* 2(2): 1–4.

Gurung, Gopal (1994) *Hidden Facts in Nepalese Politics*. B. D. Rai, transl. Kathmandu.

Gurung, Gopal (2006) *Nepali Rajnitima Mongolbad- Bahunbad-Maobad* (Mongolism, Bahunism and Maoism in Nepali Politics). Kathmandu: Prem Jimba.

Gurung, Gopal (n.d.) *Mongol National Organizationko Ghosana-Patra (Samsodhit Samskaran)*. Kathmandu: Mongol National Organization Kendriya Sabha.

Gurung, Harka (1997) State and society in Nepal, in *Nationalism and Ethnicity in a Hindu Kingdom*, D. Gellner, J. Pfaff-Czarnecka and J. Whelpton (eds). Amsterdam: Harwood Academic Publishers, pp. 495–532.

Gurung, Harka (1998) *Nepal Social Demography and Expressions*. Kathmandu: New Era.

Gurung, Harka (2003) *Social Demography of Nepal: Census 2001*. Lalitpur, Nepal: Himal Books.

Gutmann, Amy (2003) *Identity in Democracy*. Princeton, NJ: Princeton University Press.

Gutmann, Matthew (2002) *The Romance of Democracy: Compliant Defiance in Contemporary Mexico*. Berkeley: University of California Press.

Hachhethu, Krishna (2002a) *Party Building in Nepal: Organization, Leadership and People*. Kathmandu: Mandala Book Point.

Hachhethu, Krishna (2002b) Political parties and the state, in *Resistance and the State: Nepalese Experiences*, D. Gellner (ed.). New Delhi: Social Science Press, pp. 133–176.

Hachhethu, Krishna (2005) Political parties and elections, in *Election and Governance in Nepal*, L. R. Baral (ed.). New Delhi: Manohar, pp. 156–196.

Hachhethu, Krishna (2008) Local democracy and political parties in Nepal: a case study of Dhanusha district, in *Local Democracy in South Asia: Microprocesses of Democratization in Nepal and its Neighbours*, D. Gellner and K. Hachhethu (eds). New Delhi: Sage, pp. 45–70.

Hall, Stuart (1985) Signification, representation, ideology: Althusser and post-structuralist debates. *Critical Studies in Mass Communication* 2(2): 91–114.

Hangen, Susan (2001) Debating democracy at the margins: the Mongol National Organization in Nepal. *Himalayan Research Bulletin* XXI: 25–28.

Hangen, Susan (2005) Boycotting Dasain: history, memory and ethnic politics in Nepal. *Studies in Nepali History and Society* 10(1): 105–133.

Handler, Richard (1988) *Nationalism and the Politics of Culture in Quebec*. Madison: University of Wisconsin Press.

Hansen, Thomas Blom (1999) *The Saffron Wave: Democracy and Hindu Nationalism in Modern India*. Princeton, NJ: Princeton University Press.

Held, David (1996) *Models of Democracy*. Stanford, CA: Stanford University Press.

Herzog, Hanna (1987) Minor parties: the relevancy perspective. *Comparative Politics* 19(3): 317–329.

HMG (His Majesty's Government of Nepal) (1971) *The National Education System Plan for 1971–1976*. Kathmandu: Ministry of Education.

HMG (1990) *The Constitution of the Kingdom of Nepal 2047*. Kathmandu: Law Books Management Board.

Hobsbawm, Eric and Terence Ranger (1983) *The Invention of Tradition*. New York: Cambridge University Press.

Hodgson, Brian H. (1874) *Essays on the Languages, Literature and Religion of Nepal and Tibet*. London: Trubner and Company.

Hofer, Andras (1979) The caste hierarchy and the state in Nepal: a study of the Muluki Ain of 1854. *Khumbu Himal* 13(2): 31–238.

Hoftun, Martin, William Raeper and John Whelpton (1999) *People, Politics and Ideology: Democracy and Social Change in Nepal*. Kathmandu: Mandala Book Point.

Holmberg, David (1989) *Order in Paradox: Myth, Ritual, and Exchange Among Nepal's Tamang.* Ithaca, NY: Cornell University Press.

Holmberg, David, Kathryn March and Suryaman Tamang (1999) Local production/local knowledge: forced labour from below. *Studies in Nepali History and Society* 4(1): 5–64.

Horowitz, Donald (1985) *Ethnic Groups in Conflict.* Berkeley: University of California Press.

Hutt, Michael (1994) Drafting the 1990 constitution, in *Nepal in the Nineties: Versions of the Past, Visions of the Future,* M. Hutt (ed.). Delhi: Oxford University Press, pp. 28–47.

Hutt, Michael (2004) *Himalayan People's War: Nepal's Maoist Rebellion.* Bloomington and Indianapolis: Indiana University Press.

Ignatowski, Claire (2004) Multipartyism and nostalgia for the unified past: discourses of democracy in a dance association in Cameroon. *Cultural Anthropology* 19(2): 276–298.

Jayawardena, Kumari (1986) *Feminism and Nationalism in the Third World.* London: Zed Books.

Jones, Rex and Shirley Jones (1976) *The Himalayan Woman.* Palo Alto, CA: Mayfield Publishing Company.

Kaplan, Sam (2003) Nuriye's dilemma: Turkish lessons of democracy and the gendered state. *American Ethnologist* 30(3): 401–417.

Kazi, Jigme (1993) *Inside Sikkim: Against the Tide.* Gangtok: Hill Media Publications.

Kertzer, David (1996) *Politics and Symbols: The Italian Communist Party and the Fall of Communism.* New Haven, CT: Yale University Press.

Khanal, Shisir (2007) Committed insurgents, a divided state and the Maoist insurgency in Nepal, in *Contentious Politics and Democratization in Nepal,* M. Lawoti (ed.). New Delhi and Thousand Oaks, CA: Sage, pp. 75–92.

Khapangi, Gore Bahadur (2060 v.s.) Rajako Sanskritilai Gihan Gareko Hoinan, Matrai Samman Gareko Hu [I was not accepting the King's culture, I was only showing respect]. *Mato* 1(2): 28–31.

Kirat Yakthung Chumlung (2000 [2056 v.s.]) *Kirat Yakthung Chumlung Barshik Prati-bedan 2055 ra 2056 [Kirat Yakthung Chumlung Annual reports 2055 and 20560].* Kathmandu: Kirat Yakthung Chumlung Kendriya Karyalaya.

Kirat Yakthung Chumlung (2049 v.s.) *Kirat Yakthung Chumlung ko Bidhan [Kirat Yakthung Chumlung's Constitution].* Kathmandu: Kirat Yathung Chumlung Kendriya Karyalaya.

Krauskopff, Gisele (2002) An 'indigenous minority' in a border area: Tharu ethnic asso-ciations, NGOs, and the Nepalese state, in *Resistance and the State: Nepalese Experi-ences,* D. Gellner (ed.). New Delhi: Manohar, pp. 199–243.

Kunreuther, Laura (2004) Voiced writing and public intimacy on Kathmandu's FM radio. *Studies in Nepali History and Society* 9(1): 57–95.

Kurve, Marvin (1979) Nepal's ethnic groups demand better deal. *Times of India,* Septem-ber 9.

Kymlicka, Will (2001) The new debate over minority rights, in *Democracy and National Pluralism,* F. Requejo (ed.). New York: Routledge, pp. 15–39.

Lakier, Genevieve (2007) Illiberal democracy and the problem of law: street protest and democratization in multiparty Nepal, in *Contentious Politics and Democratization in Nepal,* M. Lawoti (ed.). New Delhi and Thousand Oaks, CA: Sage, pp. 251–272.

Landon, Percival (1976 [1928]) *Nepal.* Kathmandu: Ratna Pustak Bhandar.

Lawoti, Mahendra (2005) *Towards a Democratic Nepal: Inclusive Political Institutions for a Multicultural Society*. New Delhi: Sage.

Lawoti, Mahendra (2007a) Contentious politics in democratizing Nepal, in *Contentious Politics and Democratization in Nepal*, M. Lawoti (ed.). New Delhi and Thousand Oaks: Sage, pp. 17–47.

Lawoti, Mahendra (2007b) *Looking Back, Looking Forward: Centralization, Multiple Conflicts and Democratic State Building in Nepal*. Washington, DC: East–West Center Washington.

Lawoti, Mahendra (2008 [2065 v.s.]) Pariwartanko Chahana ra Dhamki-Tras [Aspirations for change and threats]. *Himal Khabarpatrika*. 16: 52–55.

Lawoti, Mahendra (in press) Bullets, ballots and bounty: Maoist electoral victory in Nepal, in *The Maoist Insurgency in Nepal: Dynamics and Growth in the Twenty-first Century*, M. Lawoti and A. Pahari (eds). London and New York: Routledge.

Lecomte-Tilouine, Marie (2004) Ethnic demands within Maoism: questions of Magar territorial autonomy, nationality and class, in *Himalayan People's War: Nepal's Maoist Rebellion*, M. Hutt (ed.). Bloomington and Indianapolis: Indiana University Press, pp. 112–135.

Leve, Lauren (1999) Contested nation/Buddhist innovation: politics, piety and personhood in Theravada Buddhism in Nepal. Ph.D. dissertation, Princeton University.

Levi, Sylvain (1905) *Le Nepal: Etude Historique d'un Royaume Hindou [Nepal: An Historical Study of a Hindu Kingdom]*. Paris: Ernest Leroux.

Levine, Nancy E. (1987) Caste, state, and ethnic boundaries in Nepal. *Journal of Asian Studies* 46(1): 71–88.

Liechty, Mark (2003) *Suitably Modern: Making Middle-class Culture in a New Consumer Society*. Princeton, NJ: Princeton University Press.

Linz, Juan and Alfred Stepan (2001) Toward consolidated democracies. in *The Global Divergence of Democracies*, L. Diamond and M. Plattner (eds). Baltimore and London: Johns Hopkins University Press, pp. 93–112.

Madrid, Raul (2005) Indigenous parties and democracy in Latin America. *Latin American Politics and Society* 47(4): 161–179.

Magar, H.B. Bura (1994) *Is Gorkhaland a Reality or Simply Mirage?* Kathmandu: Pushpawati Bura Magar.

Magar, Ujir (2060 v.s.) Bela Dasainko, Pida Hamro [Dasain Time, Our Suffering]. *Mato* 1(2): 3–4.

Majupuria, Trilok Chandra and S. P. Gupta (1981) *Nepal: The Land of Festivals*. New Delhi: S. Chand and Company.

Mamdani, Mahmood (2001) *When Victims Become Killers: Colonialism, Nativism, and the Genocide in Rwanda*. Princeton, NJ: Princeton University Press.

Mani, Lata (1989) Contentious traditions: the debate on sati in colonial India, in *Recasting Women: Essays in Indian Colonial History*, K. Sangari and S. Vaid (eds). New Brunswick: Rutgers University Press, pp. 88–126.

Manzardo, Andrew and Keshav Prasad Sharma (1975) Cost-cutting, caste and community: a look at Thakali social reform in Pokhara. *Contributions to Nepalese Studies* 2(2): 25–44.

Melucci, Alberto (1988) Getting involved: identity and mobilization in social movements, in *International Social Movement Research*, Vol. 1, K. Klandersman and S. Tarrow (eds). Greenwich, CT: JAI Press, pp. 329–348.

Mohapatra, Bishnu (2002) Democratic citizenship and minority rights: a view from India, in *Globalization and Democratization in Asia: The Construction of Identity*, C. Kinnvall and K. Jonsson (eds). New York and London: Routledge, pp. 169–192.

Mosse, George (1975) *The Nationalization of the Masses: Political Symbolism and Mass Movements in Germany from the Napoleonic Wars through the Third Reich.* Ithaca, NY: Cornell University Press.

Mosse, George (1985) *Nationalism and Sexuality.* New York: J. Fertig.

Mouffe, Chantal (1988) Hegemony and new political subjects: toward a new concept of democracy, in *Marxism and the Interpretation of Culture*, L. Grossberg and C. Nelson (eds). Chicago: University of Illinois Press, pp. 89–104.

Narayan, Kirin (1989) *Storytellers, Saints, and Scoundrels: Folk Narrative in Hindu Religious Teaching.* Philadelphia: University of Pennsylvania Press.

National Foundation for Development of Indigenous Nationalities (2003) *National Foundation for Development of Indigenous Nationalities (NFDIN): An Introduction.* Kathmandu: NFDIN.

Nepal Janajāti Mahasangh (2047 v.s.) *Nepal Janajāti Mahasangh ko Bidhan 2047* [*The Constitution of the Nepal Janajatk Mahasangh 2047*]. Kathmandu: Nepal Janajāti Mahasangh.

Neupane, Govinda (2000) *Nepalko Jatiya Prashna: Samajik Banot ra Sajhedariko Sambhavana* [*Nepal's National Question: Social Composition and Possibilities of Accommodation*]. Kathmandu: Center for Development Studies.

New Light (1979a) Tamang Jātiko Adhibeshan, 10: 2.

New Light (1979b) Tharu Sammelan, 10: 1, 6.

Nirbachan Aayog (Election Commission) (2049 v.s. [1992]) *Pratinidhi Sabha Tatha Sthaniya Nikaya Nirbachan Parinam: Ilam* [*Election Results for the House of Representatives and Local Bodies: Ilam District*]. Kathmandu: Nirbachan Aayog.

Nirbachan Aayog (Election Commission) (2054 v.s. [1997]) *Sthaniya Nikaya Nirbachan 2054 ko Parinam: Ilam Jilla* [*Local Bodies' Election Results 1997: Ilam District*]. Kathmandu: Nirbachan Aayog.

Ogura, Kiyoko (2008) Maoist People's Governments, 2001–2005: the power in wartime, in *Local Democracy in South Asia: Microprocesses of Democratization in Nepal and its Neighbours*, D. Gellner and K. Hachhethu (eds). New Delhi and Thousand Oaks, CA: Sage, pp. 175–231.

Onesto, Li (2005) *Dispatches from the People's War in Nepal.* Ann Arbor, MI and London: Pluto Press.

Onta, Pratyoush (1996a) Ambivalence denied: the making of Rastriya Itihas in Panchayat era textbooks. *Contributions to Nepalese Studies* 23(1): 213–254.

Onta, Pratyoush (1996b) Creating a brave nation in British India: the rhetoric of Jati improvement, rediscovery of Bhanubhakta and the writing of Bir history. *Studies in Nepali History and Society* 1(1): 37–76.

Onta, Pratyoush (2002) Critiquing the media boom, in *State of Nepal*, K. M. Dixit and S. Ramachandaran (eds). Kathmandu: Himal Books, pp. 253–269.

Onta, Pratyoush (2005) Assessment of policy and the institutional framework for addressing discrimination against *Ādivāsī Janajātis* (indigenous nationalities) in Nepal and a review of public discourse and action of the *Ādivāsī janajāti* social movement, in *Gender and Social Exclusion Assessment (GSEA) Study.* Kathmandu: World Bank and DFID.

Onta, Pratyoush (2006) The growth of the Ādivāsī Janajāti movement in Nepal after 1990: the non-political institutional agents. *Studies in Nepali History and Society* 11(2): 303–354.

Ortner, Sherry (1978) *Sherpas Through their Rituals.* Cambridge: Cambridge University Press.

Ortner, Sherry (1989) *High Religion: A Cultural and Political History of Sherpa Buddhism*. Princeton, NJ: Princeton University Press.

Paley, Julia (2001) *Marketing Democracy: Power and Social Movements in Post-dictatorship Chile*. Berkeley: University of California Press.

Paley, Julia (2002) Toward an anthropology of democracy. *Annual Reviews of Anthropology* 31: 469–496.

Parish, Steven (1994) *Moral Knowing in a Hindu Sacred City*. New York: Columbia University Press.

Parker, Andrew, Mary Russo, Doris Sommer and Patricia Yaeger (1992) *Nationalisms and Sexualities*. New York: Routledge.

Pathak, Bishnu and Devendra Uprety (2009) The culture of militarization in South Asia, in *Situation Update*, Vol. 81. Kathmandu: Conflict Study Center.

Pettigrew, Joyce (1981) Reminiscences of fieldwork among the Sikhs, in *Doing Feminist Research*, H. Roberts (ed.). London: Routledge and Kegan Paul, pp. 62–82.

Pfaff-Czarnecka, Joanna (2004) High Expectations, deep disappointment: politics, state and society in Nepal after 1990, in *Himalayan People's War: Nepal's Maoist Rebellion*, M. Hutt (ed.). Bloomington and Indianapolis: Indiana University Press, pp. 166–191.

Pigg, Stacy Leigh (1992) Inventing social categories through place: social representations and development in Nepal. *Comparative Studies in Society and History* 34(3): 491–513.

Pradhan, Kumar (1991) *The Gorkha Conquests*. Oxford: Oxford University Press.

Pragya-Pratishtan, Nepal Rajkiya (2040 v.s.) *Nepali Brihat Sabdakosh [Comprehensive Nepali Dictionary]*. Kathmandu: Nepal Rajkiya Pragya-Pratishtan.

Prichard, James Cowles (1848) The Natural History of Man. London: Hippolyte Baillieve.

Prichard, James Cowles (1973 [1813]) *Researches into the Physical History of Man*. Chicago, IL: University of Chicago Press.

Radhakrishnana, R. (1992) Nationalism, gender, and the narrative of identity, in *Nationalisms and Sexualities*, A. Parker, M. Russo, D. Sommer, and P. Yaeger (eds). New York: Routledge, pp. 77–95.

Ragsdale, Tod (1989) *Once a Hermit Kingdom: Ethnicity, Education and National Integration in Nepal*. New Delhi: Manohar.

Ramirez, Philippe (2004) Maoism in Nepal: towards a comparative perspective, in *Himalayan People's War: Nepal's Maoist Rebellion*, M. Hutt (ed.). Bloomington and Indianapolis: Indiana University Press, pp. 225–242.

Rastriya Gurung (Tamu) Parishad (2060 v.s. [2003]) Smarika. Pratham Aitihasik Rastriya Gurung Sammelan Mahadhivesan, Kathmandu, Nepal, 2060 v.s. (2003). Gurung (Tamu) Rastriya Parishad.

Rastriya Janamukti Party (1994) *Rastriya Janamukti Party Kendriya Karyalaya Bulletin – 1. Kathmandu [Rastriya Janamutki Party Central Office Bulletin]*, Nepal: Rastriya Janamukti Party.

Regmi, Mahesh Chandra (1971) *A Study in Nepali Economic History, 1766–1846*. New Delhi: Manjusri Publishing House.

Regmi, Mahesh Chandra (1976) *Landownership in Nepal*. Berkeley: University of California Press.

Riaz, Ali and Subho Basu (2007) *Paradise Lost? State Failure in Nepal*. New York: Lexington Books.

Richman, Paula (1991) E. V. Ramasami's reading of the Ramayana, in *Many Ramay-*

anas: The Diversity of a Narrative Tradition in South Asia, P. Richman (ed.). Berkeley: University of California Press, pp. 175–201.

Rose, Leo and Margaret Fisher (1970) *The Politics of Nepal*. Ithaca: Cornell University Press.

Sagant, Phillipe (1996) *The Dozing Shaman: The Limbus of Eastern Nepal*. Delhi: Oxford University Press.

Sasaktikaran Sandesh (2006) Loktantrik Aandolanma Mahasangh [The Federation in the Democratic Revolution]. *Sasaktikaran Sandesh* 2(1): 1, 12.

Schaffer, Frederic (1998) *Democracy in Translation: Understanding Politics in an Unfamiliar Culture*. Ithaca, NY: Cornell University Press.

Schmitter, Philippe C. and Terry Lynn Karl (1996) What democracy is – and is not, in *The Global Resurgence of Democracy*, L. Diamond and M. F. Plattner (eds). Baltimore, MD: Johns Hopkins University Press, pp. 50–62.

Schumpeter, Joseph (1962 [1943]) *Capitalism, Socialism, and Democracy*. New York: Harper and Row.

Shaha, Rishikesh (1975) *Nepali Politics: Retrospect and Prospect*. Delhi: Oxford University Press.

Sharma, Janaklal (2039 v.s.) *Hamro Samaj: Ek Adhyayan* [*Our Society: A Study*]. Kathmandu: Sajha Prakashan.

Sharma, Prayag Raj (1986) Ethnicity and national integration in Nepal: a statement of the problem. *Contributions to Nepalese Studies* 13(2): 129–135.

Sharma, Prayag Raj (1997) Nation-building, multi-ethnicity, and the Hindu state, in *Nationalism and Ethnicity in a Hindu Kingdom: The Politics of Culture in Contemporary Nepal*, D. Gellner, J. Pfaff-Czarnecka, and J. Whelpton (eds). Amsterdam: Harwood Academic Publishers, pp. 471–493.

Sharma, Sudheer (2004) The Maoist movement: an evolutionary perspective, in *Himalayan People's War: Nepal's Maoist Rebellion*, M. Hutt (ed.). Bloomington and Indianapolis: Indiana University Press, pp. 38–57.

Sharp, John (1996) Ethnogenesis and ethnic mobilization: a comparative perspective on a South African dilemma, in *The Politics of Difference*, E. Wilmsen and P. McAllister (eds). Chicago, IL: University of Chicago Press, pp. 85–103.

Shneiderman, Sara, and Mark Turin (2004) The path to Jan Sarkar in Dolakha district: towards an ethnography of the Maoist movement, in *Himalayan People's War: Nepal's Maoist Rebellion*, M. Hutt (ed.). Bloomington and Indianapolis: Indiana University Press, pp. 79–111.

Shreshta, Dambar Krishna (2004) Ethnic autonomy in the East, in *People in the 'People's War'*. Kathmandu: Center for Investigative Journalism, Himal Association, pp. 17–40.

Smith, Anthony (2004) *The Antiquity of Nations*. Cambridge: Polity Press.

Snellinger, Amanda (forthcoming) Imperfect replication: conceptions of youth and the form they take in Nepali political culture. *Studies in Nepali History and Society*.

Sonntag, Selma (1995) Ethnolinguistic identity and language policy in Nepal. *Nationalism and Ethnic Politics* 1(4): 108–120.

Sonntag, Selma (2003) *The Local Politics of Global English: Case Studies in Linguistic Globalization*. New York: Lexington Books.

Stiller, Ludwig (1976) *The Silent Cry: The People of Nepal 1816–39*. Kathmandu: Sahayogi Prakashan.

Stirr, Anna (2009) *Exchanges of Song: Migration, Gender and Nation in Nepali Dohori Performance*, Ph.D. dissertation, Columbia University.

Tamang, Mukta Singh (1999) Politics of education in Nepal: violence to an emerging polycentric nationalism. Unpublished paper.

Tamang, Mukta Singh (2005) Nepal Federation of Indigenous Nationalities (NEFIN): policy reform appeals for social inclusion, in report submitted to the Gender and Social Exclusion Assessment (GSEA) Study. Kathmandu: Department for International Development and World Bank, Nepal.

Tamang, Sita Ram (1987) *Nepalma Jan-jaati Samasya [The Jan-jati Problem in Nepal]*. Kathmandu: Sita Ram Tamang.

Tamang, Stella (2006 [2063 v.s.]) *Ādivāsī Janajāti Mahila Loktantrik Manch Awadharan Patra [Indigenous Nationalities Women's Democratic Forum Position Paper]*. Kathmandu: Adibasi Janajāti Mahila Loktantrik Manch.

Tawa Lama, Stephanie (1995) Political participation of women in Nepal, in *State, Leadership and Politics in Nepal*, D. Kumar (ed.). Kathmandu: Center for Nepal and Asian Studies, pp. 171–184

Thapa, Deepak (2003) *Understanding the Maoist Movement of Nepal*. Kathmandu: Martin Chautari.

Thapa, Deepak (2004) *A Kingdom Under Siege: Nepal's Maoist Insurgency, 1996 to 2004*. London and New York: Zed Books.

Thapa, Deepak (2059 v.s.) Jātiya Andolan ra Goreprabritti. *Ādivāsī Ekta* 1(2): 7.

Timothy, Chandra and Narayan Uprety (1995) *Our Social Studies: Book 5*. Kathmandu: Ekta Books and Stationaries.

Trautmann, Thomas (1997) *Aryans and British India*. Berkeley: University of California Press.

Tsing, Anna Lowenhaupt (1993) *In the Realm of the Diamond Queen: Marginality in an Out-of-the-way Place*. Princeton, NJ: Princeton University Press.

Tylor, Edward B. (1893) *Anthropology: An Introduction to the Study of Man and Civilization*. New York: D. Appleton and Company.

Uprety, Prem (1992) *Political Awakening in Nepal: The Search for a New Identity*. New Delhi: Commonwealth Publishers.

Vaidya, Tulasi Ram (1985) *Crime and Punishment in Nepal*. Kathmandu: Bin Vaidya and Purna Devi Manandhar.

Van Cott, Donna Lee (2005) *From Movements to Parties in Latin America: The Evolution of Ethnic Politics*. New York: Cambridge University Press.

Wallace, Anthony (1969) *The Death and Rebirth of the Seneca*. New York: Random House.

Warren, Kay (1998) *Indigenous Movements and Their Critics*. Princeton, NJ: Princeton University Press.

Weber, Max (1946) *From Max Weber: Essays in Sociology*. H. H. Gerth and C. W. Mills, transl. New York: Oxford University Press.

Whelpton, John (1997) Political identity in Nepal: state, nation, and community, in *Nationalism and Ethnicity in a Hindu Kingdom: The Politics of Culture in Contemporary Nepal*, D. Gellner, J. Pfaff-Czarnecka and J. Whelpton (eds). Amsterdam: Harwood Academic Publishers, pp. 39–78.

Whelpton, John (2005) *A History of Nepal*. New York: Cambridge University Press.

World Bank and DFID (2006) *Unequal Citizens: Gender, Caste and Ethnic Exclusion in Nepal*. Kathmandu: World Bank and DFID.

Yashar, Deborah (2005) *Contesting Citizenship in Latin America*. New York: Cambridge University Press.

Young, Iris (2000) *Inclusion and Democracy*. New York: Oxford University Press.

Yuval-Davis, Nira and Floya Anthias (1989) *Woman–Nation–State*. New York: Macmillan.

Zerubavel, Eviatar (1981) *Hidden Rhythms: Schedules and Calendars in Social Life*. Chicago, IL: University of Chicago Press.

Zerubavel, Eviatar (2003) Calendars and history: a comparative study of the social organization of national memory, in *States of Memory*, P. van der Veer (ed.). Durham and London: Duke University Press, pp. 315–337.

Index

Page references in *italic* represent tables, **bold** are figures